S0-BEB-009

The Imaginative Argument

A Practical Manifesto for Writers

Second Edition

Frank L. Cioffi

PRINCETON UNIVERSITY PRESS   PRINCETON AND OXFORD

Copyright © 2018 by Princeton University Press

Published by Princeton University Press
41 William Street, Princeton, New Jersey 08540

In the United Kingdom: Princeton University Press
6 Oxford Street, Woodstock, Oxfordshire OX20 1TR

press.princeton.edu

Cover design by Chris Ferrante

All Rights Reserved

Library of Congress Control Number 2017954047

ISBN 978-0-691-17445-7

British Library Cataloging-in-Publication Data is available

This book has been composed in Sabon Next and Replica

Printed on acid-free paper. ∞

Printed in the United States of America

10 9 8 7 6 5 4 3 2 1

For Kathleen Cioffi

whose love exceeds imagination,
and whose courage and insight
brook no argument

For it is not metres, but a metre-making argument, that makes a poem,—a thought so passionate and alive, that, like the spirit of a plant or an animal, it has an architecture of its own, and adorns nature with a new thing.

—RALPH WALDO EMERSON, "THE POET"

By imagination the architect sees the unity of a building not yet begun, and the inventor sees the unity and varied interactions of a machine never yet constructed, even a unity that no human eye can ever see, since when the machine is in actual motion, one part may hide the connecting parts, and yet all keep the unity of the inventor's thought. By imagination a Newton sweeps sun, planets, and stars into unity with the earth and the apple that is drawn irresistibly to its surface, and sees them all within the circle of one grand law. Science, philosophy, and mechanical invention have little use for fancy, but the creative, penetrative power of imagination is to them the breath of life, and the condition of all advance and success.

—JAMES CHAMPLIN FERNALD, *ENGLISH SYNONYMS AND ANTONYMS*

Contents

Preface

The Imaginative Argument is now over a decade old—barely an adolescent in human years, but ripe middle-aged for a textbook, especially in the field of writing instruction, where tastes, fads, requirements, and personnel change, it seems, month by month. Students have changed since the first edition appeared, too: they are far more wired in, on their devices seemingly continuously, all but intravenously connected to social media, and thus able to swiftly generate a wide array of communicative content. Colleges and universities, where *The Imaginative Argument* has been used as a text, have changed as well. Many courses no longer require extended writing (or argumentative writing), and some first-year composition courses even assign "nonalphabetic" works—wordless communicative endeavors that employ stickers, emojis, illustrations, and links to web content. Or they require students to write narratives—stories—rather than arguments.

So where, then, is the imaginative argument amid all this change? Simple: alive and well. Argument still perdures as the bitcoin of the so-called academic realm. Students (and their professors) still need to generate ideas and to present them in a formal, logical way and develop them within a particular disciplinary context. People who write academic prose still need to read and understand the ideas of others, and still need to take these ideas into account when constructing their own works. And further, the need remains for not just an argument but an *imaginative* argument, for as we imagine an audience we must simultaneously simply *imagine*—navigate neural pathways no one else has ventured down, and realize that despite the apparent proliferation of ideas so readily available on a variety of electronic devices—despite a seeming superabundance—we each of us can and must generate something new and even superior to what's already out there.

These are some of my thoughts in presenting a second edition of this volume. Yet I wonder: Is my claim for the necessity of imaginative argument really true? Or, more pragmatically, why do we need a new version of this book? Perhaps its ideas are simply as out of date as—what?—a cathode ray TV? I mean, do people really ever construct (or need to come up with) imaginative arguments?

My answer to this is as follows: yes and no. Lest this seem too radical a back-pedaling from my position of two paragraphs ago, let me assure you that the current socio-intellectual situation differs little from that of 2001, when I began writing the first edition. Argument, especially imaginative argument, might be "alive and well," to be sure, but it's still by no means a widespread practice. There remains a woeful lack of creativity, a distrust of imaginativeness, and an absence of originality in 99 percent of the "arguments" being advanced (that's my guess, anyway, but it might be that I've been unduly influenced by the rhetoric of a hotly contested national election). People still talk and write along well-worn routes and patterns. They try not to engage new ideas and rarely challenge their own assumptions. Now more than ever they shun media that offer viewpoints different from their own, as they have little interest in hearing, much less refuting or addressing, opposing points of view.

I'm not saying this practice is wicked or neurotic, mind you: many people would say that we have to endure so much anguish, hardship, and abrasiveness already that seeking out a relatively painless and disinterested way to deal with intellectual issues is completely reasonable and sane.

But I'm not sure that college courses are meant to make one's life painless or one's stance disinterested. On the contrary, college courses are meant to unsettle their students, to provide intellectual challenges, to induce mental struggle. When one of my teachers gave reading assignments, he used to say to his classes, "Read hard." I now know what he meant: I want students to deeply involve themselves in their work. I'm not trying to cause them pain or discomfort. I'm not striving to break them down emotionally, to bring them to the point of defeat, frustration, despair, and hopelessness. That seems to me a bit too much (though I have certainly witnessed such an attitude in some college teachers). I want students to think, to read, to write "hard"—to do these things in an engaged, vital, focused way, and if there is pain involved in doing this, they should not merely face down that pain or suffer through it, but embrace it as a sign of work being accomplished, of great effort being expended, of mental changes being wrought.

What I want is simply to diminish the widespread endemic complacency that seems to surround us. I want you to challenge yourself somewhat more than you probably do, to question orthodoxy on a more regular basis, and to think not "outside the box"—itself a cliché of thought—but *outside of* outside the box. Think of a tesseract, not a cube (a tesseract is a four-dimensional box—it's on the cover of this volume). How do you think outside of outside the box? Well, the "box" is the known, the standard, the socially determined and historically accepted ambit of possibilities. "Outside the box" is beyond that—it's seen as a way of describing the creative thinker who is not hampered by the confining limits of conventionality.

Now, to go outside this is to imagine oneself as if in another dimension altogether: it's one where the box and the notions it represents don't even exist, never existed—and even though you as a thinker cannot force yourself to forget what is in that box, you can set it aside and start anew, with new assumptions, new resources, new motivations. While the virtues of "disruptive innovation" have been touted in recent years (see, for example, books by the business theorist Clayton M. Christensen), not enough has been made of the fact that the truly innovative is always and inevitably disruptive. In short, I reject "outside the box" thinking, since the box is still in some sense the controlling element, the cubic nerve center of the issue. Let's go to thinking that is neither confined to nor immured by imagined partitions—the six walls of a box—nor focused on frantically avoiding them at all costs.

People didn't think outside of outside the box when I wrote the first edition of this book, nor do they think this way today—unless they are required or compelled to do so. This requirement and compulsion were and remain at the center of my argument.

In this second edition, I have expanded the book's scope. I wanted to add some new material. Students are often called upon to generate ideas quickly—on exams, say, or for a paper due in less than twelve hours. (Usually this situation results from their not having started working on an assignment until the last minute.) Hence I have dedicated a chapter to a practice I call "streamwriting," which, while based on and resembling Peter Elbow's "freewriting," differs from that practice in its conceptual underpinnings (writing is never "free," for example, but can be done in a continuous fashion). I have added a chapter on how to revise, that is, how to make your ideas more complex and sophisticated, and how in general to improve the gestalt of your essay. I've also included a chapter on writing and technology—inasmuch as the technological changes we have witnessed in the last decade or so have had a significant impact on all phases of our lives, including our work as writers. Finally, this second edition offers three new sample papers and a new appendix aimed at teachers who want to use this book in class.

My students in a composition class at the City University of New York recently told me that the book seemed to them rather "obsessive." Sorry. I am afraid you will have to live with that: being a conscientious, careful, meticulous, and (yes) obsessive constructor of arguments is not, ultimately, such a bad thing. We want to get things clear and straight in our own minds, and then be able to present to others a lucid version of our thoughts and ideas. The philosopher Frank Plumpton Ramsey once concluded that "there is nothing to discuss," since things could be logically proven right or wrong, or since they are facts or not, or since matters of taste are not really debatable. But at one point he amends this assertion, specifically in relation to aesthetic issues. Critics can sometimes clarify things for others, "can point out things to other people to which, if they attend, they will obtain feelings which they value which they failed to obtain otherwise" (248). The imaginative argument strives for this goal in matters nonaesthetic as well. It's a remarkably difficult enterprise, one that I have been struggling with (perhaps obsessively) for many decades. But I think the struggle has been worthwhile, and hope that in joining me, you will find it worthwhile as well.

Acknowledgments

Writing a book of this kind recalls and revivifies many people to whom I owe a debt of gratitude. Incalculable thanks to my late parents, who met in a creative writing class at New York University and aspired to be great writers. They inculcated in me and my late twin brother, Grant—to whom I also owe enormous thanks—an abiding respect for the written word and love for the literary, the artistic, and the readerly. My late uncle, Frank Salvatore Cioffi, who assumed the role of my intellectual father when my own father died in 1968, had an influence on me and my thinking too enormous to estimate. I often quote him in the following pages, and his spirit hovers in some sense above this all. I hope he would forgive me errors in my own logic, my limited scope, my too-oft-infelicitous phrasing. On him, hence on me, the influence of his wife, my late Aunt Nalini, was also profound.

Many people influenced me in college. To Scott Russell Sanders I owe thanks: his commentary on my work formed a model of superb professorial judgment. Professors Donald J. Gray, Murray Sperber, S. C. Fredericks, David Bleich, Lewis Miller, and the late Timothy J. Wiles were extremely influential and at the same time amazingly patient with me, as I tried to formulate my ideas and invent myself as a writer and member of the professoriate in the late 1970s and early 1980s. Their lucid and extraordinary writing and teaching still provide me with models toward which I aspire.

My colleagues at the Princeton University Writing Program, especially Kerry Walk, Amanda Irwin-Wilkins, Anne Caswell-Klein, and Sandie Friedman not only helped me formulate my ideas but also provided a forum and an audience for those ideas as I refined them over the course of my four years' teaching in the Ivy League.

At Scripps College, Claremont University Consortium, where I directed the Writing Program for several years, I want to thank David Roselli, John Peavoy, Nathalie Rachlin, and Steve Naftilan, all of whom were helpful to me and gave me excellent suggestions on a range of issues. Thanks also to Paul St. Amour, now at the University of Pennsylvania, but with whom I worked at the Claremont Colleges. I also thank the late David Foster Wallace, a wonderful colleague at Claremont and an extraordinary generator of ideas about how to teach writing and about what our students needed by way of writing instruction. The world is the more impoverished for being without him.

Many thanks to all my colleagues—fulltime and adjunct—in the English Department at Baruch College. I appreciate the support and encouragement they gave me during my seven years as Writing Programs director there, and I thank them for their continuing collegiality and friendship.

Thanks to my students at Princeton University, Scripps College, Bard College, Baruch College, and the CUNY Graduate Center who have used as a textbook *The Imaginative Argument* and who have provided countless suggestions and comments, many of which I found useful to incorporate into these pages. Special thanks to my students Lydia Morgan and Justin Ramon, whose recent papers appear in the second edition's appendix. These are valuable models.

Thank you also to Jurek and Justyna Limon, Andrzej Ceynowa, David Malcolm, and Beata Williamson, colleagues at the University of Gdańsk who helped me in countless ways both here and in Poland, and who supported my academic endeavors; to Patrice Caldwell of Eastern New Mexico University, who generously helped me clarify many of my ideas about writing and teaching; to Carol Cook and David Thurn, for their genuine insights into teaching and writing—as well as for providing, along with Zulema Vicens-Mortman, valuable models of teaching (*Namaste*); to Mike Tweedle and Christine Poon, who patiently listened to and helped me refine my lucubrations about writing, and who have remained steadfast companions and friends; to John Sand, Joe Powell, Anthony DeCurtis, Bruce and Kris Fredrickson, Donald W. Cummings, and Philip Garrison, who stood by me in difficult times and always engaged and encouraged my ideas; and to Jessica Kennedy Delahoy, the late Peter Gruen, and Valerie Meluskey, teachers all and colleagues who were brought together in a profoundly wonderful and I expect long-lasting way. Thank you, too, to Chuck Derry, Harvey Grossinger, Claire Barwise, Doug Kelban, Michael Robertson, and the Weymar family. You all have offered encouragement and inspiration to me over the course of many years.

Thank you also to Carole Allamand, for her insights and friendship these last two decades, and for our last bicycle ride, which she insisted on doing with me, and which literally saved my life—alerting me to the time bomb that my left anterior descending artery had silently become.

Thank you to my family, to Robert and William Cioffi, to Ann Whitehill, and to Paul Van Dyke. You have been wonderful.

And an enormous debt of gratitude and thanks to Princeton University Press's Lauren Lepow, my copyeditor and production editor on the first edition. Her attention to detail, expression, logic, and ideas was superb—indeed, extraordinary. At the Press, I also want to extend gratitude to Anne Savarese, Ellen Foos, Donna and Debra Liese, Theresa Liu, Chris Ferrante, Marilyn Campbell, Jill Harris, and Julie Haenisch, all of whom have helped me with my writing and with the publication process on either this book or my other Princeton book, *One Day in the Life of the English Language*. And great thanks and good will to Peter J. Dougherty, whose faith in this project and belief in me have been unshakable and long-lasting. I feel rewarded that he is not only my editor but now a friend.

The Imaginative Argument

Introduction

An essential part of a complex web of culture, argument shares intellectual space with analysis, evaluation, understanding, and knowledge. Yet written argument, which logically explains and defends a controversial idea, seems to be disappearing as a form of discourse. Here I offer a manifesto for the protection, for the nurturance, of this endangered species. Why? Because argument deserves to survive and flourish. It should be taught more rigorously in schools, colleges, and universities. It should more regularly enter the public conversation, informing and being informed by ordinary human feelings and actions. Unfortunately, it's too often shackled and bound by the immuring vocabulary of Greek words, life-sentenced to the dustiness of classrooms, relegated to the aerie-like confines of the Ivory Tower or cinderblock facsimiles thereof: the mad-discipline in the attic—or on the very edge of campus.

This manifesto calls not so much for revolution as for evolution, or at least reform: a reenvisioning of what writers and scholars, producers of ideas and creators of new knowledge, ought to be doing and ought to be teaching others. It also calls for you, the writer, to do something perhaps a little different from what you've previously been taught.

"Argument" and "imagination" are not usually conjoined, but doing so infuses written argument with energy and value. You as the writer need not only imagine an audience but imagine what kinds of questions that audience might raise. You also need to imagine what does not at present exist: an idea that emerges from within yourself, and that would therefore be different from anything else yet written or thought, as different as each individual is from every other. And further, if such a process takes place, you will find yourself acknowledging and taking into account the viewpoints of others. This process, I'm arguing here, will advance knowledge as it enhances your own understanding. In addition, it's a process that values and validates the individual as he or she emerges within a context of a larger, projected audience—the group to which that individual speaks, and whose influence constrains, limits, and at the same time engenders the creativity of the solitary mind.

The organizing idea behind this volume is not just the argument but the "imaginative argument." Look up "imaginative argument" in a search engine—all of the hits use the term as if it were an absolute, a summum bonum. And yet imaginativeness is oh-so-rarely taught in conjunction with argument. I make the case in the following pages that you as a writer should attempt to form not just an argument about an issue, a text, a situation, but an *imaginative* argument—one that perhaps has not been offered many times before, one that could involve a new use of language or ideas, one that might even employ a novel range or mix of source materials, what I later call a "new-write" or "newrite." Or something else—really, who knows what?—it's imaginative, hence unforeseeable. And you are not doing this just to be weird and ornery; rather, you are trying to see the issue in an innovative way—a way that will be interesting, partly because it's unexpected, but at the same time graspable and credible because it is offered in a formal, fair-minded, logically structured manner.

Here's how I would characterize the status quo: you, the proverbial student in the chair, do not want to write argument. You do not want to risk statements that could be attacked, refuted, made mockery of—or even to make strong assertions that might provide a point of vulnerability. And your timidity is not a surface timidity: it goes as deeply into your mind as it does into your educational past. You've been schooled to tread the paper-paved path of least resistance; to repeat ideas that you've been indoctrinated with; to parrot the language of authorities you supposedly value—but rarely to approach a problem from a fresh, vital vantage point, or even look at it through a quirkily inventive, eccentric optic.

Yet this stifles an important intellectual endeavor: figuring out what you genuinely feel and think about something. Don't just try to anticipate what others might want you to think—or even what people you respect and admire might themselves think or want you to think. Determine your own angle, your own true beliefs. Use some ingenuity. It is not easy to say what you think or feel about complex issues, at least not in a clear and comprehensible manner. If it were, they wouldn't be complex issues. In a way, writing argument consists of looking at evidence that supports both what attracts you about something and what you might find confusing, elusive, repulsive. It consists of trying to figure out, as you sort through contradictory evidence, what matters—not just to you, but to an audience as interested, as invested, as passionate as you are.

I admit that against me stands a long and still flourishing tradition of repeating the already-established and oft-reiterated. Indeed, much of our educational system envisions the dispensing of such truth—"facts"—as its primary goal. Charles Dickens's famous pedagogue from *Hard Times*, Thomas Gradgrind, embodies this teaching philosophy:

> "Now what I want is, Facts. Teach these boys and girls nothing but Facts. Facts alone are wanted in life. Plant nothing else, and root out everything else." (1)

Dickens has created a caricature here, of course. But now 150 years later, many people still believe in a Gradgrindian educational philosophy. Recently, when I was team-teaching a course on political theory, I was asked to lecture about writing. I basically presented (in vastly compressed form) what follows in this volume you are now holding. I explained how it was necessary to have not just an argument but an imaginative argument; how my auditors needed to form their own ideas and make their own judgments; how they needed to see the texts as being ones that spoke to them as those texts spoke from a remote past; how each generation, indeed, each individual, must come to terms with those texts and must argue why those terms matter to an audience. The professor in charge of the course, who had been looking uncomfortable for the entire eight minutes I was speaking, stood up quickly at the bell. She said, "Yes, yes, that's all true. But we also want to make sure that in your papers it's clear that you *got it*." What she wanted was ingestion and regurgitation of received ideas—and ocular proof thereof.

I know that many institutions within our culture strongly resist change, do not encourage Doubting Thomas figures, and demand, instead, just grateful acceptance. Seventeenth-century Irish poet John Denham wrote a couplet characterizing this position—the exact opposite to my own—and in the mid-nineteenth century, the grammarian Goold Brown quotes Denham with approbation:

> Those who have dealt most in philological controversy have well illustrated the couplet of Denham:
>
> The Tree of Knowledge, blasted by disputes
> Produces sapless leaves in stead of fruits. (iii)

For Denham, as for Brown, the facts of knowledge are inviolate—only damaged by debate; undermined, rendered lifeless or sterile by "gainsayers." Denham suggests here (and elsewhere in the 1668 poem "The Progress of Learning" Brown quotes from) that controversy weakens any understanding of divine creation, fatally blights "The Tree of Knowledge." Disputatiousness "blasts" away its beauty and wonder. Instead of having something we can hold on to, eat from, benefit from, we have a ravaged tree, on its way toward death. (This is an example, by the way, of the logical fallacy called a "faulty analogy." I will discuss logical fallacies in some detail in Chapter 12.) In short, Denham and Brown make a plea for the value of knowledge unencumbered by debate and controversy. Just ingest it and be happy. Or just ingest it.

This quasi-Gradgrindian conception of knowledge not only informs the philosophy of many teachers today (who want to make sure that you've "*got it*") but generally appeals to authority figures because it allows them to claim that authority as unimpeachable. I'd argue that when authority figures take this position, you probably have good reason to distrust them, whether they be teachers or writers, the media or the Supreme Court, your favorite website or presidential candidates. To squelch discussion and debate limits freedom of thought, limits freedom. Goold Brown evidently wanted just that kind of unimpeachable authority, writing for an audience that he felt needed to know the precepts—the "facts"—of English grammar, rather than all the anxiety-provoking controversies surrounding those precepts (probably my erstwhile political theorist colleague felt the same about her role in our class).

By contrast, I expect a little more than "facts." The genre of argument demands more than just evidence that you as students "*got it*"—since the facts themselves often need to be argued for, or are under some dispute, and the "truth," the "it" (of "got it")—a notoriously slippery entity—eludes, gambols, dances away at the touch of an eyebeam or the utterance of a single remark. Ralph Waldo Emerson, writing in 1838, has a contemporary conception of the "truth." He writes in "Literary Ethics":

Truth is such a flyaway, such a slyboots, so untransportable and unbarrelable a commodity, that it is as bad to catch as light. Shut the shutters never so quick, to keep all the light in, it is all in vain; it is gone before you can cry, Hold. And so it happens with our philosophy. Translate, collate, distil all the systems, it steads you nothing; for truth will not be compelled, in any mechanical manner. But the first observation you make, in the sincere act of your nature, though on the veriest trifle, may open a new view of nature and of man, that, like a menstruum, shall dissolve all theories in it; shall take up Greece, Rome, Stoicism, Eclecticism, and what not, as mere data and food for analysis, and dispose of your world-containing system, as a very little unit. A profound thought, anywhere, classifies all things: a profound thought will lift Olympus. (103–4)

The "it" of "got it" must be captured, coaxed, looked at from many angles, and possibly unmasked. Truth consists not so much of an "it," or of "facts," as of propositions based on observation, but which need to be defended and proven—within a certain intellectual context—to subsume and classify antecedent ideas.

Although this is not the place to enter the debate about the relative nature of truth, it's important to question and think about how truths are arrived at. Lewis Carroll contends, in a memorable exchange between Alice and Humpty Dumpty, that the powerful people make the truth, and can make words mean whatever they want them to mean:

> "When *I* use a word," Humpty Dumpty said in a rather scornful tone, "it means just what I choose it to mean—neither more nor less."
>
> "The question is," said Alice, "whether you can make words mean so many different things."
>
> "The question is," said Humpty Dumpty, "which is to be master—that's all." (274)

I know this might at first appear sinister, but I see it in a positive way. The power that Humpty alludes to can reside within you as the writer: you are master. You can persuade others of your position, even though you do not have billions of dollars, or enormous influence in the media, or a job in the White House's West Wing. You can establish a truth via arguing for it. It's hard work, and you can't convince everybody. But you can try.

Establishing a truth involves negotiating its terms; it involves other minds, other subjectivities. Is there a truth "out there" that you can "discover"? Maybe, maybe not. As Wallace Stevens writes, "Where was it one first heard of the truth? The the." When did we first hear of the "the" in "the truth," which implies that there is only one? Surely there are many. But just because there might be no eternal truth—or if there is, it's ever-elusive—this doesn't mean we all live in solipsistic, subjective, closed-off universes, either, worlds where we just make up whatever we want. Indeed, while our subjectivities are rarely congruent, they surprisingly often overlap, intersect, or asymptotically approach each other. Your job as a writer is to push the borders of your own subjectivity in the direction of others, just as you simultaneously determine where others' subjective worlds touch, overlap, and impinge on your own. I can't promise you that the truth you discover will be apodictic or eternal, or even that all these subjectivities neatly interlock, but your argument, your work, if it's been done honestly and thoroughly—or "sincerely," as Emerson suggests—will have the capacity to make an impact and effect change on others, on you, on your world.

A very fundamental human act undergirds and empowers this activity of arguing for truth. It's one that you see in children all the time, one that might even be annoying: the relentless asking of questions. Just as a child might ask again and again, "Why?" until an adult finally shushes him or her with a "Because that's the way it works," or "Just because. Now leave me alone!" so you as thinkers and writers should be asking question upon question. If you are perpetually curious, your questions will help you understand, assess, contextualize, make sense of a given situation, a given idea, text, or topic. And these questions should reach outward—"What have others asked and said?"— at the same time that they should delve within: "How do I feel about this?" "What do I really think?" Questioning allows you to open yourself to possibilities—an action that characterizes genuinely creative thought.

"Opening yourself" means that you must scrutinize, if you can, your preconceptions, your closely held beliefs, even your notions of good and bad, of saintly and evil, of right and wrong. You shouldn't let these notions ossify into hardened cerebral monuments, though. You should be constantly interrogating them, problematizing them—at least in your writing, if not in your life. In the process of asking questions, provided that they really probe the issues, you suddenly recognize your personal stake in the topic. No longer is writing about x or y a dry—or for that matter a wet, perspiration-inducing—academic exercise, but rather a way of discovering and inventing your "take" about something—and then it's an occasion to share that with others. It's an opportunity to transform their subjective worlds as you define and reshape your own.

What follows here is a book about how to make arguments, how to structure them in formal writing, and how to use your language to make them vivid, memorable, striking, and force-ful. It's not just meant to set out some rules that can be followed like formulas or flowcharts. Yet I hope it's a book that inspires you to want to write argument *because argument matters*. It's a book about creativity, a book about how to identify and imagine a present and a future audience for one's ideas.

Let me offer this manifesto-like assertion, which I'm hoping will be as applicable a hundred years hence as it was a hundred years ago, or as it is today: cherish your curiosity, your individual insight—even if it hurts. To adopt an argumentative way of thought is to be intellectually alive, constantly wondering; yet it's tantamount to existing in a realm of provisionality and uncertainty, to seething, almost to enduring a kind of disease. I know this is more than merely unsettling, especially since such a contingency has become an essential part of our worldview. Playwright Tom Stoppard succinctly captures this idea in his 1972 play *Jumpers*: "Copernicus cracked our confidence and Einstein smashed it: for if one can no longer believe that a twelve-inch ruler is always a foot long, how can one be sure of relatively less certain propositions, such as that God made the Heaven and the Earth?" (74). When our own confidence is cracked, it augurs loss; it provokes instability, anxiety, even alarm. That's in part why you hate to make arguments. Making arguments puts everyone under pressure. That's why many teachers adopt Gradgrind's philosophy and why so many of you remain rooted to your chairs, listening to and maybe absorbing the "facts," maybe not.

But let's join Stoppard and abandon "confidence." Instead, look toward anxiety as a tool for thought. Anxiety has a bad reputation, but anxiety about the way things work, about the way things seem to be, about how to explain a book, a person, or a universe—forms the basis for writing argument, for creating new knowledge. I wanted to write that all the important new knowledge—the new discoveries, breakthroughs, and inventions —are still to come, are yet to emerge in a distant if hazy future. I'm just not sure that's true. It might be. But think about the future, for it is your writing that will help create it, and before you can create it, you must challenge not only the present but your own capacity to supersede it.

The chapters that follow—on audience, invention, the thesis, the writing process, research, style—all strive to persuade you that having an argument is necessary, but not quite sufficient; good, but not quite good enough. You have to have an *imaginative* argument. Chapter 1 defines the genre and differentiates it from other nonfiction writing. Chapter 2, on audience, suggests that as you envision your audience, you simultaneously create it by offering readers not what they expect but what they really want: new knowledge. Chapter 3, on the writing process, strives to show how one must actively work toward creation of an essay of the kind being suggested: it's not something that emerges, Athena-like, whole from one's brain; it must be thought about, imagined, tested out, revised. Chapter 4, which covers the idea of thesis, lays out conventional thesis strategies and shows how these often function as only "pseudo-theses"—and as such are deficient. By contrast, the truly argumentative thesis is more potentiality than actuality—and serves to open up new areas of questioning. Chapter 5 examines how to develop your paper, and Chapter 6 discusses the research paper, especially as it has transformed in the digital age. Chapter 7 explores the paragraph—a "paper in miniature." Chapters 8 and 9 look at "creative" or nonstandard forms of discursive essay, and Chapter 10 presents "streamwriting" as a method of composing and a way to figure out your own ideas. Chapter 11 discusses the oft-dreaded and arduous process of rewriting.

Chapters 12 and 13 stress the need to say things in an imaginative and forceful—yet at the same time scrupulously honest—way. Chapter 12, for example, covers some figures of speech and demonstrates how to use various rhetorical patterns in order to give your language greater impact. It also lays out logical fallacies, ways of "cheating at argument" that I suggest you learn to recognize in others and avoid in your own work—they should not be used by responsible writers. Their use in fact represents, at best, intellectual complaisance; at worst, a demented version of imagination. Chapter 13, on style, offers ways to craft a distinctive, interesting style, including both prohibitions and suggestions. I provide twelve brief snippets of essays by renowned stylists and show what makes them worthy of inclusion—worthy of awe. In two concluding chapters (Chapters 14 and 15), I discuss argument in this digital era, and the need to avoid repeating the already out-there. Finally, I urge you to embrace a version of fuzzy logic that I call "fuzzy subjectivity"—a new way of thinking and imagining that has the capacity to effect change.

I

Getting Started

1 On the Writing of Essays

So much writing surrounds us that a textual environment has emerged as a complex and supremely detailed subuniverse. We as readers inhabit it as we take it in. All over the place—on cellphones, billboards, bottle caps, cereal boxes, the Internet; in magazines, newspapers, books—the written word proliferates. Yet the writing of short essays, "themes," or "term papers" has become an activity confined to students. Poor, beleaguered students. Louis Menand, an essayist and literary historian, claims that term-paper composition is "one of those skills in life that people are obliged to master in order to be excused from ever practicing them again" (92). One naturally wonders what other skills Menand has in mind—maybe the ability to do burpees?—but his point stands. Outside the college classroom, there is little direct use for writing of the kind done therein. The short, exploratory, focused, argumentative essay, though now starting to re-emerge in an abbreviated form in blog entries, still has only one secure home: academia.

But that's OK. I will contend here that the academic argument, the subject of this book, forms the central and most important kind of nonfiction writing that you should master, even if you don't get a chance to use it after graduating from college. Is this assertion "ridiculous," as one of my CUNY colleagues declared? I hope not. Argument is important because it draws on elements of all the other forms of nonfiction writing and hence allows you to move to any of those forms relatively easily. It also replicates the method by which ideas are created and tested. It teaches you to think in an intellectual way.

That's my belief, anyway. Mastering the type of writing I outline here will help not just students who want to become professional writers or professors but also those of you who work in any position that requires honest, sustained appraisal or scrutiny of issues, ideas, people, texts, or situations. It's writing that replicates the kind of thought needed to uncover, as much as possible, The Truth, though this use of the definite article, as I suggested in the Introduction, is something that we need to take with a grain of salt, or to recognize, with Emerson, as essentially "unbarrelable" (see page 5). If there is no such thing as *The* Truth, though, at least there is *a* truth that is provisional, convincing, and defensible right now. Essays seeking it look not only for *confirmatory* evidence (that is, evidence to support a given position) but for *disconfirmatory* evidence as well, and they end up using both kinds of evidence to develop their ideas. They aim to persuade yet also to provide as fair, honest, and complete an analysis as possible. For it is only such a fair and honest analysis, only such a careful appraisal of alternative and competing positions, only such a scrupulous but dispassionate scrutiny that will advance knowledge and understanding as it simultaneously opens up more questions.

While such goals are lofty ones, keep in mind too that writing such essays will also help you improve and clarify your own thoughts and insights, even about things that you thought you were already quite sure of. Sometimes, for example, you will have feelings and insights about an issue or a book or a film, but won't exactly know what they are—what they stem from, on what assumptions they might be based, or how they might connect with those of others. But writing the argumentative essay requires you to articulate these thoughts about an issue or text, and to organize your inchoate feelings and insights into a form accessible to others. Moreover, writing this kind of essay compels you to understand argumentation, a form of discourse that will be useful in any situation that requires analysis.

Once I had a position at an alternative newspaper (I was a contributing writer), and my job was to review science fiction movies. This would not have been difficult, except that I was always on a tight deadline—and I often would not really know what I wanted to say about movies like *Nightwing* or *Dawn of the Dead*. Yet I had to come up with something, maybe 1,500 words or so, and usually on the same night I had seen the film. So I had to mentally review that film first; I had to figure out what was special or striking or curious about it. And too I had to figure out if it *worked*—if I liked it. Then I wrote my review. Only by this exercise, really, was I able to determine, say, that *Alien* was a major achievement—and *Nightwing* was a flop. Argumentative writing helped me clarify both my feelings and my thoughts.

Before examining argument in detail, I'd like to look at more immediately recognizable and familiar kinds of writing. It seems to me that there are at least three discrete and historically established types of nonfiction writing, all of which differ from the kind of essay I describe here. The first might be called "essay as literature." Such a historically-established genre is quite capacious, and it can include personal essays or opinion pieces—these might resemble essays from magazines such as *Harper's* or the *Atlantic*, or from journals such as the *American Scholar, Creative Nonfiction*, or *Raritan*. This literary genre of nonfiction, sometimes called "belles lettres," forms part of our Literary Tradition. It might include the works of Montaigne, Samuel Johnson, Addison and Steele, Margaret Fuller, Thomas Carlyle, Ralph Waldo Emerson, Loren Eiseley, Richard Rodriguez, Jordan Kisner, James Hannaham, Wendy Rawlings, and many others. The essay as work of art—memoirs, autobiographies, and other kinds of "creative nonfiction"—might fall under this rubric. Courses examining (and requiring) such writing are often offered by English departments.

Other university courses (often called "Technical Writing") are widely offered on the second major type of nonfiction writing, namely, "informative writing," a type of writing that intends primarily to convey information, not necessarily in a literary or artful manner, and often of a relatively quotidian sort—instruction manuals for our gadgets and appliances, software documentation so that we know how to use computer programs, statutes, warning labels, that sort of thing. Such writing also includes some reportage—journalism. It is the language of much business writing, such as memos, reports, announcements, email blasts. Hence such writing courses are often taught in schools of journalism or in business departments.

And finally, the third main category of nonfiction has as its primary goal persuasion: this writing attempts to make you do something, take a particular position, vote for a candidate or issue, buy a particular car or beer, drug or deodorant. Such writing appears in political speeches, legal cases, and advertising: it will use any tactic imaginable—whether logic, blatant appeals to guilt or emotion, or even thinly veiled threats of various kinds—to persuade its audience. Writing of this kind often forms the subject for courses in mass communication or media studies departments.

I hasten to add that these categories are by no means as clearly separated or nonoverlapping as I've made them out. Much informative writing seeks to persuade. Journalism can be "artful" and literary. Belletristic writing is often informative, as are some political speeches or even advertisements. But the general categories hold up, I think—even if we look at the kind of writing available on the Internet, which no doubt makes up a sizable moiety of what Americans read today.

Though all of these categories differ from one another, they do share some similarities as well. For example, writers in all these subgenres aim their work at a certain audience—and heed what they think are its expectations. They all rely on a series of conventions that writers must respect—what kind of format to use, what level of formality, what tone to adopt, what syntax, language, and vocabulary to employ. They all have a readily apparent organizational structure, which should be more or less evident from the outset.

So where does the "academic argument" fit in here? I propose that it hovers somewhere in the middle, drawing on the standard aspects of nonfiction writing, in that it attends to audience, conventions, tone, language, organization. But it also shares some specialized qualities with each of these three subgenres. Writers of the academic argument pay considerable attention to the way things are stated—often striving not necessarily to "be" artistic but to present points in a creative manner, a manner that has the artist's or craftsperson's sensitivity to form, precision, and image. This type of essay also must convey some information, some facts; it roots itself in the actual. Finally, the academic argument seeks to persuade, but not to persuade at any cost—it strives to convince through the use of logical argumentation, giving as fair, honest, and complete an analysis as possible.

In fact, the essays that I require students to write in classes must do more than just impress, convey information, or persuade. They try to offer a reasonable insight or idea and try to demonstrate to a specific audience how that idea is reasonable. The staple of "scholarship," this kind of writing resembles what professors—in many disciplines—must themselves do.

What is their writing like? While an academic argument certainly does express its author's opinion, this opinion is more than "just an opinion," a knee-jerk response, or an unexplored prejudice. Rather, academic argument offers a point of view buttressed by evidence. It provides an educated, considered, and reasoned opinion—an opinion not just offered or asserted, but argued for.

Professors argue their points of view, seeking to persuade, but they additionally examine other scholars' works and situate their writing within what might be called the "dialectical discourse"—in opposition to some works and in partial agreement with others. They convey information, drawing on secondary resource material. Such writing tends to be "formal," and it almost always appeals primarily to specialized audiences, such as those for *New Literary History* (literary theorists), *Paeduma* (scholars studying medieval literature), *Urology* (medical doctors who specialize in urology), or *Behavioral and Brain Sciences* (psychologists, philosophers, neurologists).

These "presumptive audiences" consist of other specialists in the field, and scholars can take for granted that their audience dwells within what the historian Carl Becker calls the same "climate of opinion": its frames of reference will be similar, and it will share at least some notion of the value and scope of the subject matter. People in it will have read a lot of the same source material and will be interested in the argument.

The argument essay contains five key components:

1. It contains a formal statement of an argumentative position (a **thesis**), something that answers a vitally important **question or problem** in an unexpected, insightful way.
2. It develops and draws **support** for its position from external sources ("facts," "evidence," "warrants," "examples") of various kinds.
3. Its **organization** or **structure**, internally consistent and intuitive, logically and progressively shows—without using fallacious argument—both the content and complexity of its main idea and how that main idea can be supported.
4. It seeks out, examines, and answers reasonable ideas that oppose it, that would attempt to refute its thesis, or subpoints of that thesis, that is, **"con arguments"** or counterarguments.
5. Its **conclusion** amplifies and enhances the thesis—it is an idea that can be proposed once the paper has explained and explored the thesis and has dealt with the challenges that the con arguments raised. The conclusion shows a change in, an advancement over, an enhancement of, the thesis—what I call a "ΔT" (see Chapter 4).

Throughout, I want to stress that the very writing of the essay itself—the process of writing—has just as much value as the finished product. And while that finished product may well form the basis for a published article or essay, the thought, the writing, the doing, the slaving-away-at-the-keyboard effort that the finished essay required has value in and of itself. Ultimately, too, you need to realize that this effort of writing a paper is even more rewarding and meaningful than the grade or what the professor has to say about the finished product. In a variation on the expression "The spoils is the game, not the victory," I want to offer "Writing finds its rewards in the *I'm-writing*, not the *I've-written*." Now, getting you to believe this—that will be part of my challenge in this book.

The Argument Essay Defined

In a way it is unfortunate that we need to use the term "argument" to describe a kind of writing, for "argument" most typically means a heated dispute, an altercation, a verbal fight. Actual fights may indeed follow the verbal fight of an "argument" too—an argument is a serious, emotional, and confrontational experience. It's worse than a spat, angrier than a discussion, more heated than a mere debate.

But forget all that, or put it in square brackets as something that does not map directly onto the rhetorical mode of "argument." Here (and in other textbooks about argumentation), "argument" refers to a kind of discourse, an organized verbal attempt to persuade an audience through the use of *logic* and *reason*. Obviously there are other ways to persuade people— ranging from torture and coercion, on one hand, to cajolery, satire, burlesque, or advertisement, on the other. But logical argument—if you will permit a value judgment—is the most civilized, the most high-minded mode. It's the mode most valued in the Academy anyway, and it has its own system of rules and prohibitions, its own structure, and its own ontology, some of which I will attempt to delineate in the following pages.

Written argument may take many forms. For example, a *description* might strive to show a new way of looking at something, such as a poem, a system of government, or a tax loophole; a *classification* would place something in an overarching organizational matrix or system; an *evaluation* makes a judgment about something based on comparison of that thing with a stipulated ideal type; a *proposal* might suggest a future course of action or present a problem that needs to be addressed; a *comparison-contrast* might compare two different things, issues, ideas, or texts in an effort to illuminate something about one or both of them; a *cause-effect* paper might show how a situation or state of affairs could lead to or cause another; a *definition* might argue for a new way of characterizing something. In his *Rhetoric* Aristotle gives twenty-eight valid "topics" for argument, but these can for the most part be distilled into the seven modes I have suggested above.

These modes—description, classification, evaluation, proposal, comparison-contrast, cause-effect, and definition—give you the structure or subgenre of your whole paper, but they don't tell you in any detail what you actually have to do. Basically, working within these modes, your paper needs to *explain something*. Usually a paper will attempt to explain something relatively complex and difficult—something in need of explanation—but sometimes the simplest things only *seem* simple. On closer inspection, they reveal themselves as not quite so simple and hence really do need to be explained.

Let me be more specific and offer some strategies that you might use when you attempt to explain something. Although these strategies are not mutually exclusive—many in fact overlap—I nonetheless offer them as examples of what an argumentative paper can usefully do by way of explaining. Your paper might do one or more of the following:

1. *Interpret.* An interpreter usually renders one language into another, and in some sense that is what an interpretation paper does as well. It is often seen as valuable, since it argues meaning or elucidation of something difficult and perhaps obscure. It translates one version of English into a more accessible version. (Susan Sontag challenges the value of interpretation, though, in her famous essay "Against Interpretation," which ultimately concludes that we need an "erotics of art" [20]). In an interpretation, you might focus on some aspect of language, or you might look at what various "key words" mean. This involves more than merely defining them—you might conceive of what special meanings the words have in the context of the work. For example, when the philosopher John Rawls writes about "the veil of ignorance," you need to know what kinds of things he has in

mind with respect to creating a fair system of organizing a society. You also need to know dictionary definitions of words. On one exam I took in high school, I was given a poem, "The Chambered Nautilus" by Oliver Wendell Holmes, and asked to explicate it. My task was made far easier by the fact that I for some reason knew the nautilus to be a type of seashell. I was the only one in the class who knew this, so I felt like a star. Make sure that you look at all aspects of a work, including the title. For example, W. S. Merwin's short poem "Little children you will all go / but the one you are hiding / will fly" (404) makes some sense on its own, but its title, "Song of Man Chipping an Arrowhead," gives it a different meaning altogether. When Marshall McLuhan chose his famous book title, *The Medium Is the Massage*, he implied that a medium does more to "massage" than to convey any "message."

2. *Uncover assumptions.* Often a question or problem will include or imply assumptions that need to be unpacked or unmasked. Whether an essay examines a speech, a paleontological theory, a novel, or a yacht, there are underlying assumptions and elements inherent in the makeup of each of these things (speech, theory, novel, yacht), as well individual variations from novel to novel, or yacht to yacht, for example. This kind of paper would argue not just that certain underlying assumptions exist, but that they function in some interesting, elaborate, or perhaps unusual way. Sometimes an author's words themselves embody preexisting theoretical commitments. In fact, even the author might not know these implicit assumptions or they are so deeply rooted in the collective psyche that all of us might be unaware of them. But looking for these is often a useful, even sobering, task.

3. *Reveal significant patterns.* A paper might argue both for the existence of patterns of some kind (giving examples to support its assertions), and for the idea that such patterns are meaningful, important ones. These patterns can be linguistic (repetition of certain words, sentence structures, or images), thematic, or even stylistic. You might, for instance, discover some pattern that could explain how a building works—say, the use of curves or of the number six in the Chrysler

Building. Or you could find something interesting about word-patterns in a novel. For example, *Crash* by J. G. Ballard uses certain keywords many times: "perverse," "geometry," "stylized." These curious repetitions seem to suggest something about the author's sensibility, as does the fact that, for example, in Ben Franklin's very short *Autobiography*, the word "ingenious" appears eighteen times.

You might ask yourself, too, whether there is a pattern evident in the way that an author handles certain kinds of characters or situations. Is there a pattern of action that seems to predominate with reference to the way a plot unfolds? Does it remind you of other patterns of action? Sometimes such a paper can compare the patterns of the subject being examined with overarching pattern-generating schemes, such as those provided by history, sociology, psychoanalysis, feminism, or myth.

4. *Reveal pattern breaks.* This kind of paper would have to incorporate elements of (3) above, but it takes the revelation of patterns a step further, showing how the apparent patterns are not always followed and are either purposely or inadvertently violated. It might then speculate why the patterns break down.

5. *Recontextualize.* Such a paper shows how, when looked at in another context—one provided by current events, other works, a new idea or explanatory scheme—a work, idea, or artifact takes on a wholly new meaning. Simply, it views the work—poem, story, whatever—as part of a different, perhaps larger structure. For example, all movies, novels, poems, plays, or books about terrorism must be seen in a new light since the events of September 11, 2001. Financial dealings have a different, shall we say, coloration since the crash of 2008. On a less political note, you might look at a painting or sculpture, for example, in light of its initial reception, or in light of what was going on in the artist's life (or the life of his/her social class, or the life of the artist's nation) at the time it appeared.

6. *Generalize.* Such a paper argues that the system, text, artifact, or thing under scrutiny represents a more expansive univer-

sal. For example, the constantly evolving security measures at airports represent how we as citizens have in some sense lost the War on Terror. The proliferation of prescription drug commercials on television suggests a greater reliance on drug use as a way of life. Fiction can be generalized this way too: a story might be about a woman, but this story could perhaps be explained as being about the plight of every woman—or every person. A story about looking for a parking space might be seen as being about something as general as the nature of quests. A story about a boy's disappointment with his visit to a mall Santa Claus might be seen as a story about growing up and coming to terms with the alloyed quality of anticipated pleasure. Another way to think about this would be to see certain elements of a piece of writing or a situation as being metaphorical, as representing something else. (The extreme version of such a tactic is the allegorization of experience. Henry James defines allegory: "quite one of the lighter exercises of the imagination. Many excellent judges, I know, have a great stomach for it; they delight in symbols and correspondences, in seeing a story told as if it were another and a very different story" ["Hawthorne" 366]. It is a surface story that has underneath it another, perhaps more profound story, often with political or didactic intent. Almost all of *Aesop's Fables* are allegories, for example, and so are George Orwell's *Animal Farm* and John Bunyan's *Pilgrim's Progress*.)

7. *Argue for effect*. This paper might argue for how something has an impact on a reader, viewer, or participant. It tries to show how the elements of whatever is under analysis have a direct (or not-so-direct) connection to the way people respond to that subject.

8. *Extrapolate*. A paper might take the argument of an essay or the general "message" of a work and show its silliness, ridiculousness, or nonsensicality by extending it to its logical next or last step. This paper would demonstrate and explain the work's weakness, shallowness, or incoherence. (Usually people employ this strategy, called "reductio ad absurdum," to attack other arguments or philosophical propositions.

Sometimes, though, extrapolation is a valuable way to imagine a work's implications and resonance.)

Overall, you need to remember that whatever strategy you employ—and some subjects of investigation or analysis seem to be more amenable to certain strategies than others—your paper needs to argue for something *not obvious*, not taken for granted, not superficial, not readily conceded. You want to reveal something that you have in some genuine sense *discovered*. Your paper will prove why what you have discovered has importance. At the same time you don't want to "explain away" the text or subject matter: your essay will not replace or supplant what it is that you are writing about. Remember that if you feel that you've explained everything, then probably something is wrong with the angle you have taken. As the critic and writer Murray Sperber told me in conversation more than once, avoid creating a critical machine that grinds to hamburger everything in its path.

Keep in Mind That

Your own writing is not intended to be a reiteration of the class's or the instructor's ideas. Rather, your paper should be an elaboration, an extension, and an expression of your own ideas. Your own voice—your own insights—should predominate. It is, however, necessary to understand and build on the ideas of the texts, class, and instructor; to ignore these or to present them as your own (or as silly and jejune) would be a mistake. Most instructors—though not all—appreciate creativity and originality of insight rather than mere recasting or repetition of previously expressed ideas. External sources, too, should not usurp or displace your own voice in the course of an essay; rather, they should be used to bolster, to contextualize, to delineate, to challenge and sharpen your own position. This will invariably differ from class to class—some classes do require both acceptance and reiteration of the ideas of the instructor and texts: they want you to demonstrate that you "got it," to quote my erstwhile colleague. Nothing wrong with that. It's a good first step. Finally it's up to you to decide to what extent you need to go beyond it, though. You need to determine to what extent you must demonstrate that you have understood and can reproduce the various concepts (reading materials, ideas from lectures) in a course—and to what extent you are expected to be original and say something completely "new."

2 Audience: Your Projected Reader(s)

An audience—a group of people sitting in the room while we talk—usually listens, usually gives some indication of their response to what we say. They can applaud or laugh, hiss or whistle, chew gum, throw spitballs, have their own side conversations, consult their cellphones, or whip out a laptop. In one lecture class I taught, a woman who was eating a jawbreaker fell asleep, and the huge piece of candy popped out of her mouth and bounced onto the desk in front of her, waking her up. For the speaker, the feedback is often immediate.

With writing, though, the person or persons on the receiving end—also called the "audience"—cannot give us immediate feedback. I am now alone in a room. A fan whirrs overhead and cars pass by on the street below my open window. To whom might I actually be writing? Why, I'm writing to myself. But at the same time, I have to keep in mind others who might read the words that appear right now on my screen before me. Who are they? How will they respond? Will they understand what I'm saying? Find it interesting? Read to the next paragraph, even to the end of the book? Because I want them to do this, I need to respect and consider their needs and interests. Therefore, I must figure out who they might be and what they want.

When most people sit down to write, all too rarely do they deeply, self-consciously consider the variety of potential audiences, their interests and proclivities, the things that the audience will respond to (and what they might incorrectly respond to), or what the audience genuinely wants from the writing. Such considerations might be thought to border on the trivial—to be almost too obvious to bother with. But these considerations are of enormous importance, especially in the writing of arguments. You need to determine what your audience is like before you can set about persuading them of anything. And your first consideration, I think, should be the kind of language you use: the way you put together words on the page, the way you sequence, punctuate, and spell them—and also their obscurity or familiarity, even their rhythm and sound.

Language Use

When writing a personal letter or email, you probably keep the recipient in mind; if you're writing a more "professional" missive, report, or paper, though, you might think about omitting personal references, the personal pronoun, slang, abbreviations, or even contractions. But the kind of language you use, its "correctness," the level of vocabulary, the length and variety of your sentences—these should all be conscious choices. Your language does more than merely help bolster the argument you're explicitly making—it makes an argument in and of itself. If it is concise, crisp, accurate, and well edited, it carries persuasive force independent of your argument itself. If, by contrast, it contains many errors in usage and punctuation, uses short, all-too-similarly-structured sentences, employs slang, misspelled words, and other nonstandard forms, it can effectively undermine your argument.

But you need to make this rhetorical decision about "correctness." You need to control that particular variable, because whether you make this decision consciously or not, *your audience will interpret it as a conscious choice*. Your audience will respond not just to your ideas but to the way you say them. A paper rife with small errors might suggest that the writer is careless, hurried, or perhaps even uneducated. And while merely correcting the spelling and usage of a weak, empty, or old-hat paper will not turn that particular sow's ear into a Prada bag, it will nonetheless provide your work with something like entry-level credibility for an audience. Writing "correct" prose—on the sentence level—may seem a minor issue, but it is important because readers often judge a writer by the accuracy or slovenliness of usage (sometimes erroneously called "grammar"), or by the precision with which the writer follows the so-called "Rules of Usage."

Hence even if you have a very subtle and penetrating argument but use what might be perceived as inappropriate language in presenting it, your audience might automatically cover its ears. Your language use might well suggest (to some) that you don't have anything important or intelligent to say; it might, in short, stigmatize you from the onset. Let me translate this same idea into "inappropriate" (in this case, oral) language to demonstrate how it changes:

> It's like when you write, you know, it's **not** like just the *stuff* you think of, y'know, like your *ideas*, like your *insights*, like y'know, all the *content* and all, but it's, like, other things that, like, get heard too by people, y'know? It's like they see y'r writing as being, like, not just y'know, the *stuff*, dude, but like, it's like the *words*, too, that are im*port*ant. Hey, you know, I can see, like—the im*port*ant things, of course, but like, you know there are people out there who they don't, like, really *get* it, you know? It's like they don't *listen*, you know, unless you speak, like, the same way they do, and you know, here at **col**lege, it's like—dude—they don't.

Paradoxically, The Rules of Usage don't exist per se. Usage, similar in many ways to other aspects of writing discussed here, varies quite widely, adjusts to differing situations, and even within a given context involves few black/white, wrong/right issues. Perhaps you have noticed that many published, even formal essays deviate from The Rules. Writers often creatively violate the norms of "correct" usage, or they press on the margins of correctness to make a certain point or to reinforce their own distinctiveness. Hence using their writing as a model might be problematic. Keep in mind, too, that most of the writing we encounter in our daily lives does not abide by strict principles of formal usage: advertising, journalism, street signs, operating instructions, websites, poetry, fiction, "creative nonfiction," and letters or emails or texts or tweets all have their own grammar, syntax, and vocabulary ("btw," "lol," "fwiw"), their own range of the conventional and acceptable. Such writing might have considerable value, but we cannot look to it for reliable models of academic writing. Nor can we look to speech as a model for writing: things we say are typically more colloquial, more redundant, and more imprecise than things we write.

Some people have objected that I am too rigid with the level of correctness that I call for—that I should allow for an "imaginative" spelling or punctuation, one violating the norm. Although I'm sure some people advancing this argument do so a bit disingenuously, I do want to say that, yes, you certainly can be imaginative in any way that you see fit. Many great writers distort language—I'm thinking of James Joyce, Gertrude Stein, William Faulkner. Recent writers, too, such as Russell Hoban (in his novel *Riddley Walker*), David Bunch (in *Moderan*), David Foster Wallace (in *Infinite Jest*), or George Saunders (in *Lincoln in the Bardo*) use self-consciously deviant spellings, syntax, or punctuation. The Czech novelist Bohumil Hrabal made one sentence stretch out for the entirety of a 117-page novel (*Dancing Lessons for the Advanced in Age*). The American philosopher William James—himself a masterful writer—allegedly railed against people "who opposed spelling reform with purely conservative arguments" (*Letters* 2:19). He even championed, for a brief time, English "spelt spontaneously." He writes the publisher Henry Holt in a letter of 1894,

Dear Holt,—The Introduction to filosofy is what I ment—I dont no the other book.

I will try Nordau's Entartung this summer—as a rule however it duzn't profit me to read Jeremiads against evil— the example of a little good has more effect.

A propo of kitchen ranges, I wish you wood remoov your recommendation from that Boynton Furnace Company's affair. We have struggld with it for five years—lost 2 cooks in consequens—burnt countless tons of extra coal, never had anything decently baikt, and now, having got rid of it for 15 dollars, are having a happy kitchen for the 1st time in our experience—all through your unprinsipld recommendation! You ought to hear my wife sware when she hears your name!

I will try about a translator for Nordau—though the only man I can think of needs munny more than fame, and cood n't do the job for pure love of the publisher or author, or on an unsertainty. (*Letters* 2:19)

James did not continue in this vein, I feel compelled to add. In fact, how long would you continue to read this book were its spelling similar to the above? Again, everything about your writing communicates something, regardless of what you intend it to communicate. And "spelling reforms" such as those in James's letter communicate—what?—a lack of gravitas? A lack of concern with getting points across? A lack of respect for the audience? The misspellings probably serve more to distract than to reform.

Of course most of you already speak and write fundamentally sound and correct English. For example, you don't use sentences such as

*A of ran terrific inherent about plunge his the creates to.

[Throughout, I will use the asterisk to indicate a "nonstandard" sentence.]

But English, like all languages, has its own sublanguages, dialects, and variations. "Good" English in one context is not appropriate in other contexts. In this book, I try to use fundamentally "formal," correct English—not always the kind of English you might speak (or even write), but the kind that you probably want to be able to master in your academic career. And I am acutely aware, too, that experts do not always agree about what makes for "correct" English. It might be said that "formal" English serves as a default language in situations where you don't really know what kind of language your audience would consider the most appropriate. Using this kind of English will not stigmatize you—or, for that matter, automatically work to your advantage—in every situation, but it's still the safest, most neutral, for you to regularly employ.

Imagining the Audience

Now that I have you productively self-conscious (or maybe just worried) about how you use language, you have to start thinking about what you want to say and whom you are addressing. *You must spend some time imagining your audience, determining as much as possible its values and preferences.* You want to find out what that audience is like, what it expects from your writing, how homogeneous or specialized it is, and what formal and linguistic parameters you must respect. Some students feel that such audience-determination suggests dishonesty, as if they were being asked to give the audience only what it wants to hear. But that is not the case. With a hostile audience, for example, you need to present your argument in a much different way from how you would were you facing an indifferent, neutral, or friendly audience. But in no case am I recommending that you be dishonest. I'm not suggesting that you abandon your position or ideas in order to pander to what the audience wants. Rather, I suggest you assess your audience so that you might more effectively shape and present your argument.

At the same time, though, that you imagine the audience, you need to imagine (or reimagine) yourself. What image of yourself do you want to convey? Well, who are you? Here and at many other points in the writing process you will need to confront this question and do something by way of self-assessment or self-analysis. You won't, for example, need or want to project the entirety of your personality or experience in your writing. I don't want to convey to you via my writing that I'm a person who sometimes oversleeps, who tends toward compulsiveness, or who has made manifold though not fatal mistakes in his life. I'd rather not reveal these things, at least not here. (I'm working through them elsewhere.) Of course sometimes my prose unwittingly does communicate features of my personality that I am not proud of (e.g., compulsiveness, now that I think of it). But as I imagine the archaeologically constructible face I want you to see, I need to decide what that psychic mug shot should be like—keeping in mind that I'm really only in control of about (I'm estimating) 50 percent of it.

For example, I expect that many of you will be students—so I need to sound authoritative, "teacherly," in my claims, in my way of expression ("psychic mug shot"? Well, antically teacherly). I need to be someone who speaks from experience. At the same time, I want to make this book readable and interesting to you—I don't want to sound stuffy or old-fashioned or hidebound, though I know that I run this risk. Some of my audience will also be teachers, and for teachers, I also want to sound as though I know my material, but an added feature comes into play here: teachers will probably be familiar, to an extent, with much of what I'm suggesting. So there has to be something original about it, or else they won't be interested. I need to keep in mind that teachers want a new, insightful, useful, teachable angle on material that they are already "inward with," that is, understand in a very thorough way. And finally, I expect a "general audience" might read this and might want something different from the previous groups. What they want I'm not completely sure of, but I need to realize (as I write) that the personality I convey has to be one that can talk to people outside the classroom or professor's office. It needs to be someone who might engage someone in conversation on an airplane or train, at a cocktail party, at a fund-raiser, during intermission at a play, or even in casual talk at the post office.

This projected self, in rhetorical theory referred to as "ethos," permeates and informs the writing that you will do. The ethos needs to be someone that your audience will respond to immediately, the imaginary self that speaks in place of you, as your proxy, as maybe your "best" self; it needs to have a voice and personality that your audience will not only trust but also enjoy meeting and want to get to know.

Motives

Behind both the imagining of the audience and the imagining of the ideal self you want to project to that audience, however, lies one very important issue: What are all of you—all of us—here for? Why are you writing, and why does an audience pay you any heed? In some ways, for teachers and students this question seems simple to answer: you are here to do the assignment; the teacher, paid to read it, does so dutifully, or is supposed to. Yet this isn't really quite enough. You can't really write an assignment that says, "I am doing this because I have to. I want to complete this assignment, even though I would much rather be outside on the beach. I really want this to take only a few more hours." Nor could someone applying for a grant write, "I really just want the grant money. I need that grant money, so I can live comfortably and do what I want to do. My purpose here is to get that money." At the same time, I as teacher (as an audience grading a student's paper) cannot write, "I have to read this paper and I have. Now I have read it. There. It's read. I really wish I could be out on the beach rather than reading papers." I mean, these things might sometimes be true, but we have to look a little deeper for the motive and purpose behind writing—or, for that matter, behind reading, being an audience.

Actually many motives inform *both* writing and reading. Many of them are not intellectual in nature. For example, sometimes writers need to convey information that readers need to hear. If someone will meet your plane when you fly to the Coast next week, you probably need to convey flight information to him or her. Or the audience might want entertainment. They want to be amused. Perhaps your audience wants to be inspired in some way. Or your audience could want advice. They might want, by contrast, merely to assess you, the writer (say, if you're writing a letter of application). Note that these motives can blend and blur somewhat, but writers need to imagine, as they project and infer their audience, what primary purpose their writing will serve. Other motives, such as the desire just to finish what you are writing or reading—what might be called ulterior motives—clearly vie with the more explicit, more respectable ones, but you need to hold those ulterior ones in abeyance while you try to envision an audience of people who want to be there, who want to hear what you say.

Think of yourself and your audience as inhabiting a magical, imaginary, ideal space, one in which you both are interested only in ideas. At the same time, you need to imagine yourself as getting fulfillment from the act of writing itself, and to see your imaginary space and time as not subject to the problems surrounding writing or the petty annoyances of daily life. Of course, eventually the world will intrude on both writer and audience—the calls of human biology, of tight schedules, of competing claims on one's consciousness: the smartphone's ring or vibration, the doorbell, your back, your wrists, your ischial tuberosities. But for a brief time, try to imagine that you inhabit a universe of intellect and ideas rather than bodies and things, and that your audience dwells in that universe with you.

Therefore, as you write, you must in some ways serve two (imagined, projected) masters: first, the conception you have of your audience, what they are like, what they are looking for; and second, the conception that you have of your own purpose, and of what kind of personality or character you want to project. In what follows, I want to examine the two principal variables that writers need to consider with respect to this dual construction, namely, the degree of "friendliness" (or unfriendliness) of a perceived audience; and the audience's level of specialization.

Writing for a General Audience, Sympathetic or Hostile

When you don't know that much about your audience, other than that it's not composed solely of specialists, you face significant challenges. You don't really know what they expect, nor do you know how various that audience's makeup might be. For example, there might be some specialists among the audience, but perhaps they do not make up the majority. Some audience members might be more attentive than others. And levels of education will vary as well. But despite the apparently heterogeneous nature of the audience, which will present various difficulties, its degree of friendliness or hostility often emerges; and this in fact might be more useful than other kinds of knowledge as a gauge of how to direct your ideas, how to emphasize certain points and organize your argument.

Presenting ideas to a friendly audience—"preaching to the choir"—is generally not problematic. Thus many textbooks focus more on how you can present an argument to the opposite—a hostile audience. These ideas might initially strike you as largely irrelevant here, if you are a student, since your instructors are specialists, and thus they will not generally be hostile to the topics that you write about.

But differences can sometimes emerge. So how do you persuade the audience that you know will vehemently disagree with you from the outset? How do you present a persuasive argument when you think that your audience's position is flat-out wrongheaded or misguided, and when you know for certain that they will take the same antagonistic position with respect to you?

First, you need to realize that such writing entails risk. Most people, including professors, do not want to be confronted by hostility. If you must write in opposition to an audience, try to acknowledge very early in the paper that you know you are presenting a contrary view, but that you think that position has some validity and needs to be expressed. And you should take very seriously the stating of what you perceive to be your audience's values, attempting to phrase them in as exact and fair a manner as possible. Finally, keep in mind that it will be very difficult to persuade your audience. You probably won't make someone change a deeply held belief, even if your paper is tightly argued and very well written. However, if you can get members of your audience to pause in the face of something challenging their beliefs, then you have to a large extent succeeded. Of course the audience might be only demurring before rejecting your idea, but that's OK: it's the hesitation that signals success.

There are levels of success, you should keep in mind; this is not at all-or-nothing situation. Here is how I would characterize them from least to most successful:

0. Reject ideas
1. Pause, then reject ideas
2. Consider and think about ideas—neither accepting nor rejecting them as yet
3. Grudgingly accept ideas
4. Gladly accept ideas
5. Tell others about the ideas
6. Embrace ideas: do something based on the ideas, something new

The most important tactic you should use to gain this first step, this pause—to forestall the outright rejection—consists of respecting your (hostile) audience. If your audience feels its viewpoint has at least been considered, it might be slightly more open to ideas that run directly counter to its own. Remember that in disagreeing with someone, you probably don't want to suggest that the person is stupid, doesn't deserve to be in the workforce, or should be committed to an insane asylum.

Let me give you an example of an "oppositional" paper that failed to work for the very reason that the writer clearly did not respect his audience. In one class I taught, I asked students to write a proposal that argued for some change in the university, and to specify the audience to whom that proposal was directed. A student, let us call him Jim B., wrote an essay that proposed all required writing classes be discontinued and replaced with additional requirements in physical education. This did not on the face of it seem totally unreasonable, but the audience Jim B. specified (namely, me) was a person who had for many years taught required writing classes at that university. Jim B. argued that writing was a valueless skill, would never be used in his life or career ("all of my writing will be done by a low-level functionary similar to a writing professor—a secretary or speechwriter," he wrote), while by contrast physical fitness should be a lifelong commitment and concern.

I think Jim B. (though capturing an idea about writing that many people in the general public assuredly share) had confused the idea of in-your-face confrontation with that of academic argument. Indeed, he was seeking not so much to persuade as to demean his audience, hardly the kind of strategy that led to success for him on that particular assignment, but perhaps the kind of thing that fulfilled some other need—which other I will let you try to figure out. Needless to say, the audience did not feel as though Jim B. really had much respect or consideration for him, and it seems likely that Jim B. hardly thought about that audience at all, except in a fleeting, occasional, and contemptuous way. He probably still despises me. Oh well. I gave him an F on the paper. He said he thought he would get no lower than a D. But in class we seriously discussed his paper, since he openly disagreed with my evaluation of it, and his classmates in fact pointed out that he had disregarded one of the principal ideas in the course, specifically, knowing the audience.

Back to the more usual case—presenting ideas that fundamentally accord with or complement those being expressed by your instructor, your class, and your texts—let me offer this. You can be critical; you need not take for granted that any article or story or lecture is the final word or even the most accurate account of an issue. Yet you should look for subtleties and nuances in the given topic or subject, things that struck you yet were not discussed by the texts, class, or teacher. You should seek some insights that others do not have, or might not be sensitive to, or have overlooked. I don't adhere to the notion "Strive for mediocrity"—take the safe, middling pathway that shows you know the material and have a solid sense of the subject matter. You do need this solid sense of mastery, I hasten to add. It's necessary but not sufficient. You should challenge yourself to go to another level of sophistication. Find your own individual ideas, distinguish them from those garnered elsewhere, and formulate an original and insightful response to the assignment.

Writing for the Specialist Audience

Again, in classroom situations your audience will likely be a specialist. The professor will be very willing to engage your ideas and will try to look at them in a favorable light—basically, a friendly specialist audience. In classes that require writing, the audience will surely value a subtle and carefully reasoned interpretation, an original approach, precise language use, grammatical accuracy, spelling correctness, a reasonable tone, fully developed and coherent paragraphs, a logical structure, and a clear argumentative line: all these have been traditionally valued and honored in classroom situations. But it would behoove you to determine even more specifically how best to reach this audience, not only in terms of how much you need to restate or defer to his or her views, but also in terms of preferred critical approaches, political slant, or argumentative strategies.

In terms of content, most instructors look for complexity, lucidity, and depth of insight. They want (though you might not initially believe this) *to learn something new* from reading an essay. They want their understanding of an issue, an idea, or a text broadened or complicated in some interesting way. They want a new angle on an old problem. They want knowledge. Of course this creates difficulties for you, since in fact professors are usually very knowledgeable about—typically specialists in—the very topic your paper examines. But believe it or not, a genuinely new approach, a new insight, regularly emerges in student essays, and it always earns professors' respect, perhaps to the extent that it gives them pause, makes them reflect anew on issues about which their ideas might have stabilized or solidified.

At the same time that the specialized audience wants knowledge, though, it wants a range of reference and language appropriate to the subject. A biologist, for example, would have little difficulty with the following language, found in a paper from the journal *Animal Behaviour*: "The square roots of the recorded duration of immobility values were taken to lessen the effect of the outliers on the mean for each test" (Gould and Arduino 922). Nor would a philosopher or historian balk at how Andreas Huyssen, a professor at Columbia University, expresses himself in his book *Present Pasts*: "As fundamentally contingent categories of historically rooted perception, time and space are always bound up with each other in complex ways, and the intensity of border-crossing memory discourses that characterize so much of contemporary culture in so many different parts of the world today proves the point" (12). Yet a general audience would, I think, find both of these sentences difficult, obscure, jargon-clotted.

Conversely, writing for the specialized audiences that both James Gould and Peter Arduino and Huyssen project actually requires these writers to use certain language ("outliers," "immobility values," "border-crossing memory discourses") that others in the field will readily understand. In addition, the professors use the passive voice ("were taken," "are always bound up with"), which natural and social science writing requires. Using more conversational or ordinary language might undermine their credibility as specialists.

What makes writing for a specialist audience in some ways easy, though, is that that audience shares values and respects similar conventions. You know more or less the range of reference it needs. You as writer will also be able to predict the kind of language required in a given field. Gould writes appositely about the distinguishing features of scientific writing:

> The dependence on rhetoric and style is assumed to be minimal, and great suspicion attaches to papers that make overuse of the power of words. Students typically describe the style of published papers as cut and dried at best, and deliberately boring and obscure at worst. Ideally, our students should learn to make judicious use of rhetoric ... but they should also understand what sorts of assignments they are likely to encounter in science courses that may actually punish rhetorical skill in the (let's hope mistaken) belief that the writer is being frivolous in the august presence of Scientific Endeavor. ("Science Writing")

That is, there are certain conventions that attach to scientific or to any specialized form of discourse, and the specialist speaking to other specialists must heed these conventions.

Carl Becker, as noted above, calls these conventions a shared "climate of opinion," while the philosopher Frank Salvatore Cioffi labels them "we-discourse": "'We-discourse' is for 'us'; and contrasts with 'they-discourse,' which is about 'them,'" he told me many times in conversation. I prefer the term "discourse environment." As you become more specialized in an area, you come to inhabit a certain discourse environment, and you learn how that discourse operates within that environment.

Inconveniently enough, though, we all must move through multiple discourse environments, a fact that sometimes makes it difficult to navigate our lives. For example, the average person encounters wildly different discourse environments on a daily basis: the auto repair shop, an online chat room, the gym, a real estate agency, a lawyer's office. In order to understand how each operates, or make some headway in getting what you want in each, you have to at least temporarily modify what you might think of as your "natural" discourse. For students, who have to both inhabit and write within many discourse environments, the task becomes even more challenging: since writing provides ocular evidence of a slipup, it highlights flaws in their mastery of the discourse environment. And the student's specialist discourse environments are all quite distinct, and sometimes even in competition with one another: you might have courses in history, English, political science, business, and biology, each of which has its own discourse environment, but you need to intimately understand each one in order to write intelligibly or successfully—to be taken seriously.

You have a straightforward purpose in writing for a specialized audience: problems emerge in any field, and the specialist solves a given problem or problems, showing other specialists why his or her solution compels more attention and credibility than other, previously proposed ones—why it's an important problem, and how its new solution is correct. Your audience might be hostile toward you in the sense that you disagree with some long-established principle in the field. Or they might object to the way that you present your claims. But writing for a specialist audience to a large extent exempts you from having to worry about that audience's hostility: if you write for them, even if you disagree with some widely shared tenets, you still occupy the position of an insider—someone in the same discourse environment—who wants to advance knowledge in or credibility of the field. Michael Moore, for example, in his movie *Bowling for Columbine*, sought to increase his credibility with Charlton Heston by starting off (somewhat meretriciously, I'll admit) by showing Heston his National Rifle Association membership card. Moore did this to demonstrate that he was in favor of gun ownership and the sporting use of guns. He demonstrated himself to be part of the same discourse environment. And this action allowed him access to Heston's goodwill, at least until he started browbeating the elderly actor.

This is not to say that internecine disputes never develop within a field—disputes about value, importance, significance, or interpretation. Moore has a major conflict with Heston about guns, even though both men to an extent inhabit a rather specialist discourse environment. These disputes can end up fracturing the discourse environment into separate, hostile camps, such that one addressing the other must in fact face a hostile audience, people who see the specialized area in very different terms. These internal-to-discourse-environment feuds represent a somewhat unusual situation that you may not often encounter; in general it is the most difficult situation in which to make headway. Since your audience and you share so much of a discourse environment to begin with, the rift typically becomes acrimonious, even personal, and there's not much hope of bridging it.

Let me be clear, though, about the specialist audience. In order to gain entrance to it, you must inhabit its discourse environment, at least temporarily. As Gould suggests above, this involves using certain vocabulary, linguistic constructions, and conventions. But it also involves a certain assumption of shared beliefs. Often it is this very assumption that splits apart when a specialist audience fractures into competing factions. Figuring out these beliefs of your specialist audience, though, is very important, since in fact most of the writing you do will be for specialist audiences. Many problems people face with argumentative writing stem from the fact that they are actually addressing a specialist audience whose beliefs they don't really know and are treading into an alien discourse environment without knowing it. To an extent, this was the error Jim B. made: he was writing for someone who had for many years been involved with shaping and evaluating university curricula; hence when he proposed axing the writing requirement, he was inadvertently moving into the field of a specialist.

He might have been more cautious had he been writing in another discourse environment, one more obviously specialist. I think most readers would agree that James Gould and Peter Arduino's and Andreas Huyssen's prose suggests a high level of specialization, and to write within that genre requires considerable training and expertise. Most people therefore foray only with great caution into biology or historiography, since these fields require for entrance a specific modification of conversational

English. I mean, what is historiography, anyhow? However, some discourse environments subtly camouflage themselves. The following quite engaging sections from Arnold Weinstein's book *A Scream Goes through the House* do not at first blush appear specialist in nature:

> I would argue that Proust's massive *Recherche du temps perdu* is our premier exemplar for actually rendering the twists and turns that mourning may entail. (304)

And a few paragraphs later,

> There are two major deaths in Proust's book: first that of the grandmother, and then that of Albertine. They are handled differently. Proust depicts the grandmother's actual experience of sickness and dying in extraordinary detail. (306)

Nothing arcane or unusual here, or one wouldn't think so. Weinstein is merely recounting some details of the deaths as they are depicted in Marcel Proust's novel. And readers would think, too, that they could easily replicate this prose style, engage this writer in debate, or enter this discourse environment.

But in fact—and you need not just take my word for this— literary criticism has emerged as an enormously complex and difficult field, perhaps made more so by the fact that many examples often cited as exemplary use relatively conversational, accessible prose. The reader enters it, feels comfortable, and then, turned writer, tries to replicate the everyday, easily understood quality of the prose.

Yet that quality is only a sporadic and surface feature of literary criticism's discourse environment. In a recent commentary in the *Times Literary Supplement*, "J.C." opines that contemporary literary criticism has become far too removed from ordinary intellectual discourse. Here is the example he cites as representative, from *The Novel as Event*, by Mario Ortiz Robles, published in 2010 by the University of Michigan Press:

> The unresolved question regarding the coexistence of performative forces and constative objects in the middle voice, therefore, is whether the positionality of the subject gives rise

to a "something" that is itself liable to enter into patterns of substitution or whether the act of positing remains an instance within the order of performance that categorically resists constative treatment. The grammatical concatenation of subject and action is straightforward, even in the self-constitutive modality of the middle voice, but is the subject that is effected in the middle voice in any way phenomenalizable?

This is quite dense. But excerpting a section of the book is somewhat unfair, as the sentences I have quoted are only snippets of a larger argument, where terms like "middle voice," "constative," "positionality," and "phenomenalizable" are defined. Suffice it to say that the discourse environment implicit in Robles's words has a far richer and more complex makeup than the average educated reader—even the average English professor—might feel comfortable with, and if as a writer you want to enter that discourse environment, you will need as much training as you'd need were you to enter that of Huyssen or Gould and Arduino.

"The soul selects her own society—"

"Then—shuts the door—." Admittedly, you won't fully and finally know your audience for any of your writing. You'll have an idea of who they are, what their tastes and proclivities might be, and their level of specialization or sympathy with your position. But you generally won't know them that well. At the same time, though, you will need to convince them of something, argue for something of value to you and to them. In some ways this is an odd, even unnatural situation, brought about by the invention of movable type, the printing press, the computer, and the Internet. But as you imagine this audience, try also to do a little investigative work. Try to get a greater idea of what it is that they are like. What do they expect from your writing? Might you ask them what they expect? Look for models they have praised or dispraised. To what degree is this audience open to change? How much will they tolerate, even encourage, originality of form or content, experimentation in your work? To what degree will they want you to agree with them, and to what degree can you differentiate your position from theirs and still hold their attention or gain their respect? How much will they have to know in advance before they can understand you?

All of these questions need to be paramount in your mind both before you start conceiving your ideas for a written work and as you write them out, for in an important sense you actively create an audience as you write. You create in a single reader some feelings with respect to you and your work; and in a larger group of potential readers or listeners, your work "selects her own society," to borrow Emily Dickinson's phrase again.

Who will be part of that society? Who will end up listening to you? I propose that your ultimate success as a writer has at its base two audience-related factors: First, to what degree does the urgency of your purpose coincide with your audience's feeling that that purpose is urgent too? I'll ask this in other terms. What motivates your writing, what problem are you solving, what important issues have you identified, what areas of ambiguity or uncertainty does your writing aim to clear up? And second, have you successfully convinced your audience that you're the one who's capable of solving this urgent problem? How, once you have done the work of audience-assessment, can you make that audience validate your voice and accept, or at least take into consideration, what you've discovered? You're in the discourse environment: now what? You need, in short, to come up with something to say—and to say to that particular audience. How you do this is the topic of the next chapter.

3 Prewriting and the Writing Process

Invention: Strategies for Getting Started

Good writing almost always emerges as the result of a process: invention, outlining, drafting; going over that draft; revising it, rewriting it, recasting it, polishing it; then repeating this, perhaps again and again. Much good writing must be constructed over some time, like a tennis stroke or yoga pose. It finds perfection only gradually, with many small modifications and improvements made over a relatively long period.

A book such as this one can give you a few dozen suggestions, perhaps, about writing, but at some point your success will depend on a very simple factor: Can you come up with a good idea? In fact, how do you arrive at the very best idea? Oftentimes, handily, the instructor will provide you with a list of possible topics, but sometimes none of these topics will appeal to you. And sometimes the assignment requires you to invent a topic on your own and write about that. Often the assignment focuses on a specific text or texts. Or sometimes the paper assigned might focus on a theme rather than a text. But on many occasions, you'll probably have trouble coming up with something to write about. You might think, for example, that nothing you can say will be "good enough" for an expert in the field to read ... or you might have no real opinions on any of the material you have to write a paper about ... or everything you come up with seems obvious. What to do?

Ask yourself the following base-level, almost primitive questions: "Is there anything in the text (or topic of the course) that has *bothered* me?" "Did I like anything I read? If the answers to these are negative, then ask more general questions: "What am I interested in?" "What's my major going to be?" "What are my career goals?" "What kinds of things do I do for fun?" "How are things going in my other classes?" "Has the drop/add period ended?"

Such interrogation seeks to discover—or perhaps reveal—an area of *emotional response* to the material that you need to write about. That emotional response must fuel and drive any written assignment. Why did you have that strong response? Did something in the text itself spark it? What do you think of as valuable, worth striving for, in society? Were you sensitized to some area of the text that, perhaps, others would ignore or pass over? Alternatively, why did you have little or no emotional response? Do you feel that the issues of the text have been bruited about so much that you've reached your level of satiety? Do you in general feel emotionless about your work, your reading, or your life? Do you find yourself merely doing what you are told and taking no pleasure in it? Are you seeing a therapist? I don't mean this facetiously: writing involves genuine emotional commitment and often enlarges one's self-knowledge.

After deciding on the kind of writing you need to do (see Chapter 1)—and after some soul-searching or self-analysis—you might try a few possible gambits to come up with a paper topic or area of exploration:

■ *Feelings.* Look for your emotional response to an issue/text/ situation. This is the best place to begin. What is it that you *felt* when you encountered what you're writing about? David Bleich, a professor and literary critic, has advocated that we write out a statement whenever an element of the work or subject inspires some powerful emotional response. For example, if a work begins with a reference to a broken elbow, you might write about how you once had a broken elbow and the major effect that had on the way you perceived your own physicality. Or a work might have some reference to the idea of marriage and fortune, and you might have a specific strong feeling about "marrying for money," or have an interesting piece of advice that you've heard regarding this practice. When I was an adolescent, my father once told me, "It's OK to fall in love with a rich woman." I didn't really know what he was getting at. (He lifted this from William Makepeace Thackeray.) Even small things might spark an intense response—for example, you might find yourself responding keenly to a description of a particular kind of automobile, game, or kiss. After you have compiled this list of things that you have had a response to, you need to think about how they might have an impact on your interpretation as a whole: seeing those things that affected you allows you to figure out what you are actually responding to and to separate out the idiosyncratic, individual element from that which might interest a larger audience. But most of all it gets you going, gets you thinking and reacting to the most important thing: the subject matter.

- *Aporia.* This is a rhetorical term meaning "moment of doubt." Literary theory (particularly the approach called deconstruction) has employed this term quite extensively. When you read a text—a novel, essay, short story, what-have-you—where do your assumptions about its form, theme, language, or characters get called into question or become problematic? Typically, we look for patterns in a work, and we argue that those patterns are meaningful. Where does the work defy your attempts at making sense of it? And is that defiance intentional or unintentional on the part of the author? If intentional, what is the artistic/argumentative strategy the author uses? If unintentional, do you have any explanation for this apparent blindness on the author's part?

- *Disjunction.* Similar to the above, disjunction occurs when things do not fit together well, or when they seem improperly, illogically, or irreconcilably joined. Look for the places in the text—or in the society from which that text emerged—where there are fractures, and use these as a starting point for an essay examining this "lack of fit." Perhaps the most difficult feature of this strategy is limiting the number of disjunctions you examine. So many are proliferating in our society that we seem to face a near-infinite regress.

- *Nachgeschichte* (NOK-gah-shik-ta) German for "after-story" (we have no such word in English)—this is an extension from the known into the unknown. In some way, it is the prediction of a future based on what we know about the past. What if a certain text's premises or ideas could be extrapolated? How might they appear in an extended, or future, version? What elements in the story allow us to infer what follows the story proper, that is, the particularities of "And they lived happily (or not) ever after"? What does a text imply will happen in the long term? And is this something that we should fear or feel good about?

- *Backstory or Vorgeschichte (FOR-gah-shik-ta).* The back-story, prequel, or as-yet-unwritten "before-story," is what the text implies (and the reader to an extent infers) about what happened prior to the events of the story proper. Looking at the text, which typically gives multiple clues, and also using your imagination, try to figure out what the backstory would be like, either for a certain character or for a group or society. This is sometimes especially interesting when you examine the situations of minor characters, which leads to ...

- *Parallel tale.* Many times minor characters will appear in a novel, a play, or a film, and do some piece of dramatic business and then depart. What if you were to look at the story as seen from their point of view? What if you were to look at history through the eyes of a minor figure, maybe someone whose viewpoint is rarely seen? For example, in the play *Rosencrantz and Guildenstern Are Dead*, Tom Stoppard tells the story from the perspective of two minor characters in Shakespeare's *Hamlet*. Try something similar. Focusing on the minuscule figures, try to see through their eyes the majuscule events and characters of a novel, a play, or even history. Alternatively, you could comment on what the literary theorist Gerald Prince terms the "disnarrated" portions of a narrative: "all the events that *do not* happen but, nonetheless, are referred to (in a negative or hypothetical mode) by the narrative text" (qtd.by Kafalenos 3). Such an exercise could lead to an interpretation of a story, a news event, or a theory somewhat different from anything you had previously conceived.

- *Penumbral suspicions.* You might have certain unclassifiable feelings or intuitions about a work or subject, things that seem not fully logical or definable but exist as whiffs and traces, decided but near-undetectable hoverings. You might just play around with the subject, toying with its ideas and implications. You don't have to commit to any argumentative statement about it, not just yet, so feel free to follow hunches, feelings, guesses.... Sometimes this leads to startling insights.

In general, you want to be able to figure out not only the most obvious solution or answer to a given problem or topic but also one that is genuinely new. Two classic (but by no means outdated) books on creativity, *Conceptual Blockbusting* by James Adams and *Lateral Thinking* by Edward de Bono, might change the way you think. They both argue that you need to pause and question all your assumptions, question your whole project or enterprise, question how it is that you arrived at the judgments you have arrived at, and perhaps discover a different path or solution. For that matter, you could discover no path at all, or that the answer lies in multiple solutions rather than just one.

In addition, you might look for secondary sources. Reading secondary material often helps to sharpen your own point of view. See what other people have had to say about the same text or about the same or a similar problem. You can surf the Internet for a general and rather undifferentiated series of wide-ranging responses (some excellent, some awful, most somewhere in between). Or you can do work at the library, using catalogs and databases to help you find relevant books and articles. Of course your paper might not be a "research" paper per se, but often reading others' ideas will give you a point of departure, will supply some of the key issues in what might be an ongoing debate—what I have called the "dialectical discourse"—or might even give you the material for a strong counterargument or two in your own essay.

IMPORTANT NOTE!

When consulting or drawing from secondary sources, take especial care. You must scrupulously credit the author of the piece you are using if you employ any ideas, phrases, or sentences from his or her work. Even if you paraphrase that person's ideas, you must give a source and page reference.

Writer's Block

Overcoming writer's block can sometimes be done through rather "mechanical" means. For example, Peter Elbow in his book *Writing without Teachers* invents the term "freewrite" to describe a process of composition that will help you come up with ideas. Unlike its historical forebear, automatic writing, which was writing done supposedly without conscious effort of the will, freewriting consists of writing whatever comes to your mind: in some real sense you are trying to capture on the page your own stream of consciousness. (I have come to prefer the term "streamwrite," incidentally: this nicely evokes the idea of "stream of consciousness" and also jettisons the sixties-ish "freedom" that Elbow invokes—there is little "free" about doing such writing. This writing "costs" you, challenges you, tasks you. See Chapter 10.) Only one rule: you cannot stop to think about or revise what you write—just open the tap of your consciousness and let it flow through your pen. But keep that pen on the page. If you can't think of what to write, just write, "I can't think of what to write. I can't think of what to write. I can't think of what to write." This gets tiresome very soon, so generally you end up thinking of something more interesting. You can time yourself—doing this for, say, ten minutes is probably a good start—or you can just streamwrite until you come up with something that looks to you like a good idea.

Keep in mind, though, that a streamwrite does not a paper make. Free association is not usually enough for a sustained argument. While you might be able to rescue a few sentences or perhaps a paragraph from a ten-minute streamwrite, you should probably use a streamwrite just as a way to generate ideas, to generate heat if not always a great deal of light. But where there is heat, light will often follow—and when light comes, heat inevitably follows that. So once you get going, the hard part is, in some real sense, over.

You can make a streamwrite more useful, however, by dredging it: go back to what you have streamwritten and find the very best idea within it; now streamwrite on that idea, expanding what might be just a sentence or a paragraph into four or five paragraphs. (I draw this idea from Elbow.) Alternatively, you could find four or five interesting or surprising phrases in what you've streamwritten and use those as a basis for another streamwrite. You might also find that sharing streamwriting with others makes for an interesting and productive brainstorming session. Read aloud what you have written, and maybe offer commentary to one another as well.

A "newrite" (or "New-Write"), an exercise I have invented that intends to do more or less the same thing as the streamwrite, lets you take your pen off the page. In this type of writing, you consciously attempt to write something different and, yes, even weird. Just write a paper or a paragraph that you know won't fulfill the assignment, but that self-consciously experiments with language use, point of view, genre. For example, write without using any "to be" verbs. (This *is* hard.) Avoid the letters *a* and *i*. Pretend that you are someone from the distant future reading these texts or taking this course. See the issues from the point of view of a gigantic, toothless dragon hand-puppet named Smok—or one that can change sizes at will. Invent a new language to describe various things that seem to you indescribable, or invent a new emotion that you felt emerge in you after you'd read something. Use drawings, pictograms, or hieroglyphics to get your idea across. Draw out your idea on a piece of paper, and then use transparencies to draw out modifications to it, overlaying each transparency on top of the original. Translate your ideas into a musical score, inventing (if you need to) a personal system of notation.

This, too, often succeeds in getting some ideas going, but do keep in mind, again, that like a streamwrite, a newrite itself will almost certainly not stand as an appropriate response to most assignments. Now and then you can use a newrite-like paper in a course, but for the most part, such a gambit is risky, like the "hostile audience" one described above. Ideally, the "newrite" will get you thinking in different directions and perhaps will open up a way to reconsider the text or topic under consideration. On the whole these invention strategies should give you ways to begin rather than serve as ends in themselves.

Once you've decided what to do, though, once you have some ideas, you've officially begun: now what? Maybe figure out a sequence you'd like to use. Which ideas should come first, second, third? I suggest that you make up an outline.

Many experienced writers do not work from outlines, do very little revising or rewriting, and publish essentially first drafts of their work. Many of my colleagues have told me—somewhat conspiratorially—that they never use an outline and do little by way of prewriting or, for that matter, rewriting. I feel compelled to point out that most of these writers can do this only in areas where they are already expert and therefore have all-but-completely composed their writings in their heads. And they are also experienced writers whose writing production devices are as grooved as the motor skills of a professional athlete.

You yourself might write without an outline or draft. You might feel an inspiration, then sit down at the keyboard and pound out what is essentially a first draft but which superbly represents an organized version of your thoughts and ideas on an issue. On the other hand, you might have to go through something similar to the writing steps I have mentioned above and elaborate below. Obviously there are as many ways to compose as there are writers, and individual writers often use varying methods themselves. With each writing task, you will help yourself discover and refine your own "writing production device." Don't feel as if you should settle on a single process of writing your papers. Experiment. I will offer a fairly reliable pattern of composition, but I do so with the proviso that I don't

always use this pattern myself and that many other professionals use a much abridged—or much more anarchic—form of it.
Still, the stages outlined are probably those that most writers go
through either in their heads or on paper, and you would do
well to at least consider these as you prepare your work.

The Process of Writing

Reflecting

Once you have your topic, have thought about your response to
it, and after you have done some streamwriting—but before you
actually begin to draft an essay—spend some time again, in the
ways I have suggested above, analyzing the audience, the assignment, the materials that the assignment covers, and your own
motivations for writing. For example, if you have decided to
write about a theme in a certain novel, you might want to reread
and review your notes on that novel and the sections of the
novel that you will probably discuss. (This is easier than writing,
by the way.) If you have an assigned topic, you need to go over
that assignment quite carefully, making sure that you understand it fully. If you don't, you might contact your instructor to
ask for clarification and amplification. At this point, you need
to raise those "base-level questions": what is your audience for
this piece of writing—what does the audience know about your
subject? What are its prejudices? You might also examine your
own reasons for writing on this particular subject and topic: Are
you likely to be biased about it? Do you have some special qualification for writing on this topic? What brought you to it? These
issues you might think about rather than actually discuss in
writing, but they will have a major influence on the way your
essay takes shape.

At this stage, I think about the topic and make a list of all the
points worth making. This slightly haphazard collection of ideas
has no particular length limitation but usually has no more than
ten or fifteen points. Make these points as succinctly as possible,
but *in sentence form*. I urge you to put them in this form, because

in any shorthand version their impact can be lost or forgotten as the writing process continues. For example, I might write (of *The Scarlet Letter* on the topic of role-playing), "Dimmesdale becomes a better and more passionate preacher as a result of having sinned," rather than, say, "Dimmesdale's sin with respect to preaching ability," though this latter phrase might seem to capture the gist of the sentence. I don't look, by the way, for any startling or great insight just yet—rather, I just compile ideas that seem to me relevant at the time. I might use them as major points or perhaps just as evidence in support of a thesis. Only the writing itself will reveal how they might function.

Outlining

After composing this list of points, I try to group them into logical clusters. Which several ideas might belong or be discussed together? How can I take these ten ideas (say), all of which I consider important, and classify or arrange them? As you might imagine, thus begins an outline, but it's still only embryonic. I cluster my ideas into groups based on their interconnections, similarities, or family resemblance; I continue thinking about the ideas themselves, the topic, the subject; and I often think of additional ideas. (In fact, at every stage in the writing process, I am open to and seek out new ideas—new evidence, new points, new examples, new counterexamples.)

Now I try to find the point or question—what might be called the overridingly important question or problem that organizes or subsumes the others. Is there one major question the answer to which will be the point that I am making here? Is one of them a stronger, more argumentative, more striking and original point than the others? Is there an "alpha male (or female)" point? Can any of the ideas be turned into such a point? If I can find something like this, then I have discovered a tentative or provisional thesis—or one answer to the large question. I can abandon this point, or revise it if I wish, but I'm striving at this early stage of writing to find something that will organize my ideas. The tentative thesis should accomplish this.

Next, I compose the outline itself. Earlier, I've mentioned colleagues who do not outline. When they tell me that they do not outline, I always think to myself, "They may not outline on paper, but they have an outline in their head." Like chess masters who can think twenty moves in advance, such writers don't need to take notes: they see their argument as a whole and can even perceive its component parts. But I find it easier to write the component parts down and tentatively establish the order in which I think they should appear. (I guess you figured out that I don't play chess.)

At this point you might compose an elaborated outline, one that reiterates much of the thought process that went into coming up with the thesis. I streamwrite a summary of the points that I would like to make in each of the sections. Some of the language here will likely appear in the final draft, I have discovered, but much of it I will abandon. I want at this stage to see whether I actually have something to say about my topic's various aspects, points, or subpoints, that is, about the ideas my outline has isolated. Can I defend all of these ideas? Do they all seem mutually exclusive—or do I find myself simply repeating the same point in different words? If so, I eliminate the duplication. Have I addressed the possible cons? How might a reader take issue with my arguments and ideas? Have I thought of all obvious, as well as some subtle, objections?

Drafting

Drafting comes next. With my elaborated outline on the screen or next to me, I fill in each paragraph. The idea is not necessarily to develop a completely full paragraph but to get my ideas on the page as fully as I can at the moment. Again, I worry not so much about phrasing or absolute perfection as about just roughing out a version of the essay—that is, getting stuff on the page. In this phase you will feel the excitement of creativity, the passion of expressing your ideas. Here is where the lightning bolt hits and you discover your real thesis—or you discover that your tentative thesis will probably work as your final thesis, what you really want to say. One of my professors said that this stage of the writing process resembles lust: it is breathless, headlong, unplanned, even urgent—full of excitement and discovery.

As you've probably discovered, most school and professional writing, done under some pressure of time, prevents us from lingering over every stage or taking time to ponder each word or phrase. Sometimes writers have to simply push on and express themselves as best they can given the time constraints. One professional writer (a former professor of mine who shall remain anonymous) contended that every time you write something that you know fails to fully represent your idea, you *permanently damage* your prose style. Hyperbole to be sure—but this thought still hovers in the back of my mind while I compose, and whenever I write something I recognize as weak or sloppy, I stop to rewrite or rephrase.

After the draft, I recommend that you wait twenty-four to forty-eight hours. After a day or two, you will see your writing in a new light and will feel quite differently about some of the ideas you had. Certain sentences, glaringly ill-phrased or out of place, will fluoresce on the page, while others—ones that you can hardly remember having composed—might startle you with their brilliance. Just don't let their candlepower blind you to the larger task of turning all of these sentences into an argument (and an imaginative one at that).

Rewriting

Here begins the rewriting process. If the drafting stage resembled lust, this stage might embody love: here you must be careful, considerate, thoughtful—faithful to your idea. You need to evaluate your paper, first, as an entirety: does the whole argument make sense? Have you left out any crucial points or stages of argument? Overlooked any obvious and strong cons? How is the wording? Is it smooth, lucid, accurate? Does it sound right, even rhythmical, musical perhaps, to your mind's ear? Can you make it better? Here you should work on the exact form of your thesis. Here, too, you should consider carefully how you have arranged the various elements of the paper: Could it be more logically organized? Are the paragraph breaks in the right spots? Could you develop some ideas more or eliminate others that seem weak, repetitious, or lacking in originality?

Going Public

Usually, now it is best to share the paper with someone whose opinions you trust, someone who can offer intelligent and constructive criticism. You need to remember that another person will see things in your paper that you do not, and another person will also fail to see things perfectly obvious to you (and hence you'll need to rephrase or explain more). Try to take into account every one of your editor's suggestions, while still retaining fidelity to your original work. *Don't allow that editor to rewrite your work, though. That's your job.* Sometimes the comments will be about word choice or phrasing. Sometimes the editorial remarks will be much more far-reaching. Some will be wrong or silly. But whatever the case, take them into account, and, provided that your reader has done a scrupulous job, this will immeasurably improve your work.

Remember that no paper ever really reaches perfection. In some sense we don't finish our papers; rather, we set them loose and say goodbye. When I look back at some published work of my own, I always feel an impulse to revise, and I cringe at the awkwardness of the phrasing or the triteness of some metaphors. I console myself with the notion that writing can always be improved, yet the time at our disposal is always finite. To come up with as good a work as possible, though, make sure you allow yourself the time to compose it with care and plan it in as carefully sequenced a manner as possible—if not the one outlined above, then something similar of your own devising. I will examine this writing process in more detail later on (see Chapters 6–8), but here I have been trying to emphasize how important it is to see writing as process, not as some magical or genetic gift.

II

Features and Fundamentals of the Imaginative Argument

4 The Thesis

What Is a Thesis, Anyway?

The thesis stands out as the paper's most important sentence. It's the formative protein, the DNA of your essay, the compact, coded sequence that predicts the body. The thesis is an interpretation, an angle, an insight, an optic on, a perceptive view of, an analytical slant on, an evaluative synthesis of ... *something*—a text, an issue, a conflict. It explains *the most important issue*, the one most in need of explanation. The thesis makes up the precious residue that would remain if you had to boil your paper down to just twenty or thirty or forty words, if you had to distill it into its concentrated essence.

Since it is so central to an essay's power, the thesis should be something you spend considerable time and energy formulating, revising, and polishing. Some writers suggest that you start with only a provisional thesis and write the paper on the basis of it, modifying the thesis as you come to know its ins and outs. Writing in the *Chronicle Review*, Fordham University English professor Heather Dubrow quotes the architect Louis I. Kahn, whose ideas about a building can be nicely applied to a thesis. "When you have all the answers about a building before you start building it, your answers are not true. The building gives you answers as it grows and becomes itself" (B13). Exactly. When formulating a thesis, you need to realize it will inevitably change as you write your paper; it will become more complex; it will present problems that you had not been able to foresee; it will evolve. You need to leave room for these possibilities.

Another way to see the thesis is as an insight you've arrived at (about the topic) only after a lot of thought. It's a conclusion. The paper, then, explains the thought process you went through to arrive at the thesis, at the same time that it displays this very process. This recursive nature of writing can sometimes be daunting, though, since as you write the paper, you will—unfortunately—often discover flaws in the thought process you used to arrive at the thesis.

Yes, sometimes you will find that what is really original about your paper does not emerge until after you have written five pages' worth of thoughts on a provisional thesis. Of course once you have made this discovery, you'll need to go back to the beginning and start anew. (No one promised that writing was going to be easy; in fact, quite the opposite.) In a textbook on writing, the poet Donald Hall suggests you automatically reject the first four or five thesis statements that you think of, as these will be ones that would be obvious to everyone. This is an interesting idea, and one that I always allow to hover in my consciousness, but I should add that sometimes you *will* come upon an excellent thesis right away. When this happens, I think you will know it. It's unusual, but it happens now and then: each writing situation has its own structure, its own series of problems, and its own unique solutions. As I mentioned earlier, there's no single right way to compose.

Writing is hard work. And good writing, while it occasionally springs magically or bewilderingly from your frontal lobes, will more often be the result of revision, reflection, and many hours' anguished labor. "Labor" is the right word, for writing is in some ways tantamount to giving birth to something very new.

Placement of Thesis

Where should you place your thesis? Many textbook writers insist that a thesis can go anywhere, really—at the beginning, middle, or end of the paper; in fact, the whole paper can be a thesis.

Well, true enough. Such a suggestion is theoretically correct. But it fails to give enough direction. I suggest that you place your thesis near the beginning of the essay. It should probably not be at the very beginning—for the reader needs to be prepared for your idea about a given issue, and probably should know a little about the general subject and topic that you deal with. I recommend placing the thesis at the end of your introduction. This is a safe, albeit conservative positioning of it. You can experiment with placement of the thesis, putting it earlier or later, but this could generate confusion: your reader might not follow what you are arguing for, or think you are arguing something else. Worse, your reader might become bored and ask, "What point is this essay trying to make?"

Wording

Work on the wording of your thesis. Say clearly what you mean. Make the thesis forceful in its impact. Make it live in the reader's memory. Make it roll off the tongue, slide off the pen, clatter beautifully off the keyboard—or at least appear to have. Avoid using "to be" verbs and passive constructions. We all know the difficulty of coming up with a thesis that seems perfectly honed and smooth, but the effort is worth it. Avoid the clunkiness of structures such as "My thesis is that …" or "I intend to prove the thesis that …" Such verbal constructions might seem to patronize the reader or be perceived as padding. Also, your thesis should be evident without your having to signpost it. Don't discuss what you are going to do. Just do it.

Sometimes writers feel they don't want to reveal their main idea right away. Thinking that they need to "save" something for the paper proper, they cultivate a coyness. This is no place for coyness. Reveal your main idea. For example, in an essay comparing Jerzy Kosinski's *The Painted Bird* with Charles Frazier's *Cold Mountain*, the thesis, "There are several ways in which the two novels differ," fails to work. It's a vague, overly general, overly coy thesis. What are the ways that the novels differ, why are the contrasts important, and why should anyone bother to read an essay about them? Let's improve on it some: "The two novels differ in that the quest in *Cold Mountain*, while ending 'unhappily,' nonetheless enlarges the main characters' sense of love—for others, for what they are doing; while the quest in *The Painted Bird*, though one that the protagonist survives, demolishes his and the reader's sense of hope for the individual, the world, and for all mankind." You might have to define what you mean by "love" or "hope"—key thesis-linked terms—but this thesis is a great deal more specific and more argumentative: indeed, if your thesis is to live, it will live in its detail, its specificity.

Here is another thesis that could use some tuning up. This one concerns the practice of organ transplantation: "If we are going to continue accomplishing in this practice, action should be taken to diminish the increasingly unanswered demand for human organs." I have a couple of problems with this thesis. First, "continue accomplishing in this practice" sounds odd. This sentence was generated by a native speaker of English, so there's no excuse for such an unnatural, awkward formulation. Second, it uses the passive, which makes the thesis too vague: "action should be taken," it asserts, but I ask, "by whom"? And finally, what kind of action does the writer advocate? It's necessary to specify in the thesis. Here's a revised version: "Since any algorithm we invent to ascertain who should get donated organs will be a death sentence for many patients and a life extension for a few, we need to establish more than just that algorithm: we need nothing short of a court of appeals." Notice, again, that a number of the key terms need to be defined, but the thesis is a good deal more specific, and its argument is relatively clearly stated. But still more imaginativeness is needed, more of a strong and challengeable position. As it stands, I find it difficult to disagree with. It lacks, in a word, edge. Can I supply one? How about ending the thesis above with the following: "We need to establish a court of appeal based on a Rawlsian 'veil of ignorance' standard." The reader will have to know something about this concept of the "veil of ignorance," namely that decision makers have no knowledge of their own social status. And the practicability of such a plan is problematic. (The decision makers should also be ignorant of the patients' social status, I would imagine.) But the thesis has a stronger edge and seems to me a relatively promising start.

The Argumentative Thesis

An argumentative thesis is provocative, interesting, striking—so much so that it catches the reader up short. Yet it's a balancing act, too, a kind of oxymoron in that it needs to be full of competing opposites: it must be counterintuitive but reasonable; controversial but not an old debate; complex but graspable; creative but grounded in a shared reality. It should be evocative without being vague, clear and specific yet not a mere blueprint for a paper, nuanced but not ambiguous.

The argumentative thesis is not just a verbal fabrication, a manufactured piece of prose that fits a prescribed set of technical specifications. It's more than an utterance, a notion, a conception, or a proposition; it's almost a philosophy in that it represents a mode of thought, a kind of discourse, a way of dealing with the world, or, in our situation, with texts of various kinds.

To further capture the elusive construct of an argumentative thesis, I offer an idea from T. S. Eliot in his essay on Dante. Eliot declares that "genuine" poetry—and I think this also applies to the argumentative thesis—"can communicate before it is understood" (206). To be argumentative, a thesis must convey to its audience something complex, interesting, and new—"make it new"—prior to the point at which an audience fully understands it. The paper that emerges from such a thesis will give the fuller explanation, it is to be hoped, but it will be that paper's burden not only to make understood what could not initially be communicated but also to reveal why it could not be communicated instantly. If, by contrast, the thesis is totally comprehensible at the outset, there is probably something deficient with it, and the paper that follows will, typically, be predictable and ho-hum, as it strenuously argues for something that most readers would accept without proof. Of course it needs to be totally apprehensible and clear, but the genuinely new idea cannot be fully communicable at its first introduction.

"Forethought" Revisited in Light of Argument

How do you generate actively argumentative thesis statements? In the last forty years or so, teachers and professors have been emphasizing the process of writing, and have even opined that that scaffolding process—prewriting, clustering, outlining, gathering evidence, drafting, rewriting—has as much importance as the product, namely, the finished essay. One interesting way of expressing this is from the writer Lee Stringer, who in a public lecture at Powell's Books in Portland, Oregon, told an audience that writing is not just about construction but about "exploration" and "excavation."

In general, though, not enough emphasis has been placed on what one might term "forethought" about the paper's idea or thesis. Going back to Eliot, one might ask what it is that a paper's thesis communicates prior to its being understood, and part of my answer is that it communicates some of the writer's forethought. Learning what this forethought consists of can help you generate more complex, more rotund, more fresh and new thesis statements (and better papers), and can help you understand the mode of thought that writing papers such as these both teaches and requires. Elaborating on the ideas of the previous chapter, I want to propose four areas of possible forethought, though I do so only with the proviso that this is by no means an exhaustive list.

1. "Argument" implies that more than one party is involved. And people cannot be intelligent all by themselves. So there must be an audience: what is it like? Clearly, college essays are not written for a universal audience. They are aimed at quite a narrow, even parochial audience: a person professionally involved with the topic, who has read a lot of material about it, and who has doubtless repeatedly read the text or texts under discussion. As I said above, this is a specialist audience—and a sympathetic one. Yet this audience needs a lot to be surprised or enlightened. Indeed, this audience longs for surprise, is parched for enlightenment. This audience does not want, for example, simplistic answers to rather obvious questions, or, for that matter, reductive

answers to complex questions. This audience does not want a thesis he or she has read before, many—or even a few—times.

2. Forethought also needs to consider the competition: possible as well as actual competing explanations need to be looked at, imagined, or at least provisionally constructed. Just as when I decide to write a scholarly article on, say, a poet named Hilda Doolittle, or H.D., I turn to the articles that have already appeared about her (and about imagist poetry, about early twentieth-century American poetry, about women's poetry, among others) in order to determine the context for what I might write; just as I look at and read other articles in journals I want to publish in to see the kinds of approaches being used, the level of documentation, the affiliations of the authors, the length and style of the essays, so you must look to your "competition"—namely, fellow students. Of course this is in a more difficult task than mine, since you don't typically have access to your classmates' essays. You need to infer the kinds of things that scholars can more easily discern about competition.

A knowledge of the competition forms an important element of forethought—and constitutes a furthering of the notion of audience, for as the audience reads the multiple responses in a class or in a journal, that audience's expectations change: its patience with certain kinds of ideas diminishes, just as its longing for others (or maybe just for unfamiliar ones) is likely to become more acute. Of course this can be intimidating, too—but after you have finished being intimidated by the writing of your peers, and after they've finished being intimidated by aspects of yours that you probably didn't even think about, then maybe you can all sit down to do something even more worthwhile.

3. Forethought also involves determining your relation to the assignment. What does the assignment really call for? Is it looking for reiteration of the ideas of the course, or is it looking for some inventive, original idea? Is it requiring you to show that you've grasped certain concepts, that you can handle a certain technical vocabulary being taught? To what extent is the assignment actually just testing whether you've "gotten" the ideas of, say, four or five key texts? To what extent is the assignment about

the text, and to what extent is the text supposed to be used only as a pretext? Often, the argumentativeness of a thesis hinges on certain unspoken guidelines, which, not too surprisingly, vary from course to course, situation to situation.

4. Last piece of forethought, but in some ways the prime mover: You need to grapple with your own response to a work or works, or to a series of ideas under scrutiny in a class. If your reaction is muted or nonexistent, then why write anything? (When I was a freshman, I never even considered the option of telling a professor that the provided paper topics all seemed boring to me. But I should have done so when that was the case, and teachers should encourage students to take that initiative.) One teacher mentioned that there are no boring texts or topics, only boring people. I wonder.

If you have generated a thesis you are certain is correct, then why argue for that thesis? This connects both with Louis I. Kahn's idea about a building and also with the notion of "negative capability": John Keats's idea that writers should be willing to inhabit realms of abstraction and nonclarity for relatively long periods of time before responding to things. I want to suggest that inhabiting those realms is sometimes valuable insofar as doing so does not have definitive results. "The only means of strengthening the intellect," Keats declares in a letter he wrote to George and Georgiana Keats in September 1819, "is to make up one's mind about nothing—to let the mind be a thoroughfare for all thought" (515). Forethought about one's own various responses to a work suggests that writers run down many uncharted thoroughfares and byways and endure blunting up against the walls that close some of them off. Of course, blunting up against things is not a lot of fun. Keats offers Shakespeare as the example of a person "capable of being in uncertainties, mysteries, doubts, without any irritable reaching after fact and reason" (Letter to George and Thomas Keats, 21, 27 December 1817, 370). This is not necessarily a state of bliss or contentment, but it might be one from which something of value emerges. You have to learn to look for areas of dissonance, of nonfit, of possibly contradictory interpretations and ambiguities—Keats's "uncertainties, mysteries, doubts"—within a work, rather than looking only for overriding and obvious themes and problems everyone would notice, and providing superficial insights that everyone would agree with.

The "Pseudo-thesis"

What happens when you do not engage in this relatively extended forethought? You tend to generate the pseudo-thesis (or perhaps that would be soo-DOTH-es-iss). Note that these statements seriously attempt a thesis and are generally written quite clearly, such that the reader has a good idea of what the writer means. They are not grammatically confused or garbled. But they are fake or pseudo-theses because they only rarely offer any new idea or provide a genuinely creative insight or imagining. I am not going to discuss here the compacted or elliptical puzzle-like thesis, which is mysterious, vague, and ultimately meaningless: such a thesis represents a failure of language rather than one of thought. Nor will I consider the "dead-horse thesis," which appears to be argumentative but in fact is just taking an already established side in an old, never-to-be-resolved debate ("Abortion should be made a crime because x, y, or z ..."), since this kind of thesis is uncommon in text-based analyses, such as the ones I will look at here. But do keep in mind that certain issues, such as abortion, gun control, animal experimentation, and the like, invite such thesis construction: it's very difficult to have an original response to these issues anymore. They're the equivalent of television commercials you've seen a hundred times.

Text-based papers, then, often generate pseudo-theses such as the following (note that all of these should be avoided):

1. A description of research or summary of the texts;
2. A blueprint for a paper that follows;
3. A too easily conceded thesis, labeled variously the "okey-dokey thesis," the "reasonable person" thesis, the "ho-hum" thesis, or the "so what?" thesis;
4. A madcap or lunatic invention that everyone, including the author, recognizes as zany and inappropriate, and that never attempts to offer anything but that very zaniness.

All of these misinterpretations of the idea of a thesis stem from a misunderstanding of what the audience wants or expects. The first, the summarizer, thinks that the audience wants only "proof" that the student writer has read a text and knows some or all of its main features. The second, the blueprinter, feels that the audience, living in a hopelessly chaotic world, wants orderliness, organization, a plan or road map, really anything that will stave off ever-encroaching intellectual Armageddon. The third, the reasonable person, thinks all that's called for is a true and accurate statement that basically everyone will agree with, and since that's always worked in the past, why shouldn't it here? The fourth has the misguided notion that all the audience is looking for is creativity—unharnessed, unspanceled, unleashed.

Each of these positions naturally and even logically generates a pseudo-argument to back up the thesis. Not too much careful forethought goes into these. And I want to mention as a caveat or disclaimer that I don't mean to disparage the generic student-responses that I will be discussing, as these students are merely attempting to reconcile the quite alien notion of writing a paper for a university class with what they have previously been taught. They don't differ that much from you—or from me, when I was a college student.

To help illustrate some of these ideas about theses, I want to look at some thesis statements about a poem entitled "The Pool." It is quite brief, so I think you can take it all in and more or less figure out what's going on. Written by a poet who called herself H.D., a pseudonym for Hilda Doolittle or Hilda Aldington, this poem originally appeared in 1915.

> Are you alive?
> I touch you.
> You quiver like a sea-fish.
> I cover you with my net.
> What are you—banded one?

I choose this not only because I like it but because it was chosen by I. A. Richards in *Principles of Literary Criticism* as his first example in a chapter entitled "Badness in Poetry." He labels it an "instance of defective communication" (199). Ouch.

Pseudo-thesis: Summary

Here are some sample student responses to this poem. "How can I come up with something new and exciting or even interesting about this?" the first student asks in near exasperation. This student generally writes a summary or description of the text. A thesis from him or her might run, "'The Pool' is about someone who encounters a pool of water, who touches it, and watches, surprised, at the effects of having touched it." This is the "I must defer to the genius of others" position, which does have something to recommend it, some honesty and humility. But it's too timid. It shies from any real interpretation. Actually, the genuine problem is a misconception of the assignment: the student thinks assignments are just trying to get him or her to provide proof that the work or book has been read.

Pseudo-thesis: Blueprint

The second type of pseudo-thesis, the blueprint, often emerges because many high schools use it as a model. "This was the way we were taught," a student, David B., told my class. "My whole high school English department taught the same idea—that the thesis was a kind of 'road map' for the rest of the essay. What's wrong with that?" Well, what is wrong with it? I concede that probably in high school it's not a bad idea to hold up this particular ideal. I might do so myself. Why? The blueprint thesis—I take the term from Richard Marius—does force novice writers to come up with some kind of organizing principle. It does urge on them some kind of unifying structure. But the blueprint offers only a structure, a framework, a skeleton. That's not enough. You are no longer novices. I think David B. was probably trained to write what professors unaffectionately call the five-paragraph essay, namely, an introduction with a three-pronged thesis, each point of which is developed in its own brief paragraph, and then a conclusion reiterating the thesis, as in "hence, my thesis," in paragraph five.

Blueprint theses also have a tendency to turn Procrustean. Procrustes is a figure from Greek myth: he lived in a hut in the woods, and when travelers stopped at his house, he would offer them a bed to sleep in. Little did they know that if they were too tall for the bed, he would cut them down to fit, and if too short, their host would use some diabolical device to stretch them to fit. (We won't get into the other ways that Procrustes dealt with unwary wanderers, such as those who fit his bed perfectly.) My point here is that when you have a blueprint, you tend to modify the evidence so that it fits the blueprint perfectly. Such modification is Procrustean—or, in a word, fatal. You need in your papers to be more open to possibilities of things that don't fit, and you need not only to deal with them but actively to seek out areas of "non-fit." Blueprints offer only a plan that will be followed to the letter.

A blueprint thesis for "The Pool" might look like this. "In her poem 'The Pool,' H.D. depicts an individual who addresses nature—represented by a pool of water—disrupts it briefly, and then marvels at the changes she has wrought." There is the start of an analysis here, and it's slightly more than just a summary as well. This student has a much better idea of how to fill up a paper (probably five paragraphs too), than the previous summer-upper. One hopes that the blueprint builder will in fact come up with an argument. Sometimes they do. The student has found something to generalize about (pool suggests nature) and has found a narrative, a sense of change undergone by the poem's speaker. There is even a "marveling" going on.

It's a start, but the tightly controlled blueprint argument will probably limit or prevent much change or growth of thesis—it's too tidy, this thesis; it leaves no room for surprise, discovery, and excitement. It's exactly what Kahn is alluding to when he talks about having all the answers to a building before you build it. The blueprint contains all the main points of a paper—on page 1. Again, it might be a good idea in secondary education, but I don't recommend it; in fact, it's really only a form of elaborated outlining.

Pseudo-thesis: "Okey-Dokey"

Creators of the "okey-dokey" or the third kind of pseudo-thesis feel not so much betrayed by their previous education as suspicious of what I'm offering in its place. "Why do I have to come up with what you call an 'argumentative thesis'?" (usually accompanied by air quotes). "I can find plenty of good, solid evidence to back up a thesis, and then you say that's not argumentative. Or I can come up with a thesis that doesn't have much potential support, and I can invent b.s. to back it up. Is that what you want?" A student named Scott G. asked me this, and yes, he really used the term "b.s." Here is my response to Scott G. "If you can find plenty of good, solid evidence for a thesis, then probably others can too. Probably that thesis is just a bit too obvious, too easy to support. As for coming up with a thesis that you can find only b.s. to back up—well, I don't recommend that. These are not the only two choices; it's not an either/or situation. You need to find a subtle, complex thesis that you can back up with evidence that's not b.s. The evidence for it should also be 'good' and 'solid,' but you have to argue for its goodness, prove its solidity. The evidence should back up what's essentially a new idea—an imaginative 'take' on the issue or text."

Scott G. and many others are arguing for what I term the "reasonable person thesis." It might be called the "oh-so-reasonable person thesis," now that I think of it, or the too-easily-conceded thesis, as well as the "okey-dokey thesis." Here's an example of a thesis in this genre: " 'The Pool' shows the difficulty of connecting with nature and the impossibility of knowing how one's intervention into natural events will affect them and us." OK. In fact, okey-dokey.

Many times you will be tempted, I think, to look for a very reasonable middle ground. There are perhaps two quite radically opposed positions, neither of which might seem suitable, so why not split the difference and argue for an intermediate position? It does seem a reasonable, evenhanded gambit. Maybe, though, it's a bit too reasonable. And the paper that will emerge from this rhetorical tactic generally is so reasonable that it puts the reader to sleep.

One more example, though I could give you many more from what seems to me a too-oft tapped resource of rhetorical strategies: "The natural language of the poem mirrors the naturalness of the pool of water." This kind of thesis suggests that the paper's argument won't matter. Again, it's a reasonable enough statement, but in short, if I weren't being paid to read the paper that follows these pseudo-theses, I'd be off to the gym.

Pseudo-thesis: Zany

The final genre of pseudo-argument, at least that I want to offer right now, grows out of a kind of madcap pseudo-thesis. "You wanted something argumentative, didn't you?" students who come up with such pseudo-theses typically ask. In a newspaper column, the humorist Dave Barry suggested that the best way to write papers in college writing courses was to make the most outlandish comparisons possible. He said that as soon as he did this, he started getting high grades. For example, he said that he compared Herman Melville's *Moby-Dick* to the Republic of Ireland. His professors loved that kind of thing.

Here are some zany thesis statements about H.D.'s poem. "The Pool" is about a tiger lying in its own pool of blood. It's about a pregnant woman touching her swollen belly. It's about swimming laps and watching the lane lines painted on the bottom of the pool. As one tires, the lines become hazy, confusing.

I know that feeling of lines becoming hazy. These are explanations that I have actually seen offered. Here, too, each writer has misconstrued audience, purpose, and relation to subject matter but, even worse, has in some sense cut the cord that grounds his or her explanation to the text itself. Your papers and the interpretations they offer are not versions of patients' responses to inkblots: they must be constructs that others—an audience—can be swayed to finally perceive as sound explanations, not merely private reactions that one either sees or does not, depending on mood, personality, receptivity, and the like. In short, these pseudo-theses emerge from the idea that a thesis need only be asserted. In fact, it actually has to be proven. And that's the hard part.

A version of the zany thesis is what I term the "wampyjogged thesis"—namely, the verbal construction that is so dense and/or metaphorically expressed that it *sounds* complex, elaborate, and smart, but in fact is, at worst, just plain b.s., to use Scott G.'s term. Or at best, okey-dokey. I've written some of these myself, so I sympathize with the impulse. "H.D.'s poem recounts the unknowability of the natural world, suggesting that when one submits to it, the mind, reduced to near-autistic cerebration, attains to reptile-status." This sounds pretty highfalutin', but the writer is only arguing that the speaker has a somewhat simplistic or childlike response to the depicted world. Ho hum. Or another: " 'The Pool,' with its staccato imagery suggestive of the trench warfare that surrounded H.D. herself, makes words into weapons with which the newly armed woman of the world can engage nature red in tooth and claw, or in all its pervasive, embryonic wetness." This writer, alluding to Tennyson, has greater confidence, but I just don't know what her point is. Words are weapons? Is this an allusion to Amiri Baraka? I'm just not sure. Both of these thesis statements seem impressive at first, but they sound new only because they're couched in such ornate language. Ornate language doesn't constitute an argument; it's just a flowery writing style attempting to disguise the fact that the writer has no real argument.

Some Actual Arguments

What, then, is a solidly argumentative—and provable—thesis about "The Pool"? Actually, this is an amazingly difficult poem. In fact, it seems to me that coming up with a genuinely argumentative thesis about it is an excellent exercise. I. A. Richards's above-mentioned thesis is a strong one, namely, that the poem lacks any emotional content. But that doesn't seem likely to be something a student working on only "The Pool" would generate, for its understanding depends on the context set up by the entire book. Here is Richards:

> Not the brevity only of the Vehicle, but its simplicity, make it ineffective. The sacrifice of metre in free verse needs, in almost all cases, to be compensated by length. The loss of so much of the formal structure leads otherwise to tenuousness and ambiguity. Even when, as here, the original experience is presumably slight, tenuous and fleeting, the mere correspondence of matter to form is insufficient. The experience

invoked in the reader is not sufficiently specific. A poet may, it is true, make an unlimited demand upon the reader, and the greatest poets make the greatest claim, but the demand must be proportional to the poet's own contribution. The reader here supplies too much of the poem. Had the poet said only "I went and poked about rocklings, and caught the pool itself," the reader, who converts what is printed above into a poem, would still have been able to construct an experience of equal value; for what results is almost independent of the author. (200)

In short, Richards finds the poem too easily paraphrasable, and the paraphrase—as well as the poem—is about a fundamentally exiguous experience. I disagree; and I disagree with his paraphrase. In fact I think his argument is ridiculous. But it is an argument.

It seems to me that a useful way of thinking about how to come up with an argumentative thesis is to think of a major, overriding, important—and ultimately unanswerable—question about the work or issue. Richards seems to be asking, "Why is it that this poem does not excite any response in me?" and he comes up with the idea above regarding the absence of a significant experience behind H.D.'s poem.

Here is an excellent student response to the poem, one that taught me something about H.D. and her transgressiveness. The curious thing about Nina B.'s response, in fact, is that it assumes H.D. to be male, an assumption that seems defensible. And the student's thesis suggests that the poem's speaker manifests a very typically male attitude toward the pool itself:

By entitling his poem "The Pool," H.D. thrusts [an] image of human interference upon readers. The poem itself, however, does not limit itself to discussion of a pool, but has a broader, more generalized focus. Building on this allusion to human tampering, H.D. explores the instinctive, human response to any encounter with "the other." When faced with some foreign entity that defies comprehension, be it an element of the natural world or a member of an alien race, humans reveal a need to draw this entity into their respective sphere of control. Through attempts at classification or physical exploitation, man betrays an intolerance for the unknown, which is grounded in a fear of overthrow; to avoid domination, humans dominate. In "The Pool," brief though it may be, H.D. depicts some encounter with "the other" and uses it to exemplify the human need to suppress, coupled with an inherent unconcern for the object of subjugation.

Nina B. has developed a highly argumentative position, even though—or maybe because—she mistook the author for male. The idea of dominating so as not to be dominated, and the lack of consideration for the object being dominated, take on a different slant if one assumes a male speaker as opposed to a female one; H.D.'s poem reveals itself as a highly "gendered" statement. Maybe Richards actually resented the poem and the poet because H.D. was a woman adopting a male point of view? It seems that taking an argumentative stance can often lead to sudden, unexpected insights.

Let me offer my own interpretation, expanding on the arguments offered by some of the student writers I cited above.

H.D.'s short 1915 lyric poem "The Pool" resists definitive interpretation. As I. A. Richards contends, "The experience invoked in the reader is not sufficiently specific." And such non-specificity makes one feel the poem could "mean" almost anything, provided it's sufficiently abstract, ethereal, or amorphous. In fact, the poem's simplicity, coupled with the conventional notion that a short lyric typically reflects a moment of special insight or beauty, makes for an interpretive field day. Anything goes. Almost. " 'The Pool' is about memory"; " 'The Pool' is an anti-war poem"; " 'The Pool' is a sports car's internal monologue when a driver gets into it" (one of my students, Sam F., came up with this idea). All of these are arguable. Even zany interpretations seem plausible, a fact that evidently bothers Richards. "What results," Richards concludes, "is almost independent of the author." Yes, perhaps so.

In fact, arguing the poem is only about memory, sex, war, or a car's ruminations too narrowly limits its evocative power. **This wild proliferation of possible readings should be set** aside, I propose, in favor of one that might subsume them all: **the poem is about the interpretive act itself, the cerebral activity of trying to understand something, maybe even something as ordinary as a pool of water.** "The Pool" presents a structure of interpretive/intellectual activity: wonder, exploration, observation, change, renewed wonder. And this structure, which can engine a near-infinite number of specific experiences, constitutes the armature around which the poem revolves.

To describe this structure in more detail, the poem examines the encounter with something other than oneself—it could be anything, really—but it's something that is or has become alien to one's understanding, what Emerson calls the "not-me." The poem dramatizes how such an encounter starts in wonder ("Are you alive?"), and then, as the individual seeks to understand this not-me on the most basic level— via touching—that tiny investigative foray effects a change: "I cover you with my net." Trying to understand the "other" transforms it, adds to it some element of the probing mind itself. Yet another transformation soon takes place, making that other more alien still, a transformation that brings us full circle, back to wonder once again—wonder at the change that was wrought: "What are you, banded one?" The very act of investigating the pool, the "other," of "touching" it, fundamentally alters its essence—twice. Thus understanding lurchingly accumulates. H.D.'s poem anticipates Werner Heisenberg, who contended that we could not observe a phenomenon without fundamentally altering it (the so-called "Heisenberg Uncertainty Principle"), an idea that didn't emerge until over a decade later, in 1927.

This opening to a paper seems to me fairly promising, though by no means perfect. There is a thesis present (in boldface), and it does have an argumentative edge, even if it's a bit blunt at present. But what's positive about the thesis is that it stirs things up. It does not seem to be an obvious endpoint or easily conceded idea. A good thesis should spark controversy, rather than shut down conversation. I haven't yet written the whole paper on "The Pool," so I don't know how this will play out. But before I wrote it, I would need to project a context, infer an audience, and also reexamine my own interpretation of the poem. I'd have to do a lot more by way of forethought, asking the above questions and ones like them.

The Δ-Thesis

And as I imposed on my thesis pressure from actual counterarguments offered by other critics, as well as from ones I might anticipate, as I brought more evidence to bear both for my thesis and against it, I would notice the thesis beginning to mutate or change, so much so that by the end of the paper, I could not simply reiterate my thesis but would actually have come to a new point, an enhanced version of the thesis, an idea I could not have started with but might now assert because I have been putting my thesis under pressure for five or eight or eighteen pages. The thesis has evolved, has become the equivalent of a second, a changed, thesis, the "Δ-Thesis" or "ΔT."

I'll go even further. If you've actively and creatively supported your thesis, if you've genuinely sought out and engaged counterarguments, and at the end you repeat your thesis exactly as it was initially formulated, it will have acquired a new, different meaning. What it was initially communicating is now understood, or better understood. In your ΔT, you should explain and reflect on that new idea.

We have a familiar word for ΔT—a conclusion. And while such an evolution of the thesis is a desideratum, any conclusion is ultimately never "right," or "definitive," or "final." It is not incontrovertible. Eliot says that poetry communicates before it is understood; a thesis should do the same, but by the end of an essay generated by that thesis, an approach to understanding should also have emerged. And that's OK; that's the point.

Only approaching understanding? Yes. It seems to me that knowledge in humanistic discourse is always only asymptotic: it approaches a truth but never actually touches it. As the philosopher Frank Ramsey remarks, "meaning is mainly potential" (1); that is, the search for it opens up types of understanding that lead to new, often interesting questions, which then open outward to more questions, rather than answering them and shutting down discussion. We don't really ever discover "the" truth—"the the"—what or how a poem means, for example; there's no "Aha!" experience by which all aporias and perplexities of a work are suddenly resolved.

What you're doing consists of asking progressively more difficult, probing, pointed questions and not being satisfied with the answers you come up with. Finally, you will arrive at a question and at an answer that you know most people aren't going to accept, at least not initially, but it's one that you deeply believe, and you want to show how you arrived at it. That's your thesis. You develop this idea as you show your thought process. You know that what you write represents only a series of successive approximations of a truth. And after you've demonstrated that thought process—you've laid it out in the entire paper—your conclusion shows something novel. It's not so much that you've been unable to solve or answer all problems. Rather, the thesis, now that you've explored and explained it, opens up new areas of inquiry (if it's an argumentative thesis); it raises still more questions. In fact, one can start with a paper's conclusion and use that as a thesis (I recommend you try this, by the way) or use someone else's conclusion and develop that idea. By the end of a paper, you might rightly ask, looking at your own lines on the page, "What are you—banded one?" or maybe, "Are you alive?"

5 Developing an Argument

Most argumentative essays have a similar organization, which is often called a "structure" or "shape." While I don't want to straitjacket you with a fixed form, I do want to suggest that certain elements of the essay are essential:

1. Title
2. Introduction and thesis
3. Body
4. Conclusion

Most essays, that is, include a title; an introduction of some kind, which includes a thesis statement (or a "claim"); a "body" providing support for that thesis (examples, evidence, elaboration, classification, qualification, distinction, definition, division), as well as "con" arguments that the paper addresses in some way, either refuting them, dismissing them, or partially accepting some of them and incorporating them into the thesis; and a conclusion (what I have termed a Δ-Thesis). I want to emphasize here that argumentative essays have a tight interconnectedness: just as a sentence is not merely a heap of words, an essay isn't merely a piling up of elements. Just having the component parts is not sufficient. Working in unison, the separate parts are successful only insofar as they are part of a whole.

Another way of thinking about paper structure could be one that uses "thesis" in some form to describe each part. While this is atypical, let me present the idea at least provisionally. (Note that you need not include all of these elements. One or two of those with an asterisk might be omitted.)

Title	[pretextual-thesis]
Introduction	[Pre-Thesis]
Background information	[Arche-Thesis]
Thesis	
Support	[Sub-Thesis]
*Counterargument₁	[Counter-Thesis]
Support	[Sub-Thesis]
*Counterargument₂	[Counter-Sub-Thesis]
Summary of argument	[Syn-Thesis]
*Counterargument₃	[Counter-Syn-Thesis]
Support	[Sub-Thesis]
Conclusion	[Neo-Thesis]

You can probably see why this particular nomenclature has never caught on, but it does give an idea of the unifying, near-hegemonic power a thesis should have in a paper.

Individual Parts of the Essay

At the same time that you conceive of the paper as an entirety, you should consider the component parts of its argument: the title, the introduction, the body, and the conclusion.

Title

Your paper needs to be titled. The title should answer the question "What is this paper going to be about?" It should describe the paper's content. Make the title brief and descriptive. It should invite the reader in. It's more or less the pretext for the paper itself: it comes before the text (pre-text), and it's a pretext for the discussion and analysis in the paper proper. Try not to hide what the paper will discuss or analyze; try not to be obscure or punning or condescending.

The punning title, for example, of a paper on Henry David Thoreau's work *Walden*, "Thoreau-Up," is both too childish and too mocking: it does not suggest a serious or analytical essay is likely to follow. I don't think the writer has given us enough information to transform this into a good title, but here's an attempt: "The Lack of Economy in Thoreau's *Walden*"; "How Thoreau's Works Were Made Trite by 1960s Popular Culture"; or even something as simple as "How Is Thoreau Still Relevant?" In a similar vein, one of my fellow graduate students entitled his paper on Clifford Odets's 1935 play *Paradise Lost*, "*Paradise Lost*: A Loser," a title impressive only in its failure. A more effective title, one implying a more balanced, scholarly analysis, might be "Narrative Discontinuities in *Paradise Lost*." Another title (which I encountered in a graduate seminar on the works of Henry James), "Why Henry James Does Not Quite Cut It as a Novelist," also does not work, I feel, largely because of the dismissive tone it sets up, which places the reader (in this case, the professor who assigned the work by Henry James) on the defensive. "Does Not Cut It," I feel obliged to add, does not itself stylistically "cut it" as appropriate, formal English.

Remember that since the title is the first piece of information encountered, it not only gives the initial clue as to what the paper will be about, but also conveys your tone, that is, your relation to the subject matter. A good title should be informative, concise, and straightforward. In scholarly essays, it's best not to use a title that angers, offends, or assaults the reader—unless that is your intention and you are self-consciously writing a broadside, diatribe, or screed: not typical assignments. Strive more for *captatio benevolentiae*: self-consciously capturing the goodwill of the audience, getting them on your side before they have even read your paper.

Introduction, and the Thesis Therein

A tension exists between the title you have chosen and the first words of your essay. You have given your readers two new pieces of information, and they must process them both. Hence there should not be too great a disjunction between these two elements. Your introduction should probably expand on some of the ideas of the title, but most of all it must continue to invite the reader inside: it must be engaging and interesting. Some people call it a "hook"; this is a crass expression of the same idea. I would not recommend a long first sentence, for example, as that could be off-putting or confusing. An excellent first sentence comes from Scott Russell Sanders's essay on the lack of character development in science fiction, "Invisible Men and Women: The Disappearance of Character in Science Fiction": "Science fiction is the home of invisible men and women" (14). This more or less repeats the idea of his title, but it does so in an engaging and interesting manner. Notice, for example, the double entendre. The characters can be literally invisible, as in H. G. Well's *The Invisible Man*, or they can be "invisible" in the sense of unmemorable, flat, underdeveloped. Try to excite your readers' interest and imagination; give them credit for being smart and observant.

As you proceed into the introduction, keep in mind that it needs to continue presenting information to the reader, basic background material, such as the subject, topic, and thesis of your paper. The subject is usually the thing—book, poem, principle, idea—being analyzed; the topic is some aspect of the subject; the thesis is an argumentative "take" on the topic. For example, in a paper called "Public Secrets: Confession in *The Scarlet Letter*," your subject might be Nathaniel Hawthorne's novel *The Scarlet Letter*; your topic might be the public confession of sin in the novel; and your opening paragraph and thesis might be the following:

> Although Hawthorne's characters and narrator claim that the best way to live one's life is to confess openly to one's sins and shortcomings, the dramatic structure of the novel suggests that such a confession is not only impossible but also self-destructive and counterproductive. Those who confess, like Hester, are ostracized by society, and those who harbor secrets (the two male characters, Dimmesdale and Chillingworth) discover that doing so gives them power and effectuality. It is significant, too, that the male characters die before their time, while Hester lives a long, if lonely, life. Yet the novel implies that Hester has something of an afterlife: the embroidered "A" that she wore most of her life is still hot, electric to the touch almost, many years after her death. Divulge your worst secrets, and you can live forever.

Notice the complexity of this. And note, too, that you might not agree with it right away. Don't be afraid of the possibility of counterexamples. For example, your essay might acknowledge that Chillingworth is somewhat elderly, and decide whether he really does die "before his time." In addition, you might admit that Hester never really, fully "confesses," since she never names her child's father. "Confession," a thesis-driving term, will need to be parsed and unpacked in the course of the essay. In some ways, the thesis raises more questions than it answers—and this is a virtue for a thesis.

Here's another good thesis on the novel, by the late David Van Leer, who was an English professor at UC-Davis:

> Everywhere in the tales, the philosophical assumptions of Hawthorne's narrators are as important as the moral judgments they make. So, in *The Scarlet Letter*, a narration that at times seems indecisive—an intellectual cacophony—is itself part of the book's characterization of the problem. (57–58)

This is an imaginative look at the novel, taking something that might be construed as a negative feature of its art, something perhaps defective in the novel's composition, and suggesting that Hawthorne self-consciously built that in so as to increase his novel's impact.

In addition, your introduction needs to set up something of the context for your discussion. It needs to suggest why your topic or subject is really worth writing about. Is it something that has recently been in the public eye? Is it something controversial and potentially explosive? Is it something that automatically would interest any reader—and if so, in what way? You don't want your essays to be just dry academic exercises; instead, you want them to elicit recognition of their importance, immediacy, even drama. What brought you to write about this? And if there are many articles or essays about the same topic, what kinds of issues do they offer as the crucial ones that you will reconsider?

You need to set your ideas within a field of discourse and at the same time distinguish your own insight, angle, or interpretation from those that have preceded it. Yours is not a disembodied voice discussing some recondite issue that interests no one. No. Your voice has importance; your topic, immediacy. And your thesis about the topic will offer something new and controversial—or at least striking.

Most introductions are rewritten several times, in fact often after the rest of the essay has been finished. So while it's nice to draft a satisfying opening paragraph, you probably shouldn't spend a great deal of time on it in the first draft or two since you will return to it repeatedly. But in the end, you do ultimately need to get the introduction just right: it needs to be precisely composed and well balanced. Extra time spent on it will inevitably be well spent.

Body of Essay

Just as the human body—everything south of the head—is the bulk of a person, so too is the "body" the bulk of your paper. In this metaphor, the introduction is akin to a human head, and the thesis is sort of like the brain, which controls and directs the body.

But the metaphor breaks down, since in the body of your essay, you will attempt to prove your thesis, use evidence to support its controversial assertions, and deal with possible counterarguments. The body must actually present the evidence and do the arguing. Such evidence might include relevant facts that you have encountered in books or articles, quotations from the text that you might be analyzing, logical inferences of various kinds, or explanations of what you mean. Many writing courses use the following terminology: your thesis is a "*claim*," and to support your claim, you must provide in the paper various "*warrants*." More plainly, the idea is that you must do more than just assert: you must convince; you must persuade.

I think it's often useful to imagine an essay's body as being divided into sections. These can be titled separately, or they can remain untitled, with the essay smoothly flowing from one to another. Some of these sections will explain in detail what exactly you mean by certain words or concepts. It's important to explore terms that are politically charged, technical, or ambiguous, like "confession" in the example above. But it is up to you to figure out what terms are being used in ways that your audience might not grasp intuitively. In fact, many arguments hinge on just such definitions: an essay about abortion, if it defines human life as existing from the moment of conception, predetermines its argument: in this case, it's the very definition of key terms that must be argued for most strenuously. What, for example, constitutes human life? A fertilized egg? A fully formed fetus? A newborn child?

Evidence should appear in other sections of the body. This will typically be in the form of quotations or references from a variety of sources. Keep in mind that such presentation of evidence is done only to support and develop your thesis; it should not be offered as truth in and of itself or as proof of the author's immense erudition. Oftentimes students will suggest an idea and then quote an authority who, in print, says essentially the same thing. A strategy such as this does not prove your assertion to be true. Instead, it might suggest that you lack originality and invest complete credence in an external source.

A better strategy involves differentiating, if ever so slightly, your own position from that of the person you are quoting. (It probably will be different, but if you find that you cannot do this—that is, if someone already came up with the exact idea you have—you probably need to find a new idea or develop it in a different direction.) You should present evidence only insofar as it functions as part of your argument. Then your paper will evaluate and comment on that evidence in order to clarify and expand your own position. At the same time you need to realize that various positions "talk to" one another, and you want, in your essay, to both enable that conversation and be part it.

Keep in mind too, that certain details often will help you make your point. A vivid image will occasionally carry more weight by itself than the whole argument has. For example, labor attorney and law professor Bruce Fredrickson mentioned to me how powerful were a couple of images from the speeches at the 2016 Democratic National Convention. Bill Clinton gave a speech about his wife. Clinton was making the argument that his wife is a good person and would be a great president. But an image he used conveyed this as powerfully as anything else: when he and Hillary dropped Chelsea off at Stanford, where she was an entering first year student, Bill talks about how he remembers Hillary working the last minute, on her hands and knees, putting liner paper in the drawers of Chelsea's desk. Michelle Obama also used very powerful images. She described how on their first day of their school, the Obama children were taken off in security SUVs ("with big men with guns"), and she recalled seeing the children go, their worried faces pressed against the inside of the bulletproof glass windows. She wonders, "What have we done?" Like Bill Clinton's, Michelle Obama's imagery lingers powerfully, helping an audience remember the argument in some detail.

Extension of your thesis will also be a part of the body—possibly in titled sections. Your aim is not to elaborate on or give evidence for only a single idea but also to expand, complicate, and extend your thesis to cover other, related areas, ones that your reader might not have been able to predict. You want to surprise the reader. Going in slightly unexpected directions can keep your reader engaged with your ideas and at the same time can demonstrate, hone, and clarify your thesis. Throughout the essay, your thesis must grow and evolve, sometimes in ways that you yourself might not have been able to predict or anticipate. For example, in my essay on "The Pool" (pages 77–78) I came to a new idea when rewriting, namely the poem's anticipation of the Heisenberg Uncertainty Principle.

But at the same time the evolution represents a logical progression of thought. If you discuss, say, three books or essays, you don't want your discussion of each to repeat the same ideas or analytical pattern; rather, you want to arrange the paper so that each discussion builds on what went before. The points you make about the second text emerge from points you made about the first, and the points you make about the third text could not be made without the foundational analyses of the first two.

The topic sentence in each paragraph typically advances the thesis to a new stage. At the same time, the topic sentence must do the work of controlling the ideas of its own paragraph. Hence you should very carefully think about and clearly phrase your topic sentences. A reader should get a clear conception of your argument by reading the introduction, the topic sentence of each paragraph, and your conclusion. Such a schematic reading won't capture all the complexity of your argument, nor will it allow the reader to evaluate the evidence that you use, but it should provide a relatively complete notion of your paper's shape. And sometimes, the topic sentence of a paragraph might relate more directly to the preceding paragraph than to the thesis, but since the preceding paragraph is closely linked to the thesis, the overall organization will still make sense.

Development of an Argumentative Essay

I have been beleaguering students for decades with the idea of an argumentative thesis. But I'm aware that you probably don't really believe that a good argumentative thesis will "solve the problem" of producing a paper since you quite pragmatically see papers in quantitative terms. A thesis is one sentence, maybe two, which is easy enough to write; why all the hassle over just one sentence? What's more worrisome is filling up the following five or ten or however many pages. Thus I have been trying to adopt a two-pronged approach. I'm striving now to present development in such a way that it bolsters the idea of an argument, so that in fact you will be able to develop your essay if and only if you have an argument. Describing development in that particular way might, I'm hoping, nurture or even compel an argumentative approach.

Essay as Dialogue

Envisioning the entire paper as a kind of dialogue—as a series of provisional answers to imagined questions—might demonstrate the attractiveness and appeal of written argument. I want to use some foreign words to delineate this dialectical conception: *erotesis* and *prolepsis*. Specifically, I'm proposing that you propel your argument forward erotetically, by opening up a wide variety and a large number of questions of all kinds. Yet in order to rein in and organize this interrogative proliferation, you also need to employ forethought about what your audience is like. Specifically, I propose this forethought consist largely of prolepsis—anticipation—predicting what kind of questions, and even exactly what questions, might interest the audience.

I first encountered the term *erotesis*, hijacked from classical rhetoric, and used in what I think is probably an eccentric but nonetheless a valuable manner, in *The Philosophy of Horror, or Paradoxes of the Heart*, by the philosopher Noël Carroll. (Typically *erotesis* refers to questions that imply strong affirmation or denial [Lanham 46.]) Erotetic narrative, according to Carroll, is a staple of the frightening, engrossing, breathless horror story that most of us are familiar with. Such narratives, he suggests, use erotesis—namely, raising all kinds of questions as to what's going on, who's doing what, and what will happen next—in order to draw in the reader and make the narrative frightening, engrossing, and breathless. Carroll writes,

> Popular novels are often called "page-turners" in honor of the way they keep their readers obsessively entranced. As well, it is commonly thought that this is a function of the heavy emphasis that they place on narrative. The erotetic model of narration, applied to popular fictions, suggests ... the nature of the connection between the page-turning phenomenon and the kind of narration being employed in popular fiction: viz., the reader is turning pages to find out answers to the questions that have been saliently posed. (132)

Such a narrative asks questions for which the reader needs answers, and the reader does read on, must read on, is compelled to read on, will read on even if a bear were to appear at the campsite where the reader sits, engrossed—because the reader craves those answers.

But in some sense the questions do depend—even in Carroll's model—on a certain kind of audience, an audience sensitive to the questions being raised. While erotesis moves the narrative forward, prolepsis or anticipation places limits on the erotesis such that the audience's point of view, interests, and predilections are taken into account. It's an interactive dialectic in horror stories, but Carroll has also suggested that erotesis and prolepsis drive many popular television shows and movies. And I think the two concepts at once complicate and clarify what we mean by development of an academic essay.

The Example-Supportable Assertion

Such advice markedly varies from standard advice, which might be that after presenting a thesis, a paper should probably clarify what that thesis means, following up with examples of the claim put forth. I'm not suggesting that this structure is entirely wrong-headed. One does want to make a claim of some sort and then back up that claim. This claim needs evidence of some kind—some support, some examples—which makes up the bulk of the paper's body.

But a problem emerges with the suggestion that only "examples" can prove or support a thesis, because examples can be used to support a pseudo-thesis as well as a genuinely argumentative thesis. Thus many writers, using examples to support their pseudo-theses, automatically think they are doing the right thing. In fact, examples often provide a great deal of (the wrong kind of) comfort: examples nicely fill up pages. I'm not suggesting that we throw out the idea of the "example," which is obviously a staple of scholarship, something we use all the time in our writing: I'm using examples here; this whole section is an example. Rather, the example can be dangerous to rely on as the primary or sole method of development of a thesis or, especially, as the only principle behind development. You can too easily think that if you can find examples of what you mean, you have done enough. In fact, generalizations for which examples can be readily found are frequently boring and simplistic, while generalizations of greater value are often ones for which examples are not immediately, readily available.

It might just be that example-supportable assertions are not necessarily the right place to begin. Example-supportable assertions, I'm suggesting, tend to be too easy and tend to invite summary. But on the other hand, assertions that are not example-supportable might seem too airy, too unsubstantiated or inferential, to be really grasped. So we can't abandon the idea of the example altogether. But it seems to me that to get you to make the startling or insightful inference, I need to show you that you must do more than merely give examples of what you mean.

The Development of Your Essay

Let's look in more detail at what erotesis and prolepsis can provide in addition to (or in place of) the example-supportable assertion. An erotesis generator and a prolepsis sensor, taken together, might be said to constitute a kind of demon—a heuristic similar to Maxwell's Demon, which James Clerk Maxwell (in a markedly different context) proposed as being able to group fast-moving molecules on one side of a dual-chambered vessel and slow-moving ones on the other (hence apparently refuting the second law of thermodynamics). Out of a sense of good taste I propose that we *not* call our demon "Cioffi's Demon." Instead, substituting the everyday terms "question" for "erotesis" and "anticipation" for "prolepsis," I suggest that an ever-questioning, anticipation-sensing demon might be useful. If you want to give it a name, call it the "Development Demon." Like Maxwell's Demon, this entity also has two major roles: (1) imagining manifold, multifarious questions; and (2) anticipating what the audience would conceive of as useful questions.

Using this Development Demon might help show you how your writing must do more than just reflect and chart your interpretation, thoughts, insights, ideas, or the like. Besides doing these things, your papers must also take, in some real sense, a second essayistic journey: you must also subject your thesis to the machinations of the Demon, namely, to constant questioning of all kinds, and to a parallel conscious anticipation of an imagined audience response, in order to see not only how much of the thesis survives the ordeal but also how it changes—develops, deforms, enlarges—as it's subjected to this intense interrogation.

This Demon, I should point out, is an androgynous entity. I am reminded of Virginia Woolf's somewhat aphoristic statement in *A Room of One's Own*: "Some collaboration has to take place in the mind between the woman and the man before the art of creation can be accomplished. Some marriage of opposites has to be consummated" (136). The Demon, then, must be something that does not take a position either exclusively male or exclusively female. Its questionings, its forecastings, must come from an as-if-sexless, as-if-two-gendered, entity. Its ever-questioning stance must "embrace multitudes," as Walt Whitman put it in his famous poem.

Of course academic papers are supposed to be not just posing questions but asserting things. True enough. But I want to persuade you that if your assertions are not calibrated to an audience's interests and wonderings, readers tend to perceive them as irrelevant or obvious. Yet if you carefully attune your assertions to what you expect your audience is interested in, then suddenly those ideas become suffused with importance and significance.

An essay composed as I'm suggesting would not have to reproduce the actual questions—these would remain tacit—but it would answer them as if they were being asked by an imagined, an inferred audience: the audience anticipated by the Development Demon. A version of the "reader over your shoulder," to use the title of a book by Robert Graves and Alan Hodge, this entity functions as an invisible and slightly prickly but relatively willing-to-be-persuaded interlocutor. It isn't out to hurt your feelings or belittle or demean you; it aims, rather, to help you discover something akin to truth. This entity really wants to know something about the topic or subject, is a being driven purely by curiosity, by a craving for *ideas*. It is this entity's questions and anticipations and the writer's answers to them that drive the paper forward. In some way the Development Demon is an ideal version of the professor reading the paper, but in fact it should form part of your consciousness, should be an imaginative projection that guides you as writer through the composing process.

What Kinds of Questions?

A large question, typically unspoken, precedes a thesis. I want to call this a "macro-question," a term coined by Noël Carroll, "a means for organizing whole narratives" (135). This is the big question that really produces the whole paper. Wayne Booth calls this a "problem"; Gordon Harvey, a "motive." In any event, it resembles the question in a reader's mind after the first page of a whodunit. Who, exactly, has done it? In a horror story, What is the monster like? Or, more urgently, How do we stop it? How can we get away? The need to find out the answer gives velocity to a narrative that follows. Again, Carroll's ideas apply to narrative and not specifically to the expository, argumentative essay. But I think we might present the argument essay as a kind of narrative, for in some sense it is a narrative of a thought process, of a kind of verbal jousting with a perceived but often largely inferred, imagined audience.

How do we come up with the macro-question? What activity should you engage in before formulating it? There are a variety of options when the subject is literature, and the process would vary somewhat in the case of an argument about a political issue or a historical event. But in terms of textual analysis papers, I suggest that before writing at all, you try to generate a wide variety of other questions, opening gambits—ones somewhat similar to the "discussion questions" teachers sometimes prepare for a seminar or class. These typically look for areas of confusion, dissonance, bafflement, perplexity—for things about the text or the reading experience that are enigmatic and worth exploring. Do any details of the text-world fail to make sense? Are there any striking changes in characters' personalities—especially between the beginning and the end of the work? Are there areas of especial intensity in the story, places where the author seems to be working especially hard, or stepping out of one voice into another? Are various themes of the work handled in an odd or interesting, a provocative or controversial manner? What does the work seem to be suggesting about them? Are there curious or startling patterns—of imagery, event/action, or language use, for example? And finally, though I know this cannot be an exhaustive list, how does the work make you, the reader, feel? Do you have any strong emotions in response to it, or especially any conflicting emotions? Why so? Can they be connected to something within the text?

These opening-gambit questions can even be contextual: Why was this text assigned? Were you in a particularly bad or good mood when you read it? What in the world could (insert the name of a person—professor, friend, relative, reviewer) see in this? I don't recommend that you mechanically go through this list one question at a time, but rather that you use it as a way to open up possibilities about the issue or text, identify questions that might help you formulate a macro-question, and, perhaps most importantly, figure out just what you really feel about a work, how you have internalized it, what you think is "going on" in it—what questions it leaves unanswered, evocative; what lingers with you like a pleasant aftertaste or, for that matter, a noxious eluate or residue.

From your opening-gambit questions you should choose a macro-question, or create one that's a composite, perhaps, of several questions, an activity that the Development Demon should assist you in. What's the audience like? What might interest them? What is really "new" here, really "original"? What might be worthwhile and interesting to explore in a whole paper? Admittedly, there's a bit of magic here—well, I've already invoked a magical entity—and we have to concede that the writer's experience helps make the Demon more capable of making a good judgment. But in general, a viable macro-question has to be one that compels the interest and enthusiasm of both the writer and the inferred audience. And it's probably best to generate a lot of opening questions, ones of all stripes, all shapes, all sizes. Some of the thought behind these questions might go into the introduction. But the most important questions generated will function as or help make up the macro-question, which would then be answered, at least provisionally, by the thesis.

A macro-question has the effect of not only providing impetus for the thesis but also subsuming the whole argument—it does this by sparking still more questions—what Carroll calls "micro-questions." "Micro-questions," Carroll suggests, "organize the small-scale events of the plot, even as they carry forward the macro-question in the story" (136). In the case of academic argument essays, I think these micro-questions fall into four major categories. First, they call for clarification: What do you mean? (in my idiolect, "Huh?"). Second, they can call for development, contextualizing ("And—?"), or even, *though not exclusively*, examples ("F'r'nstance?"). Third, they can ask why something is significant or important ("So?"). Finally, the micro-question can be an actual objection to some stage of an argument ("What?" or "What about *x*?").

To a certain extent, some micro-questions are always available for the writer of an argumentative essay. Such micro-questions might well achieve the status of macro-question, though this is something you might have to decide only after you have done quite a bit of writing. The extent to which you use these will vary, depending on the way that you have assessed your audience's interests and background, but here are the standard ones:

1. What is the background on the issue under scrutiny? Typically this micro-question will be posed (tacitly) and answered toward the beginning of the essay. Background might be necessary for the reader unfamiliar with the issue discussed.
2. Why does this issue have importance? Again, this would be an early micro-question, though it might also appear throughout the essay. As your argument develops, new aspects of an issue emerge. And these details could well have an importance that the reader would not have been sensitive to or aware of at the opening of the essay.
3. What is the definition of your major, thesis-driving concepts? Are they sufficiently precise and well defined?
4. Is the evidence you are using interpretable in other ways? Can it be used as evidence for alternative, competing thesis statements?
5. What are some positions that others have taken, or solutions that others have offered? Typically, this kind of micro-question is posed and explored in a research paper. If no research is necessary, however, the writer might pose hypothetical other positions, and this leads to perhaps the most important micro-question, namely . . .
6. What arguments might be deployed against yours?

Here, then, are some micro-questions that might help develop the thesis about H.D.'s "The Pool," which I advanced in Chapter 4: **This wild proliferation of possible readings should be set aside, I propose, in favor of one that might subsume them all: the poem is about the interpretive act itself, the cerebral activity of trying to understand something, maybe even something as banal as a pool of water.**

- Questions about context: For example, one might look at biographical material to see if H.D. had some specific metaphor in mind when she wrote this poem; this information might seriously undermine the thesis—or it could support it. Was she in the midst of a love affair when she wrote it? Had she just experienced some great grief? Did she know anything about particle physics and the work people were doing in the field? Seems unlikely, but some research would be helpful here. H.D.'s biography won't be the ultimate determiner of meaning, of course, but knowing something about the poet will help us gain a fuller understanding of her sensibility and her concerns. H.D.'s other poems, and poems by other "imagists" writing about the same time, might also help flesh out an understanding of "The Pool."

  What about social context? The poem appeared in March of 1915. To what extent is this a poem about war? Is it perhaps the poet's way of talking about World War I, which was raging at the time of composition?

  What do other literary critics have to say about this poem? Do you agree or disagree with what's written?

- Questions about the consciousness of the poem's lyrical ego or speaker: Note that this need not be the same as H.D. the poet. Why is this poem in the second person, if it's about interpretation? How can the lyrical ego know words like "quiver" and "sea-fish" but not know whether a pool could be considered "alive"? Maybe "alive" has some kind of special meaning here? In fact, is this supposed to be an average person speaking, an everyman/everywoman figure, or is the poem's speaker neurotic, psychotic, or brain damaged (someone who doesn't know if a pool is alive, for example)? If the speaker is supposed to be mentally or psychologically challenged, then any picture of his or her interpretive act would be atypical.

- Questions that challenge the adequacy or viability of the thesis: For another interesting con argument, one might simply ask, "Isn't this poem really more about ensnaring and capturing ('I cover you with my net') than it is about interpretation? Or is it suggesting that capturing/ensnaring and interpretation are on some level similar activities? Do we ensnare things in order to interpret them? Does interpreting things make them alive or only give them the semblance, the superficial appearance, of life?"

- Questions that might clarify or enhance the thesis: What does this thesis imply, finally? If the poem is about interpretation and the relative impossibility thereof, is it suggesting that we not ever engage in that activity? Do we inevitably only infect the examined thing with our own ideas and actions and thus distort its essence? Seems a sort of negative view of a basic human action, doesn't it? And does the speaker really make any headway in her or his understanding of the pool? Is there any evolution or advance from "Are you alive?" to "What are you—banded one?"

- On a related topic, here is a specific question: is the "wonder" that the poem evinces ultimately convincing? Or does it seem sort of manufactured? If one wonders, the way the speaker does, about something as everyday as a pool, how does that person deal with somewhat more complex issues and situations, like having relationships with other human beings? Maybe we need a different word from "wonder"—maybe it's a poem about the temporary assumption of a totally innocent perspective.

- Finally, it's often revelatory to look at the original publication of an older work. Does it contain anything that differs from the current text? If so, then the writer has revised, and usually that will provide some insight into what she was attempting and will affect our understanding. For example, I was very surprised when I looked at the original publication (in *Poetry* magazine, 1915). The second line is not "I touch you," but "I touch you with my thumb." Subsequent printings have omitted the final prepositional phrase. Why so? What did H.D. think was "wrong" or misleading about it? And does the thumb refer to the thumb of the hand, or perhaps the thumb of the foot, namely the big toe? (I got this idea from a student, Justin Broomfield, and his idea is corroborated by the *Oxford English Dictionary*, which lists "big toe" as one definition of "thumb.")

The Counterargument; Infeeling

Generated by the Development Demon in its crankiest incarnation, this last micro-question—audience objection—genuinely drives forward a paper's development. Strong objections— commonly called counterarguments—must be raised and dealt with. John Stuart Mill discusses this notion in *On Liberty* (1859), and he is worth quoting at length. Mill contends that

> when we turn to subjects infinitely more complicated, to morals, religion, politics, social relations, and the business of life, three-fourths of the arguments for every disputed opinion consist in dispelling the appearances which favor some opinion different from it. The greatest orator, save one, of antiquity, has left it on record that he always studied his adversary's case with as great, if not with still greater, intensity than even his own. (35)

Mill claims here that 75 percent of an argued opinion should deal with counterarguments, but typically in my classes, despite my emphasis on the counterargument, the papers submitted rarely spend more than a paragraph on the counterargument— and when even that much is included, it's a rarity.

Why is the counterargument such an alien concept? Students ask me all the time, "Why bring up arguments against your own?" Or "Isn't bringing up these arguments just going to be prejudiced anyway?" a question that I think means something like, "Isn't inventing counterarguments a false contrivance, since you are bringing them up only to show they're weak?" If you have presented the paper's development, though, as emerging through erotesis and prolepsis, some of these objections can be easily headed off. You have anticipated what the audience needs by way of explanation, elaboration, and significance, and you have also anticipated what kinds of objections they might raise. Alternative explanations, possible objections from an inferred audience, are welcome, not necessarily hostile, since looking at them might help you further interrogate the issue raised by the argumentative thesis.

But you need more than to merely "look at" counterarguments or give them a passing nod. You need to engage them in a deep and serious manner. Mill says of the writer:

> Nor is it enough that he should hear the arguments of adversaries from his own teachers, presented as they state them, and accompanied by what they offer as refutations. That is not the way to do justice to the arguments or bring them into real contact with his own mind. He must be able to hear them from persons who actually believe them, who defend them in earnest and do their very utmost for them. He must know them in their most plausible and persuasive form; he must feel the whole force of the difficulty which the true view of the subject has to encounter and dispose of, else he will never really possess himself of the portion of truth which meets and removes the difficulty. (35)

I suggest that the way you "know them in their most plausible and persuasive form" is to empathize with your opposition, even attempting perhaps to inhabit its consciousness. This mental-emotional extension of self also informs (though to a lesser degree) the conception of audience throughout the whole paper. I had first thought to describe this by using the German word *Einfühlung*, which was translated as "empathy" after Theodore Lipps and others proposed using it in reference to aesthetic and philosophical issues in the late nineteenth century. But *Einfühlung* carries some contradictory or mismatched philosophical baggage (Chismar). Let me introduce a word that seems to convey better what I mean, and that might be a more adequate translation of *Einfühlung*: "infeeling." I think this is the concept I am trying to get across—you have to strive for infeeling your opponents' positions, trying to experience and to an extent even inhabit those positions.

The advantage of "infeeling" over "empathy" is that with "infeeling" there exists a possibility that the writer will in fact turn around and side with the opposition, will take some material, some perspective, some insight, some ideology from the "other side." With empathy, there's always a sharp split between the me and the "other": one puts oneself in another's shoes, but only temporarily, only contemplatively. Like empathy, infeeling requires an extension of self, but unlike empathy, this extension of self can result in a modification of self, or at least of one's ideas. Infeeling is bidirectional, is done not just for comprehension of another's state or position, but for the purpose of allowing that state or position to influence, undermine, even resituate one's own.

What if no actual opposition exists? In this case, you either lack an argumentative thesis, or you need to invent, to imagine, an opposition. As Mill remarks, "So essential is this discipline to a real understanding of moral and human subjects that, if opponents of all-important truths do not exist, it is indispensable to imagine them and supply them with the strongest arguments which the most skillful devil's advocate can conjure up" (36). Through the work of the Development Demon—an interrogative, anticipatory mode of thought—as well as through the act of infeeling with a perceived (or actual) opposition, you should, over the course of the essay, arrive at a new idea, one that represents an evolution of the thesis, a three-dimensionalization of its initial form. More than just making explicit what the paper has implied, the conclusion enables you to ask a macro-question about that newly explicit notion. It is a widening outward—a familiar idea—but it is also a kind of "second thesis," a conclusion, to the paper: one animated by the Development Demon's metaphoric stretching of the original.

Looking closely and infeelingly at the opposition not only complicates the argument, allowing for a conclusion that advances the original thesis, but also lends credibility to the writer's ethos, which appears the more trustworthy for its willingness to address opposing viewpoints, its readiness to abandon apparently adamantine positions, its willingness to negotiate multiple truths. Such a rhetorical strategy helps differentiate the idea of academic argument from ugly dispute or verbal altercation: indeed, you can't infeel with a person you're arguing with or about to punch in the jaw—or who you fear is about to unload a haymaker on you.

6 The Research-Based Argument in the Digital Age

A research paper, long a staple of writing courses, is only a beefed-up, fortified, as-if-on-steroids version of the argumentative essay as I have been defining it here. You need to keep this in mind as you do research and write this paper. The most important thing about it isn't how many articles, websites, or books you consult. It's not the form of your references or works cited. It's not how long it is. These are certainly significant surface features, but no matter how much research you do, no matter how many references you include, you need to harness this work to the task of helping you make your argument. If you don't do this, you risk submitting not a research paper but a data dump. The most important thing about your paper is simply you, your ideas, your argument, your "take" on the research about a given topic.

Furthermore, I want to propose (realizing all the while that you are going to be slightly skeptical) that writing a research paper can be valuable in and of itself—that is, by virtue of its own merits—because it will help you discover things about the world, the culture, and yourself. As an undergraduate, I had several research paper assignments, and now, decades later, I can still remember the topics I wrote about, some of the sources I used, and some of the insights I gained. Herbert Aptheker, a famous historian who wrote about slavery in the United States, provided me with much to think about regarding the U.S. slave system. And when I read about riots and revolts in other countries, or about social unrest in our own country, I think of one of my professors, Ted Robert Gurr, and his "theory of relative deprivation," which I applied to an analysis of slave revolts in the United States and ancient Rome. When I was doing research for and composing that paper, I remember thinking, "No one has ever seen this before; no one has ever made these connections," and that insight was empowering, maybe even intoxicating.

Specifically, what happens to you as you do research papers? I'd like to focus on one psychological transformation that typically takes place: you become a splitter rather than a lumper. A splitter makes fine distinctions, classifies things with great care into many differing categories, and sharpens differences rather than smoothing them out. By contrast, a lumper levels differences and sees only similarities. A lumper might see a wristwatch and say, "It's just a wristwatch," while a splitter might say, "It's an Audemars-Piguet tourbillion minute repeater—in platinum." Of course, you might say, what's the difference? In this case the difference is significant. According to Statisticbrain.com, an average Swiss wristwatch costs $739, while the Audemars-Piguet would run you about a quarter of a million. So the difference is $249,261, to be exact. Plus tax. But you wouldn't know this until—until when? Until you'd done some research, until you became "inward with the material." I have noticed that people are almost always splitters with respect to the things they really like. And the material in your course—well, you can be certain that's something about which your professor is a splitter extraordinaire.

Invention and Research

Let me outline the basic pattern of a research paper. First, you will need to find a topic. Usually, you'll be writing within a given subject area or field—the one specified by your course, that is—which should help define your options. Check with your professor, and reread several times the description of what you have to do for your paper, since you don't want to invest a lot of time doing the "wrong" thing. You might not really know what you want to write about. But that's OK. Part of the initial writing process involves discovering what's sufficiently interesting to you, and what has already been written on a given issue or problem.

That brings me to the next issue. Your motivation for writing the paper should probably revolve around solving a problem—answering a macro-question—of some kind. I have mentioned above that "dissonance" often forms the impetus for a paper; similarly, when you do a research paper, you need to find something to talk about that's not been resolved or settled or talked to death. This problem needs to relate to the course, and, more explicitly, to the assignment.

In a way, this is the most interesting part of the research paper, because during this initial phase, you can basically read all sorts of material, even that which is only tangentially relevant to your topic. This is also the time for revisiting the course texts; going to Google, Bing, DuckDuckGo, and other search engines to see what range of materials the Internet has to offer; exploring the library's resources; talking with other students about their topics; and consulting with your professor and with librarians about possibilities for your research.

At this stage it is useful to gather and put in computer files (or if you prefer the old- fashioned way, to photocopy or print out) all the potentially useful sources you consult. Typically, after photocopying an article (or a book section), I used to staple it into a manila folder, making sure to include a photocopy of the title page or pages that include the source's bibliographic information (author, title, journal or publisher, date, volume). I then annotated these sources directly on the pages themselves, either using a highlighter or just underlining with a pen. This annotating stage, however, can be replicated using computer files: on Adobe Reader or Acrobat, you can use the highlighting or notes functions on the Comment menu to make notes on the electronic versions of articles. And having them all easily available for you on your computer or device is extremely valuable. I think you also might take advantage of a program like EasyBib. com, which will format your bibliography or works cited for you in exactly the style and format that your discipline requires.

I do not recommend that you copy quotations out onto note cards. You might have been taught in previous courses or in high school that note card use was the preferred way to keep track of information during the research process, but photocopying is cheap and readily available now, and the Internet has made accessible much material that is easily printable or storable. Many libraries and offices now have photocopy machines that will copy to a pdf, which you can than download and convert to Word, if you want. The fact is that if you use note cards to record material from sources (via direct quotation), there is the chance that you will mistranscribe it, be unable to read your handwriting, or—worse—think that the words you have written out are your own. (Several scholars have been accused, in widely publicized cases, of using others' words as their own. It seems to me most likely that they simply misread their own notes.) Using photocopied or downloaded sources keeps it clear whose words are whose. If you are wedded to the use of note cards to organize your research materials, you might just photocopy material and then paste that onto the note cards. The less longhand copying that you do, the better.

At this stage, too, as you search around on the Internet, you need to determine which on-line sources are credible and sound, and which are not. Here is a quick series of guidelines that I use. The first four concern "provenance," that is, where the site originated—and hence ask the questions "Who has created this site and what is its purpose?"; the next five have more to do with the content and organization of the site itself:

1. In general, you need to figure out the contextual information which, quite clear when you are dealing with hard-copy resources, often fails to appear on web pages. When you pick up a book, you can easily determine the author, title, publisher, and date of publication. You have a sense of the book's seriousness of purpose by its use of a bibliography, an index, and references. You might have a biographical blurb about the author, or even snippets of quotations from reviews of the book. All of these factors suggest to you the level of a book's seriousness, and the degree to which it can be trusted

as a source. With web pages, a little more detective work is often required.

2. In examining websites, first figure out if there is an author. That is, do you know who has put the site together? If not, this is a bad sign, though it does not necessarily mean that you should discard the information from the site. You need to be careful, though, how much credence you place in it. If an author's name does appear, put that name into a search engine to find out about him or her or them. Does she or he have a Wikipedia page? A website?

3. Is this author connected with any institution of higher learning, a governmental agency, a church-related organization, or a business of some kind? If academically or governmentally connected, the website has potential for being good material. Some academic websites are promotional in nature, though, so be careful when using these for information. If the site is connected to a church or a business, the likelihood of its being good is somewhat lessened. Sources that were once print-only have now moved online, but they are likely to have the same criteria for academic honesty and completeness that they had when they existed in their print-only format, so they can still be trusted. Some businesses have academic integrity, though: the sites of major corporations tend to be reliable if inevitably somewhat tendentious. Church-related sites can also be helpful (e.g., the Mormon church is very helpful with genealogy), but again, you need to attempt to evaluate them using some other (internal) criteria before automatically accepting what they are offering.

4. Remember, under a 2017 law, internet service providers may now legally collect and sell any data about your internet use.

5. What is the language of the site like? Are the words correctly spelled? Does the site use appropriate, fundamentally accurate grammar, spelling, punctuation? If not, the site's credibility suffers, to my mind. I would still scan through the site, however; a few spelling and usage errors do not necessarily constitute a fatal flaw. (However, be forewarned. I've noticed that on eBay, for example, those product descriptions that are most ill-spelled, ill-conceived, and illiterate have provided me

with the most problems as a buyer. Admittedly that is anecdotal evidence, but it also strikes me as powerful. I know this is an ad hominem argument [see Chapter 12], but sometimes ad hominem arguments are logically sound.)

6. Does the site seem to be current in its allusions, research materials, and the like? Often sites will remain for years on the web but will never be updated or revised.

7. Are there "pop-ups" of any kind? These diminish a site's seriousness, I think, since the site is being used to generate income; still, it may be a solid reference tool. You also might check to see whether the site has implanted any "cookies" into your hard drive—a bad sign, if it has, since this suggests a commercial motivation for the site. Often sites will warn you that they use cookies. I appreciate the full disclosure.

8. What banner ads appear on the site? These will tip you off somewhat to the kind of site you're visiting. The site's links are helpful in enabling you to figure out its value. And sometimes in fact the links will be more valuable than the site itself. Then, too, if you have advertisements that tout an end to wrinkles, a simple solution for impotence, or a way to lose forty pounds in a month—well, you get the idea. The examples are almost literally endless, but the wilder the claims made by the site, the more likely that site is a sham.

   If there is any pornography on the site, or any links to same, you should probably be cautious about using that site as a credible reference tool. If you are asked to provide your credit card number in order to access information on a site, do not do so: there's a good chance the information you want will be available elsewhere, free. You will need to go beyond the first screen or two or any Google search you do, but a lot of material is available, and often it's only a matter of looking harder for it to locate what you need.

9. Finally, although the site may be only a popularized account of an issue you are seriously exploring, or though it may be principally a vehicle for selling something, don't completely dismiss it. The Webster's Dictionary site has a lot of clickbait in its margins, but it offers excellent definitions.

10. Try to look at a variety of sites; don't rely on just one or two.

Web-based searches are easy ("Google it!"), but the real key to discovering good material is using the databases available at your library. For most topics, these are more valuable than the web, because they contain not only online material but also material that is not (yet) available on-line. More importantly, they have organized the data in accessible ways. It is available, at present, only to institutions or individuals who subscribe to a given database. The companies putting together such databases (ProQuest, Lexis-Nexis, Medline, Ebsco, MLA International Bibliography, etc.) have hired people to scan an amazing variety of articles from books, magazines, newspapers, and other periodicals; these are available (in full-text or abstract-only format) to subscribers only. Most students, therefore, have access—via their university or college computer terminal—to a whole additional virtual library of information, which is almost always superior to the material available via Google and the Internet: its provenance is clear and its authoritativeness as easy to verify as that of the hard-copy publication that the database reproduces or sends you to.

You will probably end up using databases to locate hard-copy material, such as journals and magazines (and books). Of course, you can also use the catalog in your library (typically available on-line, now). These computer/web-based resources will lead you to the old-fashioned books, newspapers, and magazines, whose provenance is easily discoverable. Some teachers will in fact require that a sizable proportion of your sources be hard-copy materials.

Often, you'll find there's just an enormous amount of material on the subject you've chosen. Some students take this as a positive sign, choose five or six sources at random, and go from there. You should see this surplus of information as a sign that a subject or topic is too broad. How can you narrow it down? Is there some subtopic that you might look at? You need to become more of a splitter here, if for no other reason than that you have to divide up the lump of material you've located.

Here are six ways to narrow down a topic:

1. Subdivide its content. If you are looking at, say, euthanasia, break it down into euthanasia for terminally ill infants (thus

not having to deal with euthanasia for adults or animals, for example).

2. Subdivide by geographical scope. Look at euthanasia for terminally ill infants in Western Europe, say.
3. Narrow the time span. Look at what happened in just the last decade, or by contrast during the 1930s.
4. Narrow by kinds of author. Look just at articles by medical doctors, perhaps, or just at accounts by parents of terminally ill infants.
5. Narrow by kind of source. You might look only at those articles that are not in mass circulation newspapers or periodicals, that is, only at articles in journals or in published books.
6. Narrow by language: you might choose to look only at English-language sources.

Yet keep in mind that even as you narrow your topic, you don't have to ignore material that could function as an overview. You should read some of this as well, since it will help you make better sense of the subtopic, as well as the entire area of research that you are exploring.

Fake News in the Post-truth Era

Doing research now, though, we confront a significant problem: We have entered an era of "fake news," that is, material which is flat-out untrue, and which most people know is untrue, but which is being presented as if it were the actual honest-to-God truth. So you need to make sure you are not being "taken in" by a site. How do you know this? The trouble is that most of this fake news has some element of truth to it, some connection with what might be possible, if not plausible. That connection is what keeps you guessing, or at least keeps you reading on. But here are some ways to determine if you should credit what you're reading:

1. Tip-off opening phrases: "In a surprising recent reversal ...," "Amazingly ...," "Defying all predictions and odds ...," "Contrary to all expectations...." Admittedly some news can

be genuine even following such hooks as these tip-offs. ("Defying all odds, Donald Trump has won the presidency," for example, is actually a true statement.)

2. Obviously counterfactual claims. If a putative news article claims to have discovered a perpetual motion machine, it's probably a put-on. If it claims that by "playing" the furniture in a room, one can recover all the sounds that the furniture was witness to, that's probably made up. If it claims to have used computer techniques to highlight the Zapruder film of President John F. Kennedy's assassination and discover three men in the background, wielding rifles, that's not to be trusted.

3. Any calls for unusual forms of payment are suspect. Sometimes you will have to pay to look at an article on-line, and that's a piece of genuine information you are purchasing. But what if the site asks you to pay in bitcoin or in iTunes gift cards? (Some do. I'm not making this up.) In general, you probably should not have to make any payments for the information you are gathering, aside from the cost of your computer and its connection.

4. If the "news" or information on offer seems on the face of it somewhat astonishing (see 2, above), you need to confirm its veracity by looking at other sources. Usually real news is picked up by multiple news sites, and those sites are not just sharing the same wording and information; they each should have their own spin on the events described.

5. Humor. A lot of times what fake news reports have going for them is that they are somewhat funny and ridiculous. Most news is not.

6. Source. Are you reading this news on your "news feed" from Twitter or Facebook or some other social media site? Is what you are reading just another piece of click-bait?

It has become increasingly difficult to sort the actual from the fake. But I think that you can train yourself to be able to make the discrimination. One problem is that oftentimes readers cannot recognize satire or irony. Unfortunately, not all fake news is satire. Some is constructed to resemble the real, and succeeds in hoodwinking many readers. You want to be able to sort fact from fiction, real news from "fake news," truth from what's become known as "post-truth." That is to say, you need to get a bead on things as they actually are, rather than be taken in by attempts to confuse or deceive you. Trying to sort through an increasingly complex maze of information, information that is instantly and readily available to us on our phones, our computers, our tablets, our television and radio is more and more difficult.

What, then, are we to do when writing research papers? We are trying to find out the actual truth, I should add, not "post-truth," not "fake facts." How do we know which sources are real and which fake?

I think that the key here is verifiability. If you read something that appears on-line, and it seems to you somewhat shocking or labels itself as "strange but true," or even as "earth-shattering," it could well be true. These things happen sometimes. But you need to be skeptical. "A wise skepticism is the first attribute of a good critic," as James Russell Lowell memorably declared. You need to be skeptical. This is the opposite of gullible.

Many groups prey on the gullibility of the general public. These groups know that there is a hard core of people who will believe the most ridiculous nonsense in the world, so they don't have to worry about that group. That group is on their side. Then there is also a segment of the population who, with Lowell, remain skeptical about all kinds of things. They don't buy into the latest conspiracy theory, fad, fraud, or outrageous claim. They look for verification. The fake news fomenters don't usually target that group; since it's small and impervious to the fake claims, there's no need to bother with them. But you want to be in that group, a group that one hopes will get larger and larger. You want to be perpetually skeptical, so that when people make claims such as that the Twin Towers were actually destroyed by the U.S. government, that vaccination is actually a way of infecting a large segment of the population, that the Kennedy assassination was engineered by the CIA—these and myriad other claims that we come across almost every week—you don't just accept them because they prove, upon investigation, to be completely unfounded in any consensus-based reality.

Why would anyone believe them, then, you might ask. Well, in addition to the two groups I mention above, the gullible and the skeptical, there is a large segment of the population that is neither. This group has some suspicions about what things are genuine and what fake, and they have worries about how the world seems to be taking shape around them. For many of these people, fake news serves as a way to confirm their worries, fears, and suspicions: sometimes these wacky theories will articulate and thus give solid form to various anxieties and hunches. People in this group will then desperately grasp such theories, since they reify or make real subarticulate thoughts and feelings. Sometimes gullible, sometimes skeptical, people in this group are the ones that the fake news fomenters want to capture—sometimes they will be taken in, and they will believe in things that have no basis whatsoever in factuality.

So what is a researcher to do? You need to verify information that you get from the web. You need to find reputable sources. You need to be skeptical, especially of wild claims, of conspiracy theories, and of explanations that explain everything. After he was apprehended, Edgar Welch, who attacked a pizzeria in Washington, D.C., where he believed that children were being held hostage, told a *New York Times* reporter, "The intel on this wasn't 100 percent" (Goldman). He probably should have done a bit more research before he drove 350 miles to rescue the supposed hostages. You need to get good "intel."

Discovery

As you read, annotate, and sort through the material you've gathered, look for some patterns: how do the various writers present the background, facts, issues, flashpoints, and their own positions? You are trying to get an overview of the issue or topic, and even though you will have narrowed your topic down somewhat by this point, you will probably not have decided what you want to say. Don't push yourself yet to take a position. You are scanning what's out there; it's as if you are trying on for size various positions and perspectives and ideas. As you read and gather information, you will notice that your ideas become more complex as well as more informed.

Often, students will become very distressed at this stage of their research; they feel overwhelmed by the material and don't think there is enough time in the world for them to really understand the whole range of opinions and positions on a given topic. Everyone feels this at some point. Don't despair. You need not read every word of every article that you come across. In fact, you should really limit yourself to ascertaining the thesis statements—the main ideas—of the material that you encounter. In these initial stages, read broadly but selectively (in a wide range of materials but only portions of each), rather than in a focused or comprehensive way. Get a sense of where the authors come down on a given issue, but don't try to capture or understand all the nuances of their arguments, not just yet.

In fact, 80 to 90 percent of what you read will turn out to be material that you do not directly cite in your paper. But it is useful to have read it just the same: it gives you the equivalent of what stereo enthusiasts call "headroom"—an ability to perform at much higher levels than necessary. Used as a justification for the purchase of very powerful equipment (speakers, receivers), even though it might never be played at louder than living-room level, headroom is the gap between the maximum capacity of a piece of equipment and the typical requirement. For example, if a speaker is using only 10 percent of its capacity at any given time, it typically performs effortlessly and flawlessly. The same principle applies to your research; the more that you've done, the more "headroom" you have, the more easily you are able to handle the ideas and resources that you do cite. Having the 90 percent in abeyance, or not actively used, makes the 10 percent you do use more credible, more informed, more crisp, sharp, and solid—the best 10 percent maybe.

Here's your goal at this point: you need to gather some information and sort out what is most important to you. That is, you need to flesh out some background and some details about the topic you're investigating. Another way to put this would be to say that you're trying to familiarize yourself with the range and terms of the arguments that have already been made. Or to use the language I am using here, you're trying to discover what sorts of macro- and micro-questions other writers and researchers are attempting to answer, and you're trying to decide which ones you might need to address in your paper. Remember that your paper should not merely summarize existing research or try to reproduce the range of opinions or insights on a given issue. That's called a "report," not a paper. You are instead trying to contribute to the universe of knowledge by saying something new. You want to generate original, imaginative ideas that differ in some ways from what you have read, for, finally, your idea is the most important one, not the ideas of others.

Essentially, what happens as you read widely is that you become familiar with the topic, internalizing its issues and complexities. And this will be reflected in the next stage of writing, which involves moving from the position of an outsider viewing issues articulated by others to that of an insider who has something original to say about these very issues. In fact, you are ultimately trying to discover what it is that you feel about a given issue. You are doing research in order to determine your proclivities, inclinations, beliefs, and ideas. You'll find some authors you come to agree with and others that you think are wrong. Some will appear to you wrong in some places and right in others. But as you read—and this is the exciting thing about doing research on something you find interesting—you will discover that no one's position *exactly matches* your own. Thus the more you read, the more you will clarify your idea of what it is that you really feel, and why you feel it. This is what I mean when I say that doing a research paper is a discovery of self.

Beliefs and Paradigms

Some things about you will never change, though, no matter how much research you do. If you are a genuine believer in, for example, the flat-earth theory, or in astrology, or in creationism as opposed to evolution, your research is probably not going to reverse these deep-seated beliefs. As the philosopher Noël Carroll remarks, "Belief is not something that is under our control.

We cannot will our beliefs.... Rather, belief is something that happens to us" (65–66). Hence researching our beliefs is a pointless task: we won't be open to change at all.

Or is this true? It seems to me that a large middle ground exists—a ground for research that will allow you to change or even reverse your position, which might be something quite close to, but perhaps not as strong as, a belief. This is the arena in which you will do your work. Exploring it will neither undermine nor threaten deeply held beliefs you don't want to part with (or cannot part with) In this arena, you are not quite sure of what you will discover—you have some idea, but not a complete one—and you are open to various suggestions, various interpretations, various angles of inquiry. You have some hunches, suspicions, and predilections, to be sure, but these are not so strong as to inhibit exploration. Some of your hunches will turn out to be wrong, or ill-informed; some of your predilections, you'll note with chagrin, will reveal themselves as prejudices. But that's OK. That's what doing research should entail.

What's interesting, too—and this is my final point about allowing research to change one's mind—is that once you have a firm idea about a topic, once it has rooted itself in your consciousness, you might initially be incapable of seeing disconfirmatory evidence. You are to an extent hampered by your predilections, personal theories, and beliefs. I guess my point is that you have to be constantly on the lookout for things that might seem not to be explicable by your own theory, idea, suspicion, or even belief. You have to be looking not just for things that conform to what you expect, but also ones that do not, that even go so far as to undermine the entire structure of your expectations.

The philosopher Thomas Kuhn, in *The Structure of Scientific Revolutions*, reports how test subjects who were shown playing cards and asked to identify them would get the identifications wrong if the cards were nonstandard, for example, a red ten of clubs or a black jack of diamonds. It seems that the subjects had subconsciously established a theory for the situation—it was a "normal deck" they were being shown, and the experimenter was basically honest, trustworthy, not out to trick them in any way. Hence the subjects simply could not perceive the anomalous cards:

> For the normal cards these identifications were usually correct, but the anomalous cards were almost always identified, without apparent hesitation or puzzlement, as normal. The black four of hearts might, for example, be identified as either the four of spades or the four of hearts. Without any awareness of trouble, it was immediately fitted to one of the conceptual categories prepared by prior experience. *One would not even like to say that the subjects had seen something different from what they had identified.* With a further increase of exposure to the anomalous cards, subjects did begin to hesitate and to display awareness of the anomaly.... Further increase of exposure resulted in still more hesitation and confusion until finally, and sometimes quite suddenly, most subjects would produce the correct identification without hesitation. Moreover, after doing this with two or three of the anomalous cards, they would have little further difficulty with the others. (63, my emphasis)

To use Kuhn's terms, the subjects established a "paradigm" of how the experiment worked, and it took considerable disconfirmatory evidence—multiple showings of anomalous cards, in this case—for them to reshape their paradigm. Paradigm reshaping did not happen with the first piece of disconfirmatory evidence, nor typically with the second or third. Yet it did finally happen with most subjects; that is, the paradigm was susceptible to change and hence not a belief so strong it could not be abandoned.

Once you have discovered a field or arena in which you can be open to the anomalous, you are in the position of being able to do some good, relatively disinterested research in it. If you have a theory of how something works, or of why something happened, or about the value or importance of an idea, issue, or individual, try to force yourself to seek out evidence that will challenge that theory. Of course, with Kuhn's experiment, the subjects were tricked—they thought that they were dealing with a "normal" pack of cards. Similarly, sometimes the unspoken assumptions about a given issue will be the very ones on which you've established an erroneous theory.

But only truly imaginative research seeks to uncover those false unspoken assumptions or challenge prior paradigms. Your research will involve reading, digesting, and internalizing the material available on your topic—making it your own—and doing so with as open a mind as possible. Ideally, you will have some surprises as you do your research, as you will discover things that you had no idea of. You will discover and maybe demonstrate how your paradigms have been reshaped.

Documentation and Quotation

Even though you will be dealing with a variety of source material, your writing process should resemble the writing process for any other academic essay: you have to do prewriting, outlining, drafting, and rewriting similar to what I suggested in the early portions of this book. However, you need to deal not only with additional actual points of view—ones that both support your own and that disagree with your position—but also with the issue of how to document the material that you cite.

What do you need to document? And what can you merely assert without having to offer a source to back it up? These questions are often troublesome to students, partly because no easy answers exist. But I want to provide a brief guide here, and to suggest that if you have any questions, ask your professor. In general it's better to overdocument than to underdocument, but overdocumenting can convey an uncertainty that might detract from your credibility.

1. Things that do not need to be documented:
    a. Common-knowledge facts. George Washington was our first president. The Earth is the third planet from the sun. The United States is composed of fifty states. That sort of thing.
    b. Opinions of your own. You are offering an opinion, though I expect it will be an informed opinion, since you

are doing research, and that does not itself have to be given documentary support.

c. Your personal experience. If you are drawing on an experience of your own, this does not have to be documented, unless perhaps it is a lecture that you attended (this can be documented—give date, place, and speaker), or an interview you conducted.

2. Things that are often documented, but need not be:
   a. A meaning of a word. I avoid quoting a dictionary; this seems to me a somewhat childish ploy. In addition, connotations are usually much more interesting than denotations, or dictionary definitions.
   b. General statistics about recent occurrences, unless you are analyzing those statistics as part of your paper.
   c. Material you are fairly sure that your audience would be familiar with, even though it might not be general knowledge per se.
   d. Familiar quotations. (John F. Kennedy once said, "Ask not what your country can do for you, but what you can do for your country.")

3. Things that must be documented:
   a. Any quoted material from a source.
   b. Ideas that you have gleaned from a source.
   c. Detailed statistics.

In general, I suggest to students that if you are not sure whether to document something, you should probably do so. Published authors tend to be a little less scrupulous about this (an annoying development, I believe), but that does not allow you to be.

Documentation forms vary from field to field. Three common forms of documentation are MLA (established by the Modern Language Association), APA (developed by the American Psychological Association), and *CMS*, or *Chicago* (based on the *Chicago Manual of Style*). Some disciplines require one, some another. You should find out what style manual a given professor wants you to adhere to. Some don't care. In that case, I suggest that you find out, if you can, what writers in a given discipline prefer, and then adhere to that style. You will need to consult a handbook (such as the *MLA Handbook for Writers*), and you'll need to *follow exactly* the forms for works cited, notes, internal documentation, and even the look of a keyboarded page.

You will probably be using quotations, which are again useful in that they will often capture better than your description a certain aspect of the work that they are from. Keep in mind, though, that they are not "proof." You need to come up with your own proof, and the material you quote is part of your argument about something. It can support your argument, even provide a counterargument, but still, you must make the case and do what you can to convince a reader.

Be careful of quoting too much. How much is too much? This is your call, but realize that any quoted material is honored by being quoted and must somehow be something quite special to deserve this honor. You need not quote merely to provide an example of what you mean. And if you can effectively summarize the quoted material, there is no need to quote it. So I recommend that no more than 10 percent of the paper be quoted material. Finally, keep in mind that quoting passages from texts or outside (secondary) sources does not *prove* your argument. Just because some famous person you quote says something does not mean it's true or even correct. You need to prove your argument with your own words. Sometimes these words of yours will be an elaboration of quoted passages, but still the words need to be your own. And the paragraphs in which quoted passages appear must remain firmly in your control.

I know this sounds a little prescriptive, but my emphasis throughout, as I hope has been evident, has been on maintaining and developing your own argumentative line. If you quote extensively, you tend to fragment your paragraph's ideas. Remember, too, that if you end your paragraphs with quoted material, you have, essentially, given over to someone else the last word on a particular topic: you've ceded authority. Keep in mind that the author you quote, while likely an authority on the subject, is less important to your paper than you and your argument.

Giving Background about Source Material

I often encounter the "dropped quotation" in the student essays I read, namely, the quotation that appears, usually in support of an assertion the paper has made, but without any attribution to indicate who is being quoted or why that person has an opinion we might value. I find myself asking in the margins, "Who is it you are quoting?" "Why important?" What you need to do is straightforward, though not really that simple: you need to introduce not just your quotation, as in "Scholes remarks, 'Literature is language used to create an experience that we value for its own sake' (1)," but also something about the person you are quoting: "The well-known literary theorist Robert Scholes, writing in 1969, remarks...." Of course you usually have to do this only for the first quotation from a given source. Some textbook writers call this a "signal phrase." I used to call this contextualizing material a "source-validation protocol," or a "source protocol," since a "protocol" was initially a series of instructions printed on the flyleaf of a book, and since this particular protocol validates the source you will quote. Now, though, I have moved to a simpler phrase to describe this material: an identifier.

One of the problems with this is that you then have to figure out who it is you are quoting, why he or she is important, and how to economically fit that into your sentence. Students often protest, "These identifiers make it so wordy!" but I point out that they don't need to be. The real problem you will encounter with identifiers is not that they make your prose wordy, but that using them forces you to carefully evaluate your sources, which often involves a lot of work. In addition, when you discover certain things about these sources, you will sometimes discover that you cannot use them—they are biased, out-of-date, or written by nincompoops. This means that you will have to look for other sources.

Another problem that students often mention is that the identifiers I demand are rarely used in published scholarly articles. This is in fact true. Most scholarly articles address an audience relatively familiar with the academic field. Hence elaborate identifiers are not really needed. When I looked at an article I wrote a few years ago, I discovered that about half the quoted sources are introduced and half are not—I had evidently decided that my audience would probably need orientation of some kind for some quotations but not others. In fact, the sources I quote from outside my field of literary scholarship (that is, the sources I use from psychology, medicine, and other sciences) are exactly the ones that require the identifier.

So once again, you must decide what it is your audience knows, what they will need to be oriented in, and how much you need to tell them about your sources. In general, your audience will be the educated nonspecialist, so you won't have to use an identifier such as "The famous philosopher Aristotle writes...." But when you start doing research into areas that are rather specific and probably outside the field of your imagined audience, you will need to use more identifiers, and you will need to make them more complex.

Miscellaneous Suggestions

1. Be fair in how you characterize your sources; don't quote something that, taken by itself, misrepresents the author's opinion or position.
2. Don't just make statements that assert existing research is valid—analyze existing research.
3. Don't automatically assume your sources are either 100 percent correct or 100 percent incorrect. Some can have elements of inaccuracy and accuracy at the same time. Get good "intel."
4. Don't assume that more recent writers or sources are necessarily better than or aware of earlier ones; but don't use out-of-date material when current research has superseded, challenged, or refuted it.
5. Always make it absolutely clear what you have used—words, phrases, ideas, organization—from your sources.
6. Limit quoted material. You may summarize, but make it clear that what you are summarizing is someone else's material.
7. If you don't understand a source or passage, don't quote it. First try to figure out what it means. Then decide.

8. Remember that you want to be creative, imaginative; but at the same time, you need to stay connected to an outside world, to what's been said, written, and thought by others. These two elements together—creativity and connectedness—combine to help you become productive of ideas that aren't just different, but that actually matter.

9. You are addressing some audience and you need to figure out what that audience is like, what it wants and expects, and how to persuade it using logic and examples.

10. Finally, don't forget that in a research paper, despite the fact that you are reading enormous amounts of source material and including references as well as citing authorities of various kinds, you are still making an argument of your own. This paper needs to have a clear argumentative line. Without that, research papers turn into data dumps—no fun to read, confusing, and finally pointless.

7 Paragraph Design

Let's back up a little. You have some ideas for what you want to write, but before you commit yourself to paper, you wonder, what kind of paragraphs should I use? There seem to be all kinds of paragraphs in the textual universe surrounding us. Tweets are just one short paragraph. Newspapers use paragraphs of one or two sentences. Academic articles often have paragraphs ten or fifteen sentences in length. Which are best? How can I find the right kinds of paragraphs to advance my ideas?

A kind of paper in miniature, complete with its own thesis statement, "body," and conclusion, the paragraph is the unit that carries forward a single stage in an argument. I know some writing teachers hate this analogy, perhaps because it too severely delimits the possible forms a paragraph can take. But regardless, it is crucial to craft each paragraph such that it both makes sense on its own and fits into the entirety of the paper. So as you compose, you must keep in mind both of these notions in: how to organize the mini-paper of the paragraph, and how that mini-paper fits into or advances the entirety, the larger argument.

Topic Sentences

The "thesis" of the paragraph is often called the "topic sentence," but perhaps a better name for it is the occasionally used "controlling idea." It controls or determines the rest of the paragraph. It is the most important single point of the paragraph, the essence to which the paragraph might be reduced. Usually, but not always, this is the first sentence of the paragraph. Such a positioning is a safe one, though sometimes writers will opt for a closing sentence as a topic sentence, or will have a topic sentence in the middle of a paragraph. Some writers refer to and recommend the "hinge-structure," a structure in which the paragraph finds its true direction or reveal its thesis about halfway through. John Muir, in a 1920 essay entitled "Save the Redwoods," uses a hinge-structure for his last paragraph:

> Any fool can destroy trees. They cannot defend themselves or run away. And few destroyers of trees ever plant any; nor can planting avail much toward restoring our grand aboriginal giants. It took more than three thousand years to make some of the oldest of the Sequoias, trees that are still standing in perfect strength and beauty, waving and singing in the mighty forests of the Sierra. Through all the eventful centuries since Christ's time, and long before that, God has cared for these trees, saved them from drought, disease, avalanches, and a thousand storms; but he cannot save them from sawmills and fools; this is left to the American people. The news from Washington is encouraging. On March third the House passed a bill providing for the Government acquisition of the Calaveras giants. The danger these Sequoias have been in will do good far beyond the boundaries of the Calaveras Grove, in saving other groves and forests, and quickening interest in forest affairs in general. While the iron of public sentiment is hot let us strike hard. In particular, a reservation or national park of the only other species of Sequoia, the *sempervivens*, or redwood, hardly less wonderful than the *gigantean*, should be quickly secured. It will have to be acquired by gift or purchase, for the Government has sold every section of the entire redwood belt from the Oregon boundary to below Santa Cruz. (831)

Notice that in this longish (ten-sentence) paragraph, the fifth sentence ("Through all the eventful centuries ...") acts as a hinge. The first four sentences (about fools who kill mighty trees) serve to capture the reader's imagination and stoke indignation, but it soon becomes clear that the paragraph does not really examine the fool who destroys trees; it instead offers a suggestion that the only ones who can now save the giant trees are the American people.

Muir uses this format, I think, because his previous paragraph concluded with a discussion of how we are the guardians of the trees in our country, asserting that "the American people are equal to this trust ... as soon as they see it and understand it" (830). To follow that sentiment with the idea of the fifth sentence above, which ends, "this is left to the American people," might have struck Muir as being redundant or repetitious, so he restructured his final paragraph, opening it instead with a brief, pithy, almost epigrammatic sentence, "Any fool can destroy trees." Using a hinge structure makes his concluding paragraph overall far more powerful.

As always, the rules here will bend as you push against their limits; feel free to experiment with the placement of topic sentences. My own preference is for an initial-sentence placement, with the "hinge-structure" a close second. Sometimes alternative placements can add interest to a paragraph (and paper), offering the reader a little more variety than would a repeated structure. I strongly recommend that you do place a topic sentence somewhere in the paragraph, however; allowing your controlling idea to remain implicit or deploying the entire paragraph as its own topic sentence both strike me as risky strategies, more apt to confuse the reader than to enlighten or engage.

Succeeding sentences make up the paragraph's "body," and the final sentence, the paragraph's conclusion. One advantage to seeing paragraphs this way comes from the analogy to the parts of a paper: just as the thesis of a paper must be different from its conclusion, so a topic sentence must not be merely repeated at the end of a paragraph. A paragraph must "go" somewhere. It represents, specifically, a stage in your argument. For example, the following paragraph starts well, but I wrote it to illustrate a specific kind of paragraph problem that I have encountered surprisingly often. It goes in a circle. (This is a narrative, but the same principles apply in expository prose.)

It was a textbook example of a frightening house. The windows banged as if of their own accord. Shrill voices and shrieks that almost exceeded the power of the human ear to grasp emerged from the house's eaves. Bats flew in and out of the windows. And oddly shrouded forms, what could be just wisps of smoke or play of light from shadow and moonbeam, seemed to float behind the partially broken or cracked and cobwebbed windowpanes. It was a textbook example of a frightening house.

The paragraph has some good supportive details, but it needs to give more of a sense of progress. For example, it could end, "'Yes,' he thought, 'it's true that you never can go home again,'" or, "Yes, Hollywood movie sets do their best to embody rather than avoid cliché." Perhaps, "He couldn't believe that his grandmother had lived here her whole life." Something is needed to "conclude" the paragraph, to lead the reader in some clear direction, to help the reader figure out what the point was of having read the sentences in between the topic sentence and the conclusion.

C. T. Winchester provides us with an interesting example of how a paragraph develops and changes; it's an expository prose paragraph about the impossibility of translating poetry. The paragraph clearly "goes somewhere." He writes about the challenge of translating poetry:

> It is evident, from these considerations, that poetry can never be translated. Its finer and subtler essence always escapes in the process. Dependent for its individual poetic quality, in every instance, upon the inexplicable power of language, that quality is lost the moment the language is changed. The intellectual content of a poem, the outlines of its imagery, its more vague and general emotional effects—these may be transferred to another tongue. The translator may be content with these, and win the praise of what is called fidelity; or, if he be himself a poet, he may weave the thought and imagery of his author into a new poem of his own which shall run parallel with the original and have perhaps a similar charm. But in either case his work is seen to be something very different from the poem he has attempted to translate. (245)

Winchester actually has a two-sentence "topic sentence" in this paragraph, but it's clear that he has a definite argumentative edge here ("poetry can never be translated"). Over the course of his paragraph, though, he takes two small counterarguments into account: *some* elements of the poem may be "transferred to another tongue"; and, provided that the translator is a poet, a new poem can be created that will "run parallel with the original and have perhaps a similar charm." And yet by the paragraph's end, Winchester has made it clear that such transference to a new language or such a creation of a new poem will inevitably differ too much from the original. So he has backed away some from his topic sentence's declaration that poetry can never be translated. It can be translated, ultimately, but neither faithfully nor well. It's more like a "transfer" than a "translation." One of the nice things about Winchester's paragraph, though, is that its two-sentence controlling idea, placed early in the paragraph, allows the reader to swiftly grasp where the paragraph is going.

Transitions and the "Ooze"

An additional advantage to early placement of the topic sentence is that it will reveal when an essay has made a transition to a new stage. Not only is the paper moving to a new stage (as the paragraph break suggests), but, the topic sentence proclaims, *this is* that new stage. Such a strategy helps the reader follow the overall direction of the argument.

But sometimes an "oozing" quality emerges because students have been taught that they need to prepare the reader for the next paragraph by having an introduction to that paragraph's idea at the end of the paragraph before it. This often backfires. Yes, you do need to make a smooth transition from one paragraph to the next, and at the same time make the last sentence of a given paragraph a concluding point to that paragraph. So it's quite an important sentence. But it's more important as a conclusion to a unit of thought than as a transitional device. A signal of a new idea or of a new phase of thought, a different subject or perspective, should not displace or constitute that concluding sentence.

Your transitional device should be the topic sentence of the *next paragraph*, which at once signals a new idea and ties it in to the previous one. But to anchor it to the previous paragraph, you should probably repeat some key idea, phrase, word (or even sentence structure) from the end of that previous paragraph even as you simultaneously introduce the topic of the new paragraph. Thus the topic sentence does double duty: it logically ties the new topic to the previous paragraph, yet at the same time introduces something *clearly demarcated as new*. It's sort of like a New Year's Eve or birthday party—a link to the past but a trumpeting of the new.

A topic sentence can on occasion "control" more than one paragraph, I should point out, especially in situations in which the writer employs a classification, and each element of the classification requires a fair amount of support. But on the whole it is best to use a topic sentence for each paragraph. You are writing, for the most part, to communicate your ideas, and typically the most straightforward method of presentation will be the best. Just keep in mind that variation, while it can raise the interest level of an essay, can also muddle your meaning, so when you do attempt to innovate, you need to be especially careful that your meaning isn't being sacrificed on the altar of novelty.

Paragraph Development: The Use of Evidence

How do you fill up the paragraph? What goes after the topic sentence? Usually the paragraph "proves" or "supports" the topic sentence: it offers details, examples, incidents, logical arguments, or narrative—in a word, evidence—that elaborates on, clarifies, or explains the idea of the topic sentence. Paragraphs need to be developed just as arguments are developed in the paper proper, and as with papers, there are many methods of development. Typically, these methods are delineated as classification, cause-effect, definition, description, process, comparison-contrast, example (or some combination of these). Instead of trying to decide which of these to use in developing each of your paragraphs, it would be best simply to keep in mind that you need to expand, explore, and explain—even exploit—your topic sentence.

Some modes will be more useful in some situations than others, but in all cases, you need to offer more than just a topic sentence and a reiteration of that sentence (or its repetition in different words). Like the thesis, the topic sentence must be more than merely asserted: you need to prove it.

You prove it through the use of evidence. For some reason, much discussion of writing has taken on a legalistic or even militaristic tone—"marshaling evidence," "providing warrants," "making a case," "defending against attacks"—though the writing that you do will probably not be used in courtroom or military planning. Evidence consists of what you fill up your paragraphs with. Often thought to be the heart of argument (as Emerson remarks, "Hug your facts"), evidence usually consists of the material you have discovered or assembled that makes you claim what you claim and that you hope will persuade others of that claim. It can consist of facts, quotations, statistics, definitions—specifically, the material that you use to support your thesis, or to support some subpoint of your thesis. It can also be the material you have discovered that helps to defeat or at least answer a counterargument.

The key is this: you must find evidence that your audience will see as not only true but also somehow representative. You have to be "fair" in the selection process that you've used to uncover it, and you have to be fair as well in presenting a balanced picture of the evidence that you use. It need not necessarily be always novel or different; you can draw on material that has already been brought to light. But you may want to frame that evidence in such a way that it has a new impact.

There is no set length for a paragraph. A paragraph of one sentence can be fully developed; a paragraph of ten sentences can be underdeveloped. But what's the ideal length? I have hedged for so long in an attempt to answer this question that now I just give a suggestion. Probably the safest length for a paragraph in a student essay is six to nine sentences. Paragraphs of fewer than six sentences probably lack development; those of ten or more can typically be broken somewhere, and each resultant paragraph developed more fully. But keep in mind that some

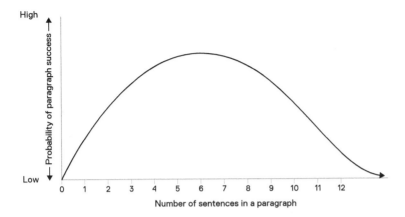

paragraphs with fewer than six or more than nine sentences will work successfully; these numerical limits represent only a very general suggestion. Your instructors will probably never count the number of sentences per paragraph. It is your goal to make sure, though, that the development of your paragraph sufficiently explains the idea of its topic sentence. (This paragraph has nine sentences, not counting this one: just made it.) (See Figure 1.)

Paragraph Coherence and Cohesiveness

One of the most difficult aspects of writing consists of disciplining yourself to discuss, within a paragraph, only the issues of the topic sentence. This concept is known as paragraph unity or coherence. A coherent paragraph limits itself to the points needed to prove the topic sentence, expanding on those as much as necessary to explain them but not so much as to stray into what might be a new topic for another paragraph.

A final idea to bear in mind when you construct your paragraphs, "cohesion" relates to how the sentences lead one into another. If the sentences connect smoothly and logically, that is, if their transitions allow them to flow into one another without a choppy or staccato effect, then the paragraph has attained cohesion.

One way to think about this concept is to envision it in terms of new information and old information. A topic sentence, as

I suggested above, has to link up to the previous paragraph—so it repeats some idea, word, or structure from that previous paragraph, what might be considered "old" information. It adds something to this "old" information, however: something "new" (thus justifying the start of a new paragraph). This kind of cohesion carries on into the paragraph itself, where new information is best introduced if it is preceded by, or introduced by, old information. As an example, the following two sentences seem to lack cohesion (the example is one that Professor Donald W. Cummings introduced me to):

> When we were on vacation, we came upon a bear. A forest ranger we encountered told us that someone had evidently shot the bear.

These are not by any means terrible sentences. But between the two sentences the reader has to pause too long, I think, to figure out the consecutiveness of thought. It seems to me an example of what might be viewed as follows: first we have an encounter with a bear, then a forest ranger. And then the bear was shot. Here it is schematically:

Sentence One:
New information1 NI_1 (vacation, bear).

Sentence Two:
New information2 NI_2 (ranger, shooting)
Old information OI or NI_1 (bear).

Or, in short form,

NI_1. NI_2, OI [NI_1].

The new information is followed by more new information, which takes a bit too long to process and might be momentarily confusing.

Ideally, the sentences should be joined in this fashion:

NI_1. OI [NI_1], NI_2.

This could be done in any of a number of ways, but the most logical might be the following:

When we were on vacation, we came upon a bear. The animal, we later found out from a forest ranger, had evidently been shot.

When the details are presented in this manner, the weakness of the whole universe of information being conveyed also becomes more pronounced. Had they come upon a wounded bear, a dead bear, or a bear that was healthy and would be shot later in the day? In short, the writer will be more likely to clear up the sequence of events if an "NI_1. OI, NI_2" format is followed:

When we were on vacation, we encountered a bear that looked a little weak. Its weakness, we later discovered from a ranger, was caused by the bear's having been shot earlier that week.

The format of these sentences is as follows:

Sentence One:
NI_1 (vacation, bear, weakness of bear)

Sentence Two:
OI (bear's weakness)
NI_2 (later encountered ranger)
OI (weak bear—cause of this)
NI_3 (shooting earlier in week)

The important cohesive links, then, are the OI ("bear's weakness") between the two sentences, and the OI ("weak bear—cause of this") between the main verb of the second sentence and its agent. Notice, too, that the two pieces of old information, the linking OIs, are rather similar to each other, thus making the cohesiveness even greater. That they are not precisely the same also is good: the sentence is going somewhere.

Here are examples of some breakdowns in cohesion. The first is from an essay by Robert Lipsyte entitled "Athletes Offer Straight Talk about Cancer." Lipsyte is writing about Lance Armstrong, the dishonored cyclist:

Armstrong, of course, is the most celebrated drug-taker in sports: the chemotherapy treatment that burned out the testicular cancer that had reached his brain in 1996 was the first step toward his amazing three consecutive victories in the Tour, starting in 1999. It happens that EPO, or erythropoietin, the blood-enriching drug prescribed to boost his chemosuppressed immune system, is also the banned drug of choice among world-class cyclists.

Lipsyte has omitted a connective between these two sentences, leaving the reader a little confused in the move from sentence one to sentence two. The first sentence describes Armstrong and the Tour de France, which Armstrong had at that time won three times. Then, with no real link, the second sentence starts discussing EPO. It would be relatively easy to segue more smoothly and with greater cohesion into that second sentence—simply by starting with OI (old information), but old information from early in the preceding sentence. Try reading the original with this sentence inserted between the first and second sentences: "Part of his chemotherapy involved taking EPO."

As you see, to avoid sounding repetitious, you don't always need to link one sentence to the tail end of the one before. Sometimes you should link a new sentence to the OI from the first portion of the one before. So instead of writing, "Janine worked in a savings bank as vice president. A vice president has a very important job. This job entails figuring out how to invest the bank's financial resources," You might write something such as the following:

> Janine worked in a savings bank as vice president. She had, in fact, a very important job, as she had to figure out how to invest the bank's financial resources.

Notice that the second sentence goes back to the beginning of the first sentence (to "Janine worked"), not to its ending.

Here is a more elaborated example that I have made up, linking the beginning of each sentence to the end of the one before, and you can see that the writing sounds immature and repetitious. It's an exaggeration of what I often encounter in both professional and student writing, but it's only a slight exaggeration:

Many commentators have noted the importance of the novel *Flatland*. *Flatland*, the creation of Edwin Abbott, remains one of the few examples of mathematical science fiction. Mathematical science fiction, that is, science fiction that concerns themes from mathematics, such as dimensionality, can usually also function as an allegory. A typical allegory that critics have seen at work in Abbott's novel revolves around the plight of an individual who, armed with some special information or some great insight into the universe, faces a disbelieving society. The disbelieving society, in the case of *Flatland*, is composed of the two-dimensional inhabitants of the world, who do not realize (as the protagonist does) that there is a third dimension. The third dimension remains mysterious and even inexplicable to them, as they lack the conceptual apparatus to understand anything outside of their own two dimensions. Their own two dimensions limit them from seeing another dimension, which would be similar to people who were prevented by their own prejudices and predispositions from seeing the "truth" of a given situation. A given situation, indeed, can have more than one "truth," however; perhaps Abbott's idea was just to suggest that surface appearance might be only one of a multitude of possible "truths."

This is clearly connection with a vengeance; it cries for something like variety. It seems to me, though, that there are enough ideas in this paragraph that it can be rather easily revised into something that resembles mature prose. I'll let you do that, if you'd like.

More typically, though, disconnectedness represents a greater and more often encountered problem—a problem perhaps with the way the writer thinks. Consider this example. It's a letter that Jonathan Franzen quotes in his essay "My Father's Brain":

We got your letter a couple of days ago and were pleased to see how well you were doing in school, particularly in math. It[1] is important to write well, as the ability to exchange ideas will govern the use that one country can make of another country's ideas.[2]

1. We need a connective here. It seems as though the writer is talking about math, and he then switches to writing skills.

2. This concept is odd—seems disconnected from the paragraph. It's possibly a hobbyhorse of the writer, something he is obsessed with? Not sure.

3. Switch to his keeping up with the reader does not quite work. The rest of the paragraph seems to be about how the reader has to keep up with or work to figure out the difficulty of the writer's prose.

4. Too abrupt switch of topic.

5. Now, we are back to the schoolwork mentioned in the first paragraph. Overall, confusing.

Most of your nearest relatives are good writers, and thereby took the load off me. I should have learned better how to write, but it is so easy to say, Let Mom do it.

I know that my writing will not be easy to read, but I have a problem with the nerves in my legs and tremors in my hands. In looking at what I have written, I expect you will have difficulty to understand, but with a little luck, I may keep up with you.[3]

We have had a change in the weather[4] from cold and wet to dry with fair blue skies. I hope it stays this way. Keep up the good work.[5]

This letter was written by a man who had Alzheimer's disease. Yet it is not so very different from many paragraphs that one encounters in writing by people who are not evidently suffering from a degenerative condition of the brain. The general point is this: work on making your sentences tie into each other so that the interstices are neither glaringly obvious nor artificially stitched close. The "stitching" of your paragraph should be neither whipstitch big and sloppy nor so tight that every seam shows.

Consider by way of contrast some writing from a medical reference book, the *Merck Manual*. I was recently stung by a bee and went to the manual for information. The author of the entry seems to have found himself in some trouble because he clearly had a very limited space to convey an enormous amount of information. Here's the entry:

Insects that sting are members of the order Hymenoptera of the class Insecta. There are two major subgroups: apids (honeybees, bumblebees) and vespids (wasps, yellow jackets, hornets). The fire ant is a nonwinged member of Hymenoptera. Apids are docile and usually do not sting unless provoked. The stinger of the honeybee has multiple barbs, which usually detach after a sting. The venom of apids contains phospholipase A2, hyaluronase, apamin, melittin, and kinins. Vespids have few barbs and can inflict multiple stings. Vespid venom contains phospholipase, hyaluronase, and a protein termed antigen 5. Yellow jackets are the major cause of allergic reactions to insect stings in the USA. (Gold 2650)

Where is the topic sentence of this paragraph? Is it really about Hymenoptera, various stingers, venom, or allergies? In such an information-choked paragraph, the reader needs more guidance, more direction as to what's important, what less so. Let me offer a rewrite:

> Stinging insects (the order Hymenoptera of the class Insecta) comprise three major subgroups: apids (honeybees, bumblebees), vespids (wasps, yellow jackets, hornets), and ants—all of which have slightly different habits and venoms. Apids, typically docile and not stinging unless provoked, nonetheless sometimes do so, and the stinger of one apid, the honeybee, has multiple barbs, which usually detach after a sting. Apid venom contains phospholipase A2, hyaluronase, apamin, melittin, and kinins. By contrast, vespids (such as yellow jackets), which cause the majority of allergic reactions to insect stings in the USA, have few barbs but can inflict multiple stings; their venom also contains phospholipase and hyaluronase, as well as antigen 5, a protein.

I combined the first three sentences into one topic sentence and tried to include within it some clue as to what the rest of the paragraph would cover. "By contrast" offers a transitional element to help guide the reader. The original author, after a brief mention of the fire ant, seems to have left it alone: that seems to me a good idea too.

If given a little more space, the author could have written three separate paragraphs rather than one, using the following topic sentences:

1. A large and diverse order of the animal kingdom, Hymenoptera includes all the common stinging insects.
2. Among Hymenoptera, the insects' stinging habits vary, as do the nature of the stingers and the chemical makeup of the venom.
3. Humans can have allergic reactions to any of these venoms, but the yellow jacket causes the most widespread problem.

I recommend this gambit because the original paragraph contains at least three major idea clusters, and packing them all into one paragraph is probably not the most efficient way to convey all the information. The single-paragraph structure works against the author: his paragraph structure breaks down, and the ideas become obscured. But it was written for a manual where space was at a premium, so the author had to compress the ideas as much as possible.

Dr. Gold apparently took my advice—or arrived at conclusions similar to my own: in the subsequent edition of this reference book, he breaks his single paragraph into five paragraphs—devoting an entire one to the fire-ant, no less—and concludes with a new paragraph about "local toxic reactions and allergic reactions." He writes, "The average unsensitized person can safely tolerate 22 stings/kg (10 stings/lb) body weight; thus the average adult can withstand >1000 stings, whereas 500 stings can kill a child" (2639). This seems to be a useful conclusion, far better than the earlier one.

With each paragraph, remember, you need to ask yourself, what is the point I'm trying to make here? How does it fit into my larger argument, yet how does it make sense within its limited confines? Your idea first has to work in its own paragraph, has to be lucid and well-developed enough to make sense on its own, before it can function as part of a larger whole.

Conclusion

So—topic sentences, the "ooze," paragraph development, coherence, and cohesiveness—these are fairly fundamental features of academic writing. You might be asking, "Where is the 'imagination' here, as in 'imaginative argument'?" or perhaps, "How can I be creative in my paragraph design?" But, like spelling (and to a lesser extent, sentence structure), paragraph shape, size, and format have become more or less standardized, so that by using the structures I offer, communicativeness can be smoothed, made more effective. Your ideas, not your spelling, sentence structure, or paragraph design, need to evince your creativity.

If you don't abide by standard forms—if you go experimental with your paragraphs—readers ignore them or seem them as flawed versions of good or normal paragraphs. For example, if you always use one-sentence paragraphs, it might make it seem as though you are jumping so very rapidly from one topic to the next that no topic is very important or needs to be considered in depth. Alternatively, if you write fifteen- or twenty-sentence paragraphs, their sheer length will be daunting to readers, but the few who stick with such monsters will internally insert break points. If you don't include a topic sentence, your reader will simply take your first sentence as the topic sentence. If you fail to make your paragraph about the same topic, readers will just assume it's all actually about the same topic and essentially infer a topic sentence that subsumes the disparate ideas. The caveat is this: you can't make your reader work too hard; you have to carefully and assiduously guide him or her as your essay moves from paragraph to paragraph, idea to idea. And you don't want to force that reader to "translate" or mentally rewrite your paragraphs into digestible units; you want instead to serve those up yourself.

The oft-repeated advice is that paragraphs are the "building blocks" of your essay, and they will be more effective at getting your imaginative point across if you abide by relatively traditional forms. Just as the spelling in William James's letter (see pages 29–30) represents a pointless and communication-diminishing aberration, so strange and nonstandard methods of paragraph design will damage your credibility and distort your message.

And we don't want that. The paragraphs need to work together to support, challenge, and develop a thesis that has an imaginative potency to it—one that its building blocks allow to shine through, as if in their supportive capacity they provide a kind of translucence, or better yet, a magnifying transparency.

III

New Forms,
Avant-Garde
Strategies

8 Different Structures, Novel Organizational Principles

The Antiargument Stance

One of the major problems with teaching argument is that students do not want to argue very much. You might see argument as a bit antisocial, really, whether we are talking about actual arguments or academic ones. A while ago, I received an email from a student, G.M., who contends that the whole basis for argument is rebarbative—at least to his generation. Here's an excerpt of what he writes in response to my ideas about the argumentative essay:

> In my lifetime I have not seen anything so polarizing as war and thus I have not *felt* the amount of momentary certainty that many past generations have. I do not want to hurt anyone's *feeling* with my ideas.... Even in writing this short idea, I try to remove much of its abrasive qualities from the final draft.... Violence is on another level ..., for I do not believe in war, but confrontation's very redeemable qualities are normally overlooked.... (My emphasis)

A cri de coeur, to be sure, which ends "thank you for being there on paper, with your essay, and in person, as a teacher." In my response to G.M., I suggested that he needs to differentiate between actual pacifism and intellectual pacifism, and that by deciding to be a student at a good university, he can no longer be intellectually pacifist.

But his point still stands. An aggressiveness suffuses academic argument; it's one of those competitive intellectual endeavors like debating or playing chess. Certainly, these are fine, admirable activities, but I just don't want to be involved with people who do them. I want to relax with my friends and colleagues. But with respect to writing academic essays, it may ultimately be impossible to throw out the whole idea of conflict, because we are dealing with a phenomenon that presumes a disrupted equilibrium of sorts, a destabilization that engenders the very writing of the essay. Perhaps seeing the essay in the terms I am suggesting—questioning, anticipating, infeeling—will diminish its inherently aggressive ontology, for the terms I propose imply reflection, rumination, and conciliation, even while they in fact require a mano a mano with ideas.

G.M. at least wanted to engage in debate. That very willingness suggests I've won him over. But what if you are not so much unwilling to assume the aggressive stance of argumentative discourse as unable to understand the whole genre—or you've opted to go into a field that does not require discursive writing, like chemistry, say, or accounting? Some of you are specific about your inability to write in this manner: "I've always been bad at English," you might confess. "I've always hated writing." You may have essentialized yourself as a weak writer, and classes requiring papers do not make up the bulk of your schedule. Some of you might be skeptical of the entire enterprise: "I have had only one English teacher mention the idea of the 'argumentative thesis.' I am unfamiliar with its principles, which conflict with the scientific-evidence-based writing that I am used to." I have been trying to demystify the writing process as much as possible, but for many of you, it might still have too much face-to-face confrontation, too much magic, too much subjectivity.

Subjective Knowledge

There, I've said it. We are seeking to discover or establish subjective knowledge. Essay writing involves manipulating subjective discourse. But it's difficult in that one does not really know what questions are important ones. And in such a situation, how do you project an audience or for that matter determine its feelings? Some people seem to be able to perform these psi-power-like mental feats—and did so all through grade school, high school, and college. It comes naturally to them; just as some people have perfect pitch, so some seem to have the aptitude for this kind of discourse. Others are tone-deaf. What help is there for those who—either innately or through personal preference—dread subjectivity, and who are tone-deaf to the music of argument?

If you are one of these students—the unwilling (G.M.), the indifferent, the anarchic—I think you need to do two things. First, you need to reconceptualize the kind of enterprise or endeavor a college paper represents. You need to use various forethought-provoking, predrafting exercises to generate ideas about the audience; questions about the issue, idea, or text; possibilities for counterarguments; and a ΔT. You need to get feedback on how your questions seem to work. You need to internalize the notion that good writing requires rewriting.

Now, I'm not sure if the terms I have introduced will interest or excite you, but I think you should envision them within a larger context of how we create and advance humanistic knowledge: asking questions, tentatively answering them; proposing ideas, imagining how an audience will respond; asking new questions. To be sure, the process has a cyclical snake-with-a-tail-in-its-mouth quality. It may even seem redundant. But it's a fertile redundancy.

Saying Something New, Take Two

Where does this not-too-terribly-redundantly bring us? We—your writing instructors—are trying to get you to look at problems, issues, ideas, or texts, and to articulate the complexity of your own response to them, to ask why, for example, they are interesting, provocative, important, urgently compelling, or dead. Yet we also want you to engage us as an audience, identifying intersections between elements of the issue and elements of the audience, just as we in the audience recognize these intersections. In a crucial sense, while the academic essay focuses on a subject, it's also simultaneously an attempt to modify the audience's perception of its previous relationship and response to that subject. We want your papers to help us recall and reevaluate what was inchoate but nonetheless strongly felt about, for example, a social issue, a historical event, a literary text. Your paper will clarify and make orderly that very inchoateness.

To put it in Aristotelian terms, we want an *anagnorisis*, a surprising recognition of some previously submerged, subarticulate response; we want something that will reorganize and explain the phenomenology of our own experience, the complexities of our own perceptions. Paradoxically, we as an audience initially resist that explanation, need to be talked, cajoled, seduced into accepting it—that's how far it is from our forebrain. And perhaps even more paradoxically, we can't say or tell just what we want explained because we don't know yet—if we could articulate what we wanted, it would be something we knew or suspected, hence not good enough. To risk an aphorism, *tell me something I know but didn't know I knew—then talk me into it.*

This might seem an impossible task. But keep in mind that writing is not merely the completion of a set series of tasks, a mechanical process anyone can teach or follow. No. We teach stages of a process, but it's the gestalt that matters most. We should really be trying to infect you with a longing, a curiosity, a desire to figure something out—a desire to explore a fundamentally unanswerable question. You may be attempting to discover "new knowledge," yet you are also trying to persuade an audience not only that what you've discovered is important, but that it logically connects with, complements, resuscitates, clarifies—makes somehow vivid or vital or special—what that audience knew before. For finally, here's what we really want: we want you to enlighten us; we want you to help us make sense of our own experience.

The Conclusion as Three-Dimensional Thesis: ΔT Revisited

Student essays, when they fail, fail most often at the outset and the conclusion. Conclusions, in particular, present problems, perhaps because these sections are composed last and often show most clearly the effects of time pressure. But try not to let pressures of time prevent you from working on your conclusion, for the ending idea, read last, is the last to impress itself on your reader's brain and leaves the most lasting impression.

What should a conclusion be like? Your conclusion needs to be a final point. It is not just the last point in a series, but *the* final point that you want to make. Hence it is not just a summary of what you did, nor a dying gasp ("That's all, folks!"), nor some totally new topic or idea. Instead, it's the point that you can finally make after having argued your thesis for three or four or forty pages. It must therefore reflect the distance that your paper has traveled, showing how your thought has changed along the way.

One way of conceptualizing this might be to see the conclusion as a second thesis: an enhanced, fortified, complicated version of the original. It cannot be opposed to or undermine the original thesis—that would be counterproductive and confusing. But it must represent an evolution over the original. Remember that you have been arguing your position throughout the paper, looking both at supportive evidence and at counterarguments; hence your thesis will have changed somewhat. If you can imagine your thesis as a steel bar alloyed and strengthened by evidence, think of how it might have bent beneath the weight of the con arguments. In your conclusion, acknowledge how that thesis has changed. Ask yourself the implications of this change. You might even go back to the opening and look at your discussion of the context for your topic. In what way does the evolved thesis redefine the context of the issues you have been dealing with? Why is your new thesis important? What impact might it have?

Your conclusion must answer the most poignant microquestion that your imaginary reader will ask, namely, "*So what?*" "That's true, but now make it interesting," one teacher I know recommends. Sometimes you will have to write several conclusions and really search hard for the best final point for your paper to present. What are the ramifications of all that you have argued? What does your proven thesis imply? Writing, you have probably discovered, is hard work, so you owe it to yourself to come up with a conclusion that will justify the effort, thought, and sweat that you've put into your paper.

What should happen in a paper is that, as you have dealt with certain examples, by the end your general idea has become more specific. Your idea has also in some way enlarged, as you have expanded its scope; and that idea has also simply changed, as your argument has offered complications, elaborations, and counterarguments. Your conclusion connects to your original thesis but differs from it enough that it's fundamentally a second thesis. This is sometimes called a "concluding thesis." I have referred to it as a change in the thesis—a ΔT—and this can happen only when you begin with a complex, a three-dimensional, thesis, and then bring that somewhere interesting and new.

Now, it's important to note that a ΔT or change in thesis can be too small or too large. If you have a very small ΔT, then perhaps you need to rethink your paper's structure and conclusion: are there implications of the thesis that you have perhaps overlooked? But if the change in the thesis is so great that it amounts to a stance in opposition to that of your thesis, or possibly a position hostile to your opening thesis, then it's fairly clear that you need to start anew, as your fundamental relationship to the subject has evidently changed.

One of my students, Jelena M., objected to this conceptualization of a paper's structure because it implies a certain contrivance. She said, "If I really *believe* in my thesis, really *believe it's true*—you know, have thought about it just as you suggest—then what can I say in a conclusion except, 'There—that just shows you that my thesis is true!'" Well, OK. But here is my suggestion about the "proven" thesis. First, college courses, argumentation, logic, and the like are not about "belief." They are about something else altogether. Second, if you have a genuinely argumentative thesis, you will have dealt with con arguments, and to some of those, you probably should have conceded something. In addition, as you wrote, you probably discovered things about your thesis that you didn't know before. That should perhaps be reflected in the conclusion.

But Jelena M.'s objection raises an important issue: what you have to do in your conclusion (even if you have "proven" your thesis) involves more than just reiterating that thesis. Instead, what you have to do is step back some from your paper, look at it, and ask yourself another series of micro-questions: "Well, now that I have proven my thesis, what can I say about that? How can I take my thought to the next level? Are there any larger issues I might now address?" You need to widen your paper's aperture by asking the "so what?" micro-question. Concluding by raising those kinds of micro-questions virtually guarantees you an interesting ΔT. You might not be able to answer them, I'll admit. But that's OK.

Another student, Will L., had an interesting story to relate about how one of his previous writing teachers composed her essays. He said, "My teacher would essentially write her whole paper, and then, by the conclusion of the paper, would finally arrive at what she realized was the actual thesis." An interesting strategy, to be sure, if a somewhat uneconomical one, in terms of time (though as you know, I sometimes recommend it myself). But I think what happened with the teacher was simply that she used the initial writing of the paper as the necessary "forethought" that precedes creation of a thesis.

And that brings me to reiterate my final point about final points. The academic argument paper's ideas do not appear on the page in the same chronological sequence in which they emerged as you wrote. That is, the sequence of ideas in your paper does not precisely replicate the thought process you went through, since you probably had to go through a lot of forethought, culling, winnowing, and predrafting in order to arrive at the thesis.

As I said earlier, your thesis, like that of Will's teacher's, is an *endpoint*—a *conclusion*. Oddly, though, in your paper, that thesis goes near the *beginning* of your essay. In the body of your essay, you essentially reveal (in organized, but abridged format) the thought process you went through—including evidence you found that was significant, con arguments that were serious, and the like—in order to have arrived at your thesis.

But then, after you've finished showing that thought process, you can't just leave your reader flat. You have to reflect on the thesis and its proof. You have to come up with a statement you can now offer as a conclusion after having proved your thesis. What can you say now that you have written the paper? How are your thesis and its proof significant?

Here is the sequence I'm suggesting:

1. Begin with forethought, generation of ideas, trying out of provisional theses.
2. Consider evidence in support of the thesis.
3. Consider con arguments, or evidence against the thesis.
4. Pin down an idea about what the thesis should really be.
5. Now, begin writing, using that thesis.
6. Tell the reader, in the body of the paper, what you did in order to have arrived at that thesis. That is, show highlights of 1–3 above.
7. Bring in other, clarifying ideas (plus necessary con arguments and supportive evidence) you think of along the way but had not thought of prior to actually writing out the draft of the paper.
8. Look at what you have written, namely, your thesis and the thought process you had to go through to have arrived at it (which constitutes the body of the paper). Now think of its further implications: ask "So what?" or "Now what can I say?" This is the ΔT or conclusion.

Other Structures/Strategies: "Creative Nonfiction"

Sometimes writers abandon the familiar shape of argument and, still staying in the general realm of nonfiction, find new ways of making their points. This is always an option, but it must be undertaken with considerable caution. (Don't you hate it when people say this? But here, it's true.) Abandoning the standard structure of argument can mean attempting to make similar points using another genre, which itself has a very different set of conventions.

For example, sometimes a parody of an argumentative paper, presenting an outrageous position but using the elements of argument, makes the strongest statement. The most famous example of this must surely be Jonathan Swift's "A Modest Proposal"

(1729), which mock-soberly argues that cannibalism (specifically, the eating of children) would end the famine in Ireland. Essentially, Swift takes on the point of view of a totally amoral individual in order to attack the quietistic attitude of his countrymen and the oppressiveness of the English. Another strikingly unusual and inhuman (though not inhumane) point of view informs Horace Miner's essay "Body Ritual among the Nacirema," which appeared in the professional journal *American Anthropologist* in 1965 and has been widely anthologized ever since. Miner describes what the reader eventually recognizes as U.S. culture seen from the perspective of an anthropologist visiting from another planet. His essay demonstrates that even a careful and intelligent observer can make hilariously incorrect inferences when attempting to understand a very different culture. It also implies that a lot of things we do in our daily lives are just flat-out ridiculous, and only an unbiased observer would be able to recognize this.

But such examples are exceptional ones, and their rarity in some sense bolsters and proves the value of the standard-format argument. In fact, when I read works written in the same vein as Swift's or Miner's essays, I often long for a standard argumentative format. (I hasten to add that I think Swift and Miner have found the perfect forms for their ideas, however.) My own suggestion is that if you wish to use some alternative structure or format, discuss it with your instructor, giving both a detailed presentation of what you want to do and a rationale for it. Such a course of action might also lead you to the discovery that you can make your points even better, perhaps, using the standard format—which, I've been strenuously asserting, allows for a good deal of creativity within its familiar structure.

The genre of "creative nonfiction" or "the lyrical essay" has also emerged as an important one in the field of writing. There are workshops, journals, graduate programs, conferences, and annual anthologies dedicated to this type of writing, and you will almost certainly encounter essays of this genre in reading either for courses or for pleasure. Of the popular magazines, the *New Yorker, Harper's,* and the *Atlantic Monthly* all regularly publish essays of this kind.

Stylistically various, thematically diverse, and generically unclassifiable, these essays differ from fiction or poetry in a single regard: they ground themselves in actual facts and a shared, historically verifiable world. Here is a succinct one-paragraph description, by Robert Scholes and Carl Klaus, of this genre, which they call the "narrative essay":

> In the narrative essay, the author becomes a narrator. But the narrative essay differs from the story itself in that it is built around a specific event or situation which has existed in time and space, and it presents itself as a kind of record of that event or situation. The story told in an essay may be highly personal, moving toward autobiography, or as impersonal as a journalistic "story" of current events. It may focus on a particular event or sequence of events; or it may concentrate on a place or person, becoming a travelogue or character sketch. But its essence lies in its telling us the "truth" about something which is itself actual or historical. The "truth" of this kind of essay includes not only accuracy with respect to factual data, but also depth of insight into the causes and meanings of events, the motives and values of the personages represented. (22)

Fiction, poetry, and drama project imagined worlds, which clearly relate to actuality, to the "real," but do not claim veridicality. The nonfiction essay does make that claim. It is a work about how things are.

There are few rules for this type of writing. Unlike the argument, which has a relatively conventional structure, including the elements I have enumerated above (thesis, development, conclusion, etc.), the "lyrical essay" or "creative nonfiction essay" may include whatever elements the author feels are necessary to make a point. Perhaps that, ultimately, is the rule: the essay has to make a point, has to have something to say, regardless of how unusual its structure or strategy may be.

Let me offer one additional suggestion to you here: this kind of essay needs to convey a point, but it also has to allow for the possibility of other views. One of its notable practitioners, Philip Garrison, mentioned to me in conversation that such an essayistic form needs to start from and demonstrate *strong but mixed feelings* about a given issue. If it shows only strong, "unmixed" feelings, then the reader might well feel excluded—as merely a witness to a prolonged tirade. If it shows weak and mixed feelings, or weak and unmixed feelings, then the reader is not likely to care. To put this into the terms introduced earlier on, this essay, despite its nontraditional form, must have something equivalent to a thesis—this might be the whole essay, or it might be implicit, or it might come as the last sentence. It also must accommodate counterarguments to the extent that it sees the thesis as not being the final, definitive word, or to the extent that it sees its own form (if you can imagine this) as not being necessarily the perfect vehicle for conveying its idea, or to the extent that its message, idea, thesis, what-have-you, ultimately resists codification and remains ambiguous, elusive, evanescent.

Many times these works take the form of narratives, as in, Here is a story; it happened to me, or to someone I know. It really happened. But usually, interwoven with these narratives are expository sections that help convey the point or idea. Often more than one narrative appears, or a narrative is nested within the main narrative. So despite their narrative appearance, these essays do more than tell a true story; they guide the reader somewhat toward an understanding. What resonates about this story? Why is it significant, not just to the author but to the reader as well? Creative nonfiction is a rich, complex, capacious art form. It resists easy definition.

9 Saying Something New: Ways toward Creativity

"How do you actually come up with something *new*, though?" People ask me this all the time. I don't actually have the secret; I also must struggle to come up with something new. It's not easy. I suggest above that you use certain strategies, such as looking for a moment of doubt—some call this a "destabilizing moment"—or running down "penumbral suspicions," or using a "newrite." But many times, while these strategies help a writer get words on the page, they don't do much to guarantee that those words crackle, spark, or even smolder with originality.

The novelist and scientist Thomas McMahon suggests that ideas just come in, as if from nowhere. "As far as I can tell, ideas always show up ... absolutely free. And very often, in a nearly final form" (qtd. by A. Becker 10). But I don't really think most people have the confidence to recognize a good idea if one appears. Theories of verbal creativity—sometimes called "invention theories"—have filled many volumes. I would like to very briefly delineate a few that might help you generate something original and striking. Ironically, these strategies themselves are not highly original or even ideas that I have myself generated, but ones that I have gleaned over the course of years of teaching. A caveat, though—sometimes originality will not compel your audience; they might be looking for something else entirely. They want the old, the "tried and true." In that case, you should probably just put this section in abeyance.

But let's say that your assignment or task requires a genuine imaginativeness; you do not want to just repeat what's been said before, but instead want to come up with something novel and original. One suggestion, in brief form, can be summarized as "Defining the Assignment in a New Way." Now, sometimes people look for writing shortcuts—templates or tricks that they can use and that will allow them to circumvent the arduous process of writing, revising, writing, revising, and then writing some more. No such shortcuts exist. Writing is simply hard work. Even McMahon, whose ideas just "show up," contends that testing ideas always requires hard work. Though ideas just emerge, he claims, "What you do have to do is test them, with your education or with your experience, to see whether they're any good. You can go to school or grow old learning how to test ideas. That takes hard work. But no one can teach you how to get them. They come for nothing" (10). While I like McMahon's emphasis on testing the ideas—developing them in some useful way—I think his own natural creativity might not be the norm. Ideas don't always "come for nothing," and in fact the hard part for most of us is to get those ideas that for him are so abundant or various.

So how do you define the assignment or task in a novel way, a way that will generate ideas? One of the most striking examples that James Adams uses in his book *Conceptual Blockbusting* involves solving the familiar nine-dot problem. Imagine nine dots laid out in a 3 × 3 grid. The task is to connect them all with four or fewer lines but without removing your pencil from the page.

Solving this typically involves going outside the actual grid a couple of times. Most people think that they must not move their pencil beyond the box created by the dots. But the instructions do not specify this limitation. It might be that this puzzle was the model for the trite expression "thinking outside the box," and typically you have to solve this problem "outside the box" from the very get-go, which makes it harder still, since we usually want to revisit well-worn paths. My students recently challenged me to solve this, as they could not. The grid was on the board. Two students had already failed. One handed me the whiteboard marker. I hate to say it, but there was an air of tension in the room.

I started at the bottom left dot and drew line number one upward through all three dots on the left column, but I extended it one "space-between-the-dots-width" beyond the box. Then, for stroke two, I angled back through the middle dot on the top row and the middle dot on the right column, down to a "space-between-the-dots-width" spot to the right of the dots on the bottom row. Stroke three was simple: I drew a line to the left, through the whole bottom row, ending on the corner dot where I'd started, and finally (stroke four) diagonally up from bottom left to right top dot. Ta da! (The students applauded.)

To expand the idea, then, one needs to determine what artificial or self-imposed boundaries stand as barricades to creative solutions. More interesting solutions Adams suggests redefine the task in increasingly "outside the box" manners. For example, one person suggested taking the piece of paper and crumpling it into a ball, then driving the pencil through that. Another suggested really huge dots and small spaces between them, so that a broad pencil would intersect them all. And my favorite example: lay the grid flat on the ground, and draw a single line through the top row of dots. Continue on around the Earth, and then pass through the second row of dots. One more circumnavigation of the planet, and the third row of dots is connected, and all this with just one line. I know that the solution lacks practicability, but I can only applaud the way that it redefines the whole assignment, evaporating various constraints (not only of the nine-dot grid but of the conventional page or pencil, or of the need for visas in order to get into all the countries one would have to gain entrance to on the way). Breaking the page rule could allow you to extend the idea even further, drawing an infinitely long line in our universe (which apparently is finite)—eventually that line will intersect every point of space, including the nine dots.

How might these offbeat solutions apply to writing? I have four suggestions, though these are by no means exhaustive:

1. Let's start with that "zany" pseudo-thesis. Offer a solution that you know is zany or outlandish, but here's the difference between what I suggest here and a pseudo-thesis: take it seriously enough to try to make it work. "Trying to make it work" is the key here—zaniness is not an end in itself; rather, you need to use zaniness to provide you with a new angle.

2. Explore contradictory feelings or evidence. Most of the time, we just gloss over, ignore, or fail to recognize contradictions—we are looking for patterns that make sense, and contradictions we more or less minimize. Actually seeking out those contradictions can often open up a topic.

3. Bring in ideas and structures from another, not obviously related discipline.

4. Invent a new form by which to express yourself, or modify your own writing in some curious, special way.

5. Do research on the issue, seeking points of disagreement among scholars.

The idea is this: You need to look for expansion joints in the seemingly solid and seamless puzzle-universe you confront. Trouble is, that puzzle-universe comprises just words and images. All words can be ambiguous, while images often produce a trompe l'oeil. Your goal is to figure out which parameters of that puzzle universe—or posed problem—can be legitimately expanded or redefined. And this goes against the grain, since most people tend to look at assumed parameters in totally conventional ways—in ways that we have lots of precedents for, but which can be too limiting and confining.

Let me explain the first four of these tactics. The fifth I discuss in greater detail in Chapter 6. Keep in mind that I'm not importuning you to be "different" just for the sake of being different. But using tactics such as these might well lead you to new, interesting insights or discoveries.

Zany and Random Thoughts

Ernest Hemingway would hand-write his stories and be pleased sometimes when, unable to make out his handwriting, he would reinterpret what it said; often that would lead him to some new angle on the narrative. For example, let's say that in the sentence above I were to reread and misconstrue one word, "pleased." Maybe I would misread this as "teased" or "plural" or "pheasant" (people who have seen my handwriting would know these are not themselves improbable misreadings). "Pheasant" and "teased" do not help much. Oh, but I typed, "does nit help much." Perhaps "nits" are relevant here? You know, as in "picking nits"? Makes me wonder how much a single sentence relies on every small detail, every nit that a nitpicker would pick. Or a peck of pickled peppers. But I digress.

How about "plural" instead of "pleased"? This suggests that Hemingway was not singular but plural. Well, that's in itself interesting for a couple of reasons. First, Hemingway has much more than just a single side to his prose. Many people work under the impression that he wrote all simple sentences and very plain stories that displayed no emotion on the part of the narrator. This is certainly not the case. He had several styles in his repertoire. And he would often use very complex sentences. He also wrote some poetry. Consider this poem of Hemingway's, "The Earnest Liberal's Lament":

> I know monks masturbate at night
> That pet cats screw,
> That some girls bite,
> And yet
> What can I do
> To set things right?
> (Hemingway 52)

Well, this seems very untypical Hemingway. This is not the disinterested, affectless recorder of atrocities, as distilled through a battle-shocked consciousness, no, not at all.

Hemingway's plurality also emerges from his having so many imitators. It strikes me, now that I think of it, that the whole "minimalist" school of American writers—Raymond Carver, Frederick Barthelme, Joan Didion, among others—all owe considerable allegiance to Hemingway. Then, too, people who preceded Hemingway (I'm thinking of Sherwood Anderson in particular, but to a lesser extent Willa Cather and Stephen Crane) formed and provided literary models for Hemingway; they pluralized in some manner the Hemingway form.

Now I'm not sure how much these spin-offs from a misreading of a word in a line really help me to get my point across or give me insights about how to generate new ideas. But here's a suggestion: pluralize yourself. How would you be different if you had grown up poor rather than rich or rich rather than poor, or middle-class rather than either of the preceding? How would you respond if faced with a much younger version of yourself? Or with a much older version of yourself? Or how about if you were faced with a version of yourself who had committed a terrible crime, or had gone into some legitimate field very different from your chosen one, or had grown up to be six feet ten inches tall—or three feet ten inches, or some height (or weight) very different from your own? Pluralize yourself as a different religion, ethnicity, gender—or as someone with none of these things, if that's possible. Suddenly you find that you have a new angle on the writing, a new set of filters through which you view the whole enterprise, the whole universe, really.

Contradictory Feelings or Evidence

In a course I teach about medical narratives, one student, Jessica C., decided that she wanted to write an essay about the pain that we as readers sometimes feel in relation to stories. She noticed that in some stories, the pain of sick or dying characters didn't bother her all that much, but in other stories the pain really hurt her. This, to her, was a contradiction. Why was she sympathetic, or even empathetic, when she read some stories, but when she read others, unmoved by the plight of suffering characters? Such a problem led to an interesting paper, which also employed the application of ideas from another field.

Another example of contradictory feelings. Let's say you want to examine some aspect of consumer desire in the United States. This topic I think most people can understand and work with, since most Americans are expert or at least experienced consumers. Does a contradiction exist in the idea of "consumer desire"? It seems to me that perhaps one does. We as consumers certainly have desires—we want to buy something or maybe a lot of things—but at the same time we have fears. We fear that those things won't be affordable, won't be available, won't live up to our expectations, will hurt us in some weird and unforeseeable way, will lead us to have to buy even more things, will require incredibly heavy maintenance, or will mark us in some way as perhaps politically aligned with the repressive regime of the country where the product was made, or as an advocate of child labor, the exploitation of political prisoners, or the brutal murder of baby seals, crocodiles, minks, or rain forest flora and fauna. So suddenly the idea of a paper about consumer desire, once the contradictions hovering around it emerge, becomes really rather complex and worth unpacking.

But let's take it to another stage of contradiction. Let's examine consumer desire*lessness*, rather than just consumer desire. The phenomenon of walking around malls or driving through shopping districts, or for that matter browsing on the Internet, palls for many consumers—to the point at which some people might lose all desire. They may find themselves suddenly flooded with so many choices, none apparently better than the rest, that they find themselves not just unable to make a choice but entirely indifferent, stunned numb by "overchoice." Looking at that feeling might help us explore the myth so heavily if silently promoted by our heavily consumer-based society, namely, that some products out there will fulfill us, will make our lives complete where they are now fragmentary, will make us happy, successful, sexy, beautiful, young, and smart. At what point in a consumer's experience does this myth break down? What must happen? Is it only a matter of age, income bracket, experience? It seems to me that these questions might be explored in an essay.

Ideas or Structures from Another Discipline

Back to Jessica C., who examined the pain of various fictional characters—she did indeed invent a provocative problem that drove forward her thesis, but I also want to cite her way of exploring this question, since it exemplifies the strategy of looking outside the discipline. After having done quite a lot of reading in and around the whole issue of feeling pain, she kept on noticing references to Elisabeth Kübler-Ross, whose work examined the social/psychological states of the dying. As background, here's a brief overview of Kübler-Ross's ideas: "Her influential *On Death and Dying* (1969) mapped out a five-stage framework to explain the experience of dying patients, which progressed through denial, anger, bargaining with God, depression, and acceptance" (*Columbia* 1558). Jessica thought that this five-stage experience might somehow mirror one's empathic experience of death, that is, how a reader feels when she or he reads the story of a dying character. She further suggested that if a narrative in some sense allowed or forced the reader to go through *all five stages* of the process, then that work was not so difficult to endure, and it did not disturb the reader. By contrast, if for some reason one or more of the stages were truncated or omitted, the reader's felt experience was painful. Of course I realize that this interpretation sees Kübler-Ross's ideas as somehow absolute truth, but just the same, Jessica's application of the five stages of dying to the reader of stories about dying seems to me a creative, striking connection.

A version of bringing a structure from another discipline, the comparison-contrast often helps generate new ideas. I don't recommend totally antic comparisons such as the one Dave Barry suggested (*Moby-Dick* and the Republic of Ireland), but I do encourage you to look beyond the obvious, the relatively or reasonably similar. For example, a paper about, say, sport-utility vehicles (SUVs) might compare Porsche Macans with BMWs and Mercedes Geländewagens. Or Range Rovers and Toyota Land

Cruisers. There are lots of possibilities, but I would suggest that going outside the SUV class might be more interesting. Comparing an SUV to a car is relatively often done, so perhaps you could compare an SUV to a tank? Or to a boat? For some reason these also strike me as too obvious, too limiting. Maybe an SUV could be compared to some sort of animal? Again, too literalist, is it? SUVs are really very much like elephants (large, lumbering, etc.). But poachers don't kill them for ivory, do they? What about dinosaurs? Maybe the SUV as a reincarnation of the extinct dinosaur would lead to new insights. Some are heavily armored, like the stegosaurus; others are relatively small but aggressive, like an allosaurus; some seem to take to water, as did others of the ancient therapods. And still others amaze us with their gigantic proportions.

I'm not sure this would get us far, but maybe an expansion to other forms would be better; let's forget about modes of transport or things that literally move outside the human body, switching our focus to things that move, or were thought to have moved, inside that body. We can then compare the SUV to one of the four humors—black bile (anger), yellow bile (depression), blood (liveliness), or phlegm (lethargy). These were thought in ancient times to dwell within each person; the idea was to seek a balance. Could our vehicles be categorized along these same lines? If so, then the SUV might be said to represent blood (liveliness), but I'd argue that this is a masquerade form, and in fact the vehicle more usually represents one of the other three humors. Again, I don't think this works, quite, since the categories of humors fail to map onto SUVs. But maybe it would be more useful to think of SUVs and vehicles on our roads in general as resembling the movement of various fluids in our circulatory systems. Cars might be the plasma that flows around everything; trucks the red blood cells, carrying oxygen and nutrients, that is, needed materials; the police cars, the white blood cells; motorcycles, invading bacteria … and SUVs would be, what? Cancer. Uncontrolled growth.

Now I don't think many people would find imaginative the idea that an SUV is just a metastatic version of a car, but that comparison might give some insight to the topic in general, and to the motives of people who buy SUVs, to the purpose of such vehicles on the roads, to the results of having so many of them. You are trying to expand your mode of thought about an issue or idea, and I think the comparison might have that effect. Of course, if you are a great lover of SUVs, you might take a different angle or paint anti-SUV commentators as absurd because they liken your favorite vehicle to a neoplasm.

But why stop with SUVs or single them out, really? Why not see all motor vehicles as cancerous? Wouldn't that be a more honest appraisal? And if these vehicles are the cancer, then what do we do to cure it? As you can see, this kind of comparison-contrast brings to light some genuinely fundamental issues—can or ought we as a society do without automotive transport? Is our system of transportation killing us slowly or even rather rapidly? And what would the alternatives be? Are the car-dependent culture and its gradual destruction of our planet as inevitable as are cancers to organisms that have evolved through a process of mutation? Suddenly the topic has opened outward, maybe itself metastasizing too wildly. But using this last-mentioned metaphor might lead to ideas about "curing" the problem afflicting the planet, through removal of the worst part of the problem, or perhaps through some version of chemotherapy, like controlling the chemicals that these cars emit.

Inventing New Forms

Since most of you are trying to write "formal" essays, reinventing the form of an essay has certain risks. You will probably need to ascertain to what extent your audience is willing to look at "new versions" of the essay or argument, and to what extent they want the more or less standard form described above. Hence you might view this section on invention of new forms as being only instrumentally valuable. It might lead you to an insight or idea about a subject, and then you could write out that idea in a more traditional format.

Let's say in a political theory class you have to write a paper about John Rawls's "veil of ignorance." Rawls, a modern political philosopher, proposed that inequalities in the distribution of wealth and power are not all evil or negative in a given society, just so long as the interests of the least fortunate are kept in mind. He invented the term "veil of ignorance" to suggest that when designing a society, we have to imagine the designers working as if they were veiled from knowing their own status, education, or even racial or gender identity, a situation that would allow for the creation of a society that granted considerable rights to the worst off—since the persons designing it realize that they could be those very people. Your paper analyzing Rawls's position will have to draw on *Theory of Justice* (1971) and Rawls's subsequent work, as well as on secondary sources. It might be that you have a prompt to answer, such as "Using Rawls's 'veil of ignorance' idea, propose how a society might implement this technique and restructure its system of equality."

You might feel somewhat stymied at this point. You will probably have read some political philosophy, but you won't really know from what angle to build a society along the lines that Rawls suggests, nor will you be able even to envision such a system, since Rawls's idea was more of a thought experiment than a proposal he saw as practicable or possible. After all, people cannot be stripped of their identities or knowledge of themselves—and if they could, would we want to listen to them, especially if it were somehow up to them how to distribute the wealth and power in a given society?

Maybe, since you feel stymied, you should try to invent a new form. You might consider writing a brief play or short story, for example, in which the society you imagine could exist. People might be given drugs, say, to make them unaware of who they were. What would human reaction be to such a system as the veil of ignorance? Your play or short story could analyze that. From there, you might in fact come up with something original as a thesis to a paper about the topic.

Alternatively, you might conduct a series of interviews with friends, family, teachers, or strangers. You might ask them questions about social inequality, about what they conceive of as an ideal society, and about what they would do were they placed in a situation such that they did not know their own status when making decisions. These interviews could well form the basis for a paper about Rawls.

Such tactics would require you to write two pieces, though—an exploratory one, and then a final copy (which itself might have multiple drafts). Could you just use some other form that would serve as the final version? Perhaps you could set up Rawls in conversation with several other political philosophers—Aristotle, Jean-Jacques Rousseau, John Locke, Karl Marx—and, using their own words, create a scene in which they discuss their ideas. Again, you will need to ascertain whether your audience is willing to accept such a deviation from the standard argument, but if they are, such an approach might well prove to be refreshing. And it might lead to new insights about the philosophy itself.

Will any of these strategies lead you to new ideas? I'm not sure. But they have one thing in common: they all require you to think about the assignment or task—the invention of ideas in writing—in some new way. Many times, I have seen students engage in self-censorship, stopping the elaboration of a thought because they feel it doesn't fit the assignment exactly, or it will move them into tangential or eccentric realms, or it will be too controversial and will generate dispute or controversy. Don't worry so much about "getting along," mimicking a party line, or fitting into a mold. Rather, think about your writing in the exact opposite terms: You want to stir things up. You want to generate debate.

Again, you need to respect your audience and keep in mind what it wants. Yet while you need to respect the interests and requirements that any audience (inferred or actual) imposes, you don't want to be in the position of being beholden to that audience. Sometimes when I speak with students about their writing, they say, "But what do *you* want?" suggesting they need a set of explicit instructions that they can follow as if they were programing a new electronic device. They will follow my guidance, do in their writing whatever it is that I want them to do. You need to discard and replace this model. What I really want is for you to think for yourself, for you to come up with an original idea that I didn't think of, imply, or program you with. Writing requires belief in yourself as a person who can generate ideas that are original, striking, creative—and at the same time fit the assignment. You need somehow to have the emotional independence to feel that you really can come up with something intellectually solid, original, and defensible, rather than kowtowing to a perceived audience's prejudices or preconceptions. You have to remember that most audiences don't want a catechism or a recitation of their own views. They would prefer something that interests them, that expands their range of knowledge, and that makes them flex and tax (and maybe change) their minds. But this willingness varies from person to person, "audience" to "audience." You have to assess how far your own imagined audience might be willing to flex/tax itself, and craft your argument accordingly.

Visual Argument, Nonalphabetic Modes

Some classes will require you not to write a paper, exactly, but rather to do a poster or to make a video presentation. Much of our experience of ideas in this digital age is via the Internet, and we are dealing with "non-alphabetic" images more and more every day. The "graphic novel" has become increasingly popular and sophisticated (I recently read a graphic version of Marcel Proust's first volume of *In Search of Lost Time*), and some novels are composed without any words at all. Xu Bing's *Book from the Ground: From Point to Point* (2013) "expresses the ideal," Bing writes, "of a single, universally understood language, and my sense of the direction of contemporary communication." It is a book beyond words, which can be understood by anyone, regardless of what language a person reads or speaks. (I'm not sure if there is or can be a Braille edition of this, however.)

Still, when you create and use a visual argument, whether a video, an illustrated work, or a poster, you need to keep in mind one principal idea: you are trying to get a point across, a point of some imaginativeness, in fact, and you can't let the technology's whizbang-ness or the illustrations' beauty distract you from this enterprise. You are still making an argument. You might not be using words, but you are trying to communicate something to an audience (see Chapter 2), and you still want to have a main idea and support for it. You might also consider graphic or illustration-based ways of bringing in counterarguments and coming up with a conclusion.

It's a challenge, to be sure. Many students complain to me, "Oh, I don't have any artistic ability! I can't draw!" but I tell them that that does not matter. You can draw stick figures and make them expressive, even if you have no artistic ability at all. And you can also snare material from the Internet, provided that you cite your sources (and if you publish, request permissions and pay for them).

The idea is simple: you are trying to master a new language, a language without words, a language of image. This takes some time. It does not come naturally to everyone (not that word use does, either). But after a little work, you can usually find a way to express yourself, even through crude or childish drawings, and to make complex points with them. An example is provided by the aforementioned Xu Bing. Figure 3 shows how Xu Bing has, through his pictures, created a "universal language."

From *Book from the Ground: From Point to Point* by Xu Bing (MIT Press). Used with permission.

Notice that all of his illustrations are quite simple ones, yet they are put together with much precision. This particular excerpt it about a man's struggle with a mosquito at 3:00 A.M. It is always interesting to try to render these drawings into words, particularly in a classroom, where others are trying to do the same. What is captivating about this particular page is that it seems to depict a moment of confusion or indecision faced by the protagonist. Why, for example, is he getting undressed in the middle of the night? Or perhaps he fell asleep, fully dressed, and is wakened by some mosquitoes, which he kills, or tries to. He then undresses, puts on a pajama top, decides to turn off the TV and light and just go to sleep. In some ways, visuals such as these often end up being as difficult and ambiguous as words.

10 Continuous Composing: Streamwriting

Back to words. It has been over four decades since the publication of Peter Elbow's groundbreaking book *Writing without Teachers*, and it seems fairly clear that his general idea of "freewriting" has reached and been accepted by a wide and diverse public. Students at all levels are and have been practicing freewriting for quite some time now. I propose that it's due for a reinvention. It's not that it's stale or has outlived its utility; quite the opposite. However, having observed its use in dozens of classrooms and workshops, I think that a wide-scale refinement is in order.

Let me start with the name, "streamwriting." Overall, using "streamwriting" terminology sets up a classroom as more efficient at generating ideas than the "freewriting" terminology does. The new term offers a different way of conceptualizing the activity, a new way of presenting it. It emphasizes the continuous flow of writing that the activity inspires. The ink flows from a pen, usually, so that particular part of the metaphor has a literal basis. The term "streamwriting" also implies a "natural" quality to what's produced. There is little intervention of synthetic things (excepting of course pen and paper) between the ideas existing, in unrealized form, in the writers' heads, and the streamwrite itself.

The term "streamwriting," has been used before. A quick Google search for it gives several hits. Blogger Brad Isaac, for example, credits Leonardo da Vinci with inventing the technique of "streamwriting," and he describes something quite similar to what I have described above (Trapani). However, the name "streamwriting" has not become very widely used or popularized.

As I said, streams have a continuousness. They don't have the entropic hit or miss-ness of "free." They're not "free"; in fact, they require quite a lot of work to generate, to manage, to make productive. Most people will have heard of "stream of consciousness," too, and like the various other metaphors that "stream" is connected to, such as "Heraclitean stream," "streaming online video," "the mainstream" (sorry to mix registers so wildly), it complements as it complicates the activity of streamwriting. While I rather like the openness of "free" in freewriting, I think many people find just that open-ended vastness intimidating—with no banks or borders or endpoints, without even a slippery or squishy place you can stand on, it's kind of a scary terrain.

Perhaps the major problem with Elbow's term is its effect on the students in a class doing freewrites. Many students seem to think that if they are freewriting, they are themselves "free" to do so in any way they wish—in fact, free not to write if they want. It's sort of like a "free pass" or a "free lunch" for them. It shouldn't be. Freewriting is an intense use of their time as well as your own; it requires very careful preparation and planning; and it taxes the creative powers of even the most inventive writer.

The Process Described

I propose that, when you want to start, prior to engaging the assignment per se, you do something else. You simply start some writing about anything you want—about your feelings, about your day thus far, about your plans for tomorrow, about the room you find yourself in. The only rule here is that you have to write continuously, without lifting your pen from the page. You can't go back to revise; you don't need to pause in order to find the perfect word. No. You just write. If you don't know what to write, keep writing, maybe just signing your name or writing:

I have no idea what to write. I have no idea what to write.

This quickly becomes quite boring, so most people naturally move on to other things that are related.

I have no idea, either, what to do about this weekend. I mean, I sort of promised my friend that I would visit him, but it's a 200-mile drive and I am really busy. Should I go? I hate to back off on a promise, but the trip will take at least three hours each way, and then, when I get there, what will I do? Will my wife enjoy the trip? Hasn't she been hinting that she in fact does not want to go at all? So I am caught between a friend's wishes and my wife's expressed preferences. What to do. I suppose I could "get out of" going, and my friend would forgive me. Or in fact my wife would put up with the whole trip, I'm sure, and probably find some enjoyment in it. But what is it that I want? Do I want to go, or is it that I just want to "have gone"? I mean, am I just kind of throwing away a weekend—and part of my rapidly disappearing vacation, I hasten to add—by doing a lot of driving to a place that's not really too terribly exciting, where I will while away an evening and afternoon and morning though not in that order and then jump into the car and get back on the road hammering back home to get my wife back in time for a hair appointment? Is that what this is all about? Just running from one place to the next? Is this what life has come down to for me? For everyone? When is it we can really just sit still and concentrate, or find something like leisure time, when we feel good about not doing anything in particular at all?

You get the idea. I usually put a timer on this, so I don't spend more than five minutes or so with this "secret spring." It's secret, in the sense that you don't typically share it with a public (I am here, I know, but I do want to give an example), and it's a "spring" in the sense that it has a kind of vitality to it. "Spring," I want to point out here, is a short form of "wellspring," which means "source" or "originary point." That's what your secret spring is—it's a covert beginning to some more extensive project. The secretness lends it a certain allure, a mystery, a specialness. And since it's covert, it can contain anything one wants—it can be a genuine and full TMI-rich verbal onslaught, if one wants.

I have invented an even more primitive version of stream-writing, if you would prefer to start even more slowly. I call this stage a "streamwrite of consciousness." In it you try to capture the nearly inchoate, rapidly shifting, often confused and non-linear flow of thoughts in your mind. It's a transcription, in short, of a stream of consciousness. One element of this then might be used as the basis for a secret spring that follows. Here is an example of streamwrite of consciousness. I wrote it in a classroom where I was running a workshop:

Sounds, stickiness, urgency. Worries dissipated since K arrived. I sweat and actually smell kinda bad. Many odd outside noises. I feel sweat slip down my abdomen. I'm still flabby, horribly so, though I'm getting better. Voices in the hallway. Circle of Hanna's water bottle. She lifts it. I wipe sweat from my brow. More sluices down my abs. Ick. Noise of people waiting. A ticking also sometimes, maybe the wall clock. Had never heard that prior to today. Motors sound on highway 9G. I feel sweat on my head. Face itches. I touch it. I can see pens move out of the corner of my eye.

There's not a lot going on here, I know, but the exercise itself is interesting—and challenging. The next writing might be a secret spring that emerges from the ideas of the streamwrite of consciousness. For example, What worries are now dissipated? Why do I think of myself as "fat"? Is this evidence of body dysmorphia?

The second stage of streamwriting, which is in fact usually done to a "prompt" from a teacher—an assignment, perhaps—is somewhat more serious. Here is where the streamwrite really has to get going, really has to make some connection to the re-quired writing that you have to do. One problem that students often have, as they struggle to come up with responses on the spot, emerges from the immediacy with which they are often compelled to invent. This kind of writing puts writers under pressure of the moment. But many students do not like to "think through their pens." They claim, often quite justly, that it's nec-essary to ponder issues; they require time to process ideas before committing anything to paper.

There is definitely something to this. Remember the whole idea of "forethought"? This can be modeled too, even when streamwriting. I suggest that you give yourself a brief bit of time for no writing at all—for "collecting" or "gathering." To sustain my water imagery, one need only think of how water, before forming into streams, first has to build up somewhere, has to exceed the absorptive capacity of whatever it falls on. This takes time. It has to collect. After an interval, though, if water is still falling (in the form of rain) or forming from ice melt, it starts moving in the direction that gravity takes it, that is, downhill: it forms streams.

"Collecting" or "gathering" has several benefits. Aside from allowing that time to collect your thoughts, it also reinforces the value of forethought in composing and inventing. During this time period, you might consider various alternatives, might come to some better understanding of the assignment, and might even experience an "aha!" moment. Sometimes such moments can end up being drowned in the rush or outpouring of a streamwriting that's following a perhaps doomed or not very promising pathway. My own experience of streamwriting is that I often have several "false starts" after a prompt. Or, worse, I will start in one direction and then realize too late that the direction was actually wrong or dead-end-headed. It would have been nice to have had just a short time to think through what I was going to write.

In addition, this "gathering" time offers a good ratio: for a five-minute streamwriting activity, a one-minute—at most—contemplative gathering of one's thoughts can be extrapolated into a one hour gathering/collecting for what might be a five-hour long task. During the gathering phase, some people might want to jot down notes. I leave this to your discretion. Certainly in the gathering phase of a five-hour writing project, notes would be needful. But for an on-the-spot five-minute streamwrite, perhaps it would be best not to touch your pen, instead internally nurturing and pooling that imminent stream.

After gathering, then you need to engage in the pen-on-the-page exercise of writing without cessation.

I realize that many people object to gathering. They suggest that you just start writing, with an idea or not. The motor process of writing will stimulate some generator of idea. There is something to this. I have to say that sometimes I long to have had the time to gather, while at other times just diving in really worked beautifully. I am reminded of the opening of Marge Piercy's poem "To Be of Use":

> The people I love the best
> jump into work head first
> without dallying in the shallows
> and swim off with sure strokes almost out of sight.
> They seem to become natives of that element,
> the black sleek heads of seals
> bouncing like half submerged balls.

You need to just write, not go back to revise, not pause for the perfect word, not cross anything out; this just involves spontaneous outpouring of ideas. It's a stream, remember, hence continuous (not continual, I might add). So you just write. You need to keep the assignment in mind, and you also have to realize, during the flow of words from your pen, that you are going to be using only a portion of this in your final draft, or maybe none of it at all. Maybe you will only use the streamwrite to come up with an idea, which then will be the basis for your paper or article.

The next stage is simple. After you have finished the initial post-gathering streamwrite, you should read it through, noting as you do when you make a good point or when you come up with an idea that might be enlarged on or clarified. This will form the basis for your next streamwrite—what I call a "meander," in the sense that a river's forks or branches are "meanders," and while these are connected to the original river, they also mark a new direction. Your goal in this next streamwrite is to explore that meander, float down it for a while, see where it leads. Then, after five or ten minutes, you might set down your pen, read what you have written, and go on another meander. This process has the amazing effect of getting you to come up with some unexpected insights.

Something else you might try involves listening to a recording of what you are writing about, or a recording of something related to it. As you listen, just write down whatever words or images or ideas come to mind as your brain processes the aural signals. I call this "mind-streaming," which has the effect of emphasizing how the writing is intended to reproduce the stream of thought being inspired by the material that that mind is taking in.

Another activity you might employ while generating ideas involves trying to figure out what underlies something you have written. I ask, using the water imagery again, "What aquifers feed into this?" Like an aquifer, which is an underground spring feeding rivers or lakes, many hidden ideas underlie a text, a commentary, a point of view, or a perspective. What are these? What might be the source of your ideas, where is it they come from, and where do you think that aquifer might lead?

One of the tenets of writing argument, as I have insisted, is that it needs to address counterarguments. It needs to have multiple points of view and not be one-sided or totally resistant to objections that could be made. Hence, in a streamwriting mode, you might take yourself to task, putting some pressure on the ideas you have advanced. I call this "testing the waters." If you are really going smoothly and powerfully, you have the verbal equivalent of "white-water rapids." And if, by contrast, your writing seems to have missed the point, seems to have gone off course or offers little intellectual momentum, or to have stalled out entirely, I think it's "run aground." You need to constantly be testing the waters, gauging where your writing is really active, turbulent, productive of something maybe new and exciting; or, by contrast, where it's hit dry land and has to be towed back on course. And getting back on course, back onto the water again, is itself a valuable activity, akin to responsibly and creatively answering the strongest of "con" arguments. It is also similar to just saying, "I need to start again."

Calling this activity "streamwriting" strips the illusions of freedom away from it. It's not free time. It's work. We are trying to create something. Starting with a "secret spring" suggests that something quiet and fragile might emerge at this point but not perhaps for long. It's a small beginning that doesn't demand anything as yet. Keeping the water metaphor, too, might prevent a "piling on" of one streamwrite after another: it's more about flow and movement than about building. And since the second or third related streamwrite is now being called a "meander," the connection to the original is maintained at the same time as the new outflow is created.

But it's those constraints—rather than simple freedom—that make for genuine beauty: as Wendell Berry writes, "The impeded stream is the one that sings" (97). In fact, unlike freewrites, which tend often to disperse their energy over large expanses into a still air, streams have banks and meanders and dams; like language, with its conventions, rules, and limitations, these are the things that keep the stream at once contained and productive, of power, of beauty, of song.

"Freewriting" was created as an invention technique and then later modified and pressed into service for classroom use, so now it's both invention strategy and pedagogy. Its continued use now—whether it's called freewriting or streamwriting—is more important than ever, as more and more teachers are moving toward in-class production of papers and ideas, given the constant press for online courses and the ready availability of potentially plagiarizable material on the Internet. We need to work together to validate the individual act of original linguistic creation—we need to give back to us our own voices. Piercy ends "To Be of Use," "The pitcher cries for water to carry / and a person for work that is real" (lines 25–26). We need to produce work that is real, and creating meaningful streams of words out of what was once just a void, a desert, a parched dry and cracked plain, is nothing short of that.

Some Examples

Here, then, is some "work" from me. I decided to look at a text that I was unfamiliar with and in a field that differs quite substantially from my own. I chose a field outside my own and a work I was unfamiliar with in order to replicate, as much as possible, the situation that you as a student often face while taking a college class. You are asked to write a paper about something you read but don't really know that much about—and which is often in a field you have no real investment or interest in. That creates a huge challenge.

Ludwig Wittgenstein's *Philosophical Investigations*, a book of philosophy, is my source here. It is written entirely in short, numbered sections, each of which contains a pithy and usually quite difficult series of statements. The task I set myself was to explain three of these statements, as a start to a paper that examined Wittgenstein's theory of mind.

> The essential thing about private experience is really not that each person possesses his exemplar, but that nobody knows if other people also have this—or if they have something else.
>
> The assumption would thus be possible, though unverifiable, that one section of mankind had one sensation of red and another section another sensation. P. I. 359

[GATHERING]

This seems to me about the problem of "other minds." We just don't really know what others are thinking, do we? I mean, we might have a really good idea of a feeling or an idea, or we might think something seems totally obvious. But then, talking to someone else about the situation reveals that he or she had a totally opposite reaction. I note that this sometimes happens when I see a movie. I find it distasteful, but my friends loved it. Or vice versa.

W. brings down the problem to the issue of perceiving color. I wonder what he means by a "sensation" of red. I don't think I get a sensation exactly, but that might be picking nits. Is my red the same as my neighbor's? Is it the same as it was a year ago, in fact? I wonder. We talk about "section" of the population seeing red one way as opposed to another. I wonder if he is implying that our notions of things are socially determined, to an extent. And I also wonder if this makes no difference at all (who cares if your red is my blue?) or makes all the difference in the world—scaffolds the heartbreak of the universe, in a manner of speaking. The disagreements arise from not just a matter of taste, say, but from some opposite sensing.

Now I reread what I have written, looking for a place I'd like to enlarge on, meander off of....

MEANDER ONE

Does the fact that our "exemplars" might differ widely, i.e., from person to person, really make all that much difference? I ask, "Who cares if your red is my blue?" but that reduces the problem to a trivial issue, really. If your red is my blue, it seems to me that maybe my good is your bad, or my courageousness is your cowardliness. That is to say, if there are wild and wide divergences from one person to the next, divergences of inner life, let's call them, these can make a major impact on social cooperation, on planning, on actions taken by society at large. W. talks about "a section of mankind," and I wonder, what constitutes a section? How do we know that we are part of a section? Are there numbers or labels on people, not as visible as Stars of David or pink triangles, but discernible to others in that "section"? Or is it sort of an intuitive understanding of a shared sense of private worlds? In short, how private are our private worlds? Maybe they are not so private after all; maybe they are worlds that we share with others in our "section," and that's why we love them—or hate them? If private worlds are shared, they aren't all that private, are they?

[I note that this exercise is intellectually challenging: one is constrained by time and also by the necessity of answering the assignment. At any rate, now I reread my first meander, in an attempt to find something about which to meander again.]

MEANDER TWO

Can there be private worlds, finally? I have been created by others (literally, that is, by my parents) and given a certain DNA, a certain already determined set of genes and chromosomes that might not fully determine who I am or what I do but that certainly has some impact on those issues. And then,

I am educated over the course of years, by my parents almost exclusively until I reach school age, and then, for twenty consecutive years in our educational system. Too, I am "educated" by reading and experiencing artifacts of our culture. In some way I am a machine that has been gobbling up knowledge and ideas, images and impressions, for decade upon decade. So it seems unlikely that any "private universe" I harbor within myself is totally "original" or at least is not in some sense plagiaristic of some element of the larger culture. Is it that I seek out people who have sort of plagiarized the same stuff, who have created their inner worlds from the same deposits of culture, the same residues of the world, that have deposited themselves in me? And I can tell this from what they say, from what they read, what car they drive, what movies they like or apps they have on their phones. Red is the same color to all of us. Other sections might see it as our blue.

Here is the second quotation from *Philosophical Investigations*:

Could a machine think? Could a machine be in pain? Well, is the human body to be called a machine? It surely comes as close as possible to being a machine. P. I. IIiv

[GATHERING NEEDS TO TAKE PLACE HERE,
FOR PERHAPS A MINUTE OR SO]

Three questions and a statement, all of them perplexing, so totally Wittgenstein. So many of his entries in *Philosophical Investigations* are similar to this one. I mean, it's full of the need, it cries out for, definitions. What do we mean by a "machine"? What do we mean by "think"? What do we mean by "in pain"? These are all very simple concepts, but their use here seems suddenly under pressure. This isn't finally a statement about A.I., which didn't I don't think exist when W. was writing, but it's a statement about the body, about machines, about thought and about pain, the latter two of which seem usually confined to living entities, and are not usually applied to machines. On the other hand I have a book by Irving Adler called *Thinking Machines*, and it came out over half a century ago. And "pain," is that only for people? Can it be something related to improper functioning, to the thing doing something that unwittingly damages itself, like a car running on a bad wheel bearing or a pump that has a clog in its line? Can't these things be said to be in "pain"?

MEANDER ONE

The body "Comes as close as possible to being a machine." I wonder. I mean, yes, there is a machine-like quality to the human body: the pump at the center, the circulatory system that keeps things running, even the cellular operations. In some ways it's all just electrochemical processes at work; these create in us what we think of as "thoughts," "feelings," "sensations." It is a fleshly machine, finally. But what does that insight give us? I mean, who cares? Does it make me feel more solidarity, say, with my food processor? Does it make me more able to deal with car trouble? Does it make doctors and car mechanics the best of friends or at least people working in the same field? I'm not sure. W. uses the expression "as close as possible," I think, because he doesn't want to come out and say, "Yes, we are machines. We think, we breathe, we love," but ultimately we are just machines. Instead, we are as close as possible to being machines, but not quite. It's that tiny difference, that subtle and necessary distinction, that makes all the difference, perhaps, in the world. Ultimately we are "machine-like," but not machines. We share many things with machines, maybe even the capacity for thought and for "feeling" "pain," but we are not machines, and machines are not humans.

MEANDER TWO

So where does accepting our essential machine-ness get us? We don't feel solidarity with machines, but we in some sense are machines, though ones made of water, carbon— flesh and blood, let's say—not of metal and plastic. Yet a lot of people, including me, have metal and plastic that have been implanted within us, that are now part of our "system." (I have titanium screws in my ankle and nylon straps holding my shoulder joint together.) Does that make us more machine-ish? I wonder, how much of one's body might be replaced before one could say that this is no longer a person but a machine? This is a question that David Bunch poses in his novel *Moderan*, now that I think of it. Is the brain, finally, where our humanness inheres, and since that can't be "replaced," then can we retain humanity even if we are reduced to the proverbial brain in a vat? It seems to me that this is wrong, too, though: a brain in a vat, a brain which can think and can be hooked up so that it can produce speech, maybe, can describe emotions or tell a story, still isn't human. Humanity requires a body as well. And if that body is machine-like, we need to expand our notion of the machine and we need to figure out what it is that makes the human machine so special.

And here is a final quotation from Wittgenstein's work:

It is in language that an expectation and its fulfillment make contact. P. I. 445

[GATHERING]

What do we expect? We expect the world to go on much as it always seems to have. We expect a certain routine course of action, namely that the trains will run on time, the building where we work will be open its regular hours, students will show up for classes, cars will travel the streets, keeping to the right-hand side of the road in the United States and obeying most traffic laws. People will walk and try not to bump into each other. Stores will accept cash or credit cards or checks in exchange for goods or services. Most people will talk when spoken to and will even be relatively nice.

These are some basic expectations. When these are fulfilled, I don't know what happens. Not anything special, really. These are just things we expect to happen, everyday kinds of occurrences, let's say, and they are mundane and predictable.

But I find that I have greater expectations. That is to say, I expect certain more contingent, less predictable things to happen. I expect to sell our house soon, and for a good price. I expect to publish a few books. I expect to lose weight and then get in good condition again. I expect to be paid every two weeks. I expect to pay my bills on time. I expect a future very much like the present. And I expect that this is a mistake.

MEANDER ONE

It's these "greater expectations" that I think maybe W. is talking about. Language is where these expectations and their fulfillment "make contact." OK—but what do we mean by making contact? Does this mean that they simply touch in some way? Expectations exist, and putting into language the way these might be fulfilled brings expectation and fulfillment into contact. Language is the necessary glue or binder.

How does this have any profundity to it? It seems to me that W. might be saying that if we can articulate the fulfillment of an expectation, we have made the first step toward actually fulfilling that. We have put the two states of affairs into "contact." And it seems to me interesting that most people do not actually articulate how their expectations might be fulfilled. They just have those expectations; that is, they expect a certain state of affairs to "happen," and sometimes that does happen but sometimes it does not. It seems to me possible that many people don't really think of or know how their expectations might be fulfilled. They might (W. might be saying) have these expectations but don't even or ever dream they'll be "fulfilled" at least not completely. They might conceive of these expectations as sort of an ongoing trial or pain, things that must be endured. And of course sometimes these expectations don't pan out. Quite the opposite often occurs; what we don't expect to happen, don't want to happen, actually does happen.

MEANDER TWO

"Expecting" something to happen differs from "having expectations," I think. The former involves simply a kind of prediction, as in a weather forecast. "I expect it will rain, since the website I'm looking at gives our chance of precipitation at 90 percent." This isn't the same as "I have high expectations of my elective classes," or "My expectation is that I will have surgery and fully recover."

And that brings me to the notion of "fulfillment," which is ambiguous as well. "Fulfillment" can mean simply "it happens," as in my forecast example above. If it rains, then my expectation is fulfilled. I'm not sure language has all that much to do in making the contact between expectation and fulfillment. But in the second example, about my upcoming elective class, it seems to me that "fulfillment" of "high expectations" does make contact in language, and what emerges too is that I don't really know what "high expectations" are. The concept is somewhat vague. In the final example, the fulfillment of full recovery is right there, joined to the expectation of it. So there is a range of language contacts between expectation and fulfillment, it seems.

Now, where might we go with these streamwrites? Can we make them into a paper, say, about Wittgenstein's philosophy? The next stage would be to possibly make some connection between the private worlds (that might not be so private), the "human as machine" (but a sort of special machine), and the connection between expectation and fulfillment. It seems to me that one might use these meanders as a basis for a paper on Wittgenstein's *Philosophical Investigations*. Here are some possible titles: "Expectation and Fulfillment in the Era of the Cyborg and the Non-Private." "Cyborgification, the Conventionality of Inner Thoughts, and Fulfilling Expectations." "Private Worlds, the Human Machine, and Language as Fulfillment of Expectation." "Inner Worlds, Machine Parts, Talking Heads: Language Fulfillment in the Era of Cyborgic Conformity." Wittgenstein set up a sort of conundrum or puzzle—do our neighbors have more or less the same private worlds as we do? Are we just sort of machines? But the introduction of "expectation" and "fulfillment"—and most importantly of all, of "language"—in some ways solves the puzzle. Or that would be my argument.

What I'm trying to demonstrate here, though, is how fruitful a composing process streamwriting can be, and also how it's not finally enough to make a complete, coherent paper. If I were to turn these streamwrites into a paper on Wittgenstein, I could use some of my already composed sentences, maybe even a paragraph or two. But I would have to do quite a bit of work to turn these ideas into an actual paper. The important thing, though, is that the process gets some ideas out there, onto the page, and often the ideas generated under pressure of time and of "keeping the pen moving" are ones that are unexpected and surprising. Perhaps it would be fair to say that in language, these ideas find a sort of fulfillment.

IV

Revising and Reimagining

11 Rewriting and Revising

You may have the option to rewrite your essay. This is not a humiliation or a signal of failure. I am typically asked (by editors) to rewrite essays that I submit for publication. In fact, I am grateful for editorial input, and I find that the essays and books I have had to rework have fewer flaws than those works accepted as submitted.

First, you must attend to the issues that the instructor or editor has highlighted on your pages. The simplest of these will be correcting typographical, spelling, format, and usage errors. If there are comma splices, repair them; if there are problems with form, consult the handbook or style guide used in the course; if there are comments you don't understand, ask your instructor or editor. You might also work with a tutor to solidify some of your ideas about usage and form, and, additionally, regularly consult a handbook of usage.

Your paragraphs might need reordering, revision, or restructuring. Do the topic sentences seem to generate the ideas of the paragraphs? Do the paragraphs focus on the ideas of the topic sentences? If they do not, you need to rewrite. As Susan Bell, a longtime editor, remarks: "Organization and clarity do not dominate the writing process. At some point, though, a writer must pull coherence from confusion, illuminate what lives in shadow, shade what shines too brightly" (49). Once you have written an essay, often the way you should have written it becomes clear.

However, a rewrite does not stop there. You also need to consider problems with thesis, structure, and conclusion. Identify the paper's weaknesses, and decide how to revise these areas. Remember that you should preserve the good things about your paper while improving those areas that seem to be weak or incorrect. So don't throw away the whole paper and start over. Instead, examine what you have done, and think of ways to explore more carefully, more deeply, and more persuasively.

You might want to figure out whether your argument is really the best one you can make, or your structure the best one that you can adopt. Take a look at your conclusion and compare it with your thesis. Do you see any development of that thesis? To recall a previous idea, is the conclusion something that you might start with rather than conclude with?

As I have mentioned above, one of the most common problems I encounter is the pseudo-thesis, or the absence of an *argumentative* thesis. Make sure that what you are trying to prove or argue for is something worth arguing for. I very often encounter the too easily conceded thesis statement. If I concede your thesis, then the subsequent "proof" does not really seem necessary or important. Emphasize or amp up your thesis—either by adding a "because" clause or by looking for ways that you can individualize your idea. Again, I suggest that you try also to see what other writers have said: check the Internet, library catalogs, and other resources to see whether your topic has been written about before. Sometimes this kind of contextualizing allows for much more complex views on an issue. (But if you use sources, be sure to acknowledge them.)

As for improving the development of your argument, try to decide whether there are key issues you are overlooking, or key objections to your argument that you have just decided to ignore. You ignore these at your peril, for if the reader can easily come up with objections to your ideas, then the essay seems a little naive or one-sided. Remember John Stuart Mill's claim that 75 percent of your paper should consist of dealing with opposing views. He's engaging in hyperbole, I think, but strive for at least 25 percent. Then too, if you have incorporated obviously weak or wobbly "con" arguments—arguments included only because they are easy to defeat and make your argument look good by comparison—you need to eliminate those "straw persons" from your paper. They only make you look bad.

In addition, attempt to make your argument grow and evolve. As you develop your ideas through the use of examples, definitions, contextualizations, classifications, qualifications, and con arguments (see Chapter 5), you'll discover that the issues you deal with inevitably become much more complex, more slippery and ambiguous, than you had first thought. This ambiguity you need to address, even cultivate, rather than ignore or bypass.

Finally, look at the conclusion. Does it have a strong impact? Is it a worthwhile way to close your paper? Again, the conclusion, the last piece of writing that your reader will take in, has to demonstrate a new idea of some kind, not just a reiteration or rephrasing of your thesis. It has to *matter*. Make sure that the conclusion shows a distance traveled, what I have called a Δ-Thesis: it should not contradict your thesis, but it needs to somehow reflect your having argued for four or five or ten pages the issues that your thesis raised. Remember: it's your last chance in the essay, so make those final words resonate, ring, and last in your reader's ears. Make that reader feel not just rewarded for having read your work but also wanting to hear more of your voice in the future.

Revision is, I know, a somewhat frightening prospect, as it often means that you must take your own writing and be critical about it, even "scrapping" some of it (I take the word from many students, who, not happy about the prospects of dismantling and reassembling one of their own pieces of writing, inevitably use that very word). Remember that there is nothing wrong or weird about this. Writing involves what might appear to be waste—wasted words, wasted effort, wasted ideas. But that's OK. It's not really waste. Once, when I showed my own writing to my students and then showed them how I had marked it up in my revision, one of them exclaimed, "You did that to your-*self*!?!" I said, "No, this isn't myself; it's just my writing. What I'm trying to do here is make it better."

Consider, for example, a sentence by Joe O'Gorman. It appeared in *The Trentonian*, a tabloid newspaper. This sentence, I would contend, does not really make that much sense. It is overly long and convoluted, and its punctuation errors further impede understanding.

> *Since the NFL went to a 16-game schedule eight teams have experienced a 1–15 as the Dolphins did last year and only two have gone on to have a winning record the next season and the last one was the 1997 Jets, coached by. .you guessed it, Parcells.

I would suggest a two-sentence revision of this, with a few small changes in punctuation (I added three commas, deleted an "and," converted the two sentences into one, and added the third dot in the ellipsis):

> Since the NFL went to a 16-game schedule, eight teams have experienced a 1–15 season, as the Dolphins did last year. Only two have gone on to have a winning record the next season, and the last one was the 1997 Jets, coached by ... you guessed it, Parcells.

I think the rewritten version better reveals the statistical detail in O'Gorman's sentence, but because his column was only casually edited (by him? by others?), its details are lost. (It's only fair to point out here that sports sections might tolerate a special version of English, and are likely edited last and most lightly.)

A Text to Revise

Perhaps revising isolated sentences is too simple, so in this chapter I'd like to take a look at a more or less complete text, one with many sentences and paragraphs (too many of the latter, I hasten to add). It appeared in the letters to the editor section of *USA Today*:

> Schools are getting blamed because they prepare students to take tests ("Schools teach for tests, instead of challenging students," Letters, Tuesday).
>
> Apparently, our schools aren't spending enough time inspiring kids creatively and academically.

In fact, the students are turning into dull, uncreative, test-taking machines—all because the system is broken.

Yeah, right. I don't understand how the idea started, but it isn't the schools' job to teach creativity or foster a love of learning. That is the parents' responsibility.

No, schools are doing exactly what they are supposed to. Schools should prepare students for standardized test-taking if we are ever to catch up with the rest of the world.

Then, at home, the parents should teach kids how to learn by providing books or promoting lively discussions.

Children learn when they are surrounded by an atmosphere of learning. Home should be one such place. It's not just somewhere to relax at the end of a day.

That can wait until after graduation. (Hwang)

"Letters to the Editor" form a separate genre of sorts: it has its own rules and conventions, and editors of various papers and magazines publish letters for a variety of reasons. Some publish letters that seem ridiculous or silly; others publish letters that perfectly epitomize or challenge the newspaper's own editorial stance. Most typically, though, letters provide a unique or contrasting point of view on a somewhat controversial topic.

I think you want, first off, to determine what your purpose is. Why are you writing the letter? Are you outraged? Are you confused? Do you think something is wrong with what the newspaper or magazine printed, something so wrong that you need to "correct" it? Or are you just blowing off steam?

Regardless, the Letter to the Editor is only a subgenre of a larger, venerable type of writing, namely, the argument. In the letter, you as writer have only about 200 or so words (at the very most; our sample letter is 162 words) to make your case, to argue for your point of view, to offer your criticism, cavil, clarification, or emendation.

Letters are usually not heavily edited, though, as the *New York Times* notes, they "may be shortened to fit the allotted space." Some letters are written by representatives of particular organizations or businesses; others come from individuals who might rarely have previously expressed their views in writing.

Rereading

Often it's clear when I receive a student's paper that I am the first human on the planet who has actually read that paper all the way through. This should not be the case. You, as the author, need to reread your work and subject it to close scrutiny. Try to put yourself in the position not of the proud creator of the "perfect piece of writing" but of the person or persons receiving what you have written: your audience. What are you offering to them?

As you review your work, keep a pen or pencil in your hand. I'll keep a pen in my hand, too, as I go over the sample letter.

Most people start with checking spelling of words, punctuation, and grammar, but I don't recommend this. Instead, determine if the idea you want to convey is getting across. That's the core issue: are you transmitting that idea? Often, we think we have conveyed our thoughts, really spelled them out completely and fully, but in fact, have not succeeded: readers will say that they just didn't get the idea, didn't know what it is we were trying to say.

What is your **thesis**? Usually, in the United States and in other Western countries, the main idea should appear early on. Readers want to know what the author is trying to state—what he or she is arguing for—and want to know it right away. The rest of the writing will back up, give reasons for, or document that thesis.

The letter's thesis is not in paragraph one, two, or three. Instead, the thesis seems to emerge in paragraph 4, the middle of the letter: "it isn't the schools' job to teach creativity or foster a love of learning. That is the parents' responsibility." But in paragraph 5 the writer claims that "[s]chools should prepare students for standardized test-taking if we are ever to catch up with the rest of the world." That also seems to me a possible thesis— or at least something worth arguing for and about.

The next two paragraphs, however, also offer a candidate for a thesis: home should be a site for learning, a place where students learn how to learn. It shouldn't be "just somewhere to relax at the end of the day." Again, this is an interesting idea, but not one that supports the ideas that come before it. Rather, it's something that needs to be proven. In a letter to the editor, just as in a research paper, simply asserting an idea is not enough. You must back up your idea, provide reasons for its truth or value, and do what you can to prove it. Ideally, you should consider arguments against your idea, showing how those are either irrelevant, incomplete, wrong—or in fact good enough to cause you to modify your initial position.

The Thesis-Audience Relationship: TAR

What, finally, is the audience of a national newspaper looking for? Generally, readers don't want to be told what they already know. They also are likely to resist something totally antithetical to their beliefs, something that undermines cherished notions or values. So you want to keep their position and proclivities in mind as you write. You need to determine as best you can the relationship between the thesis—your main idea—and your audience. Like this book, most books about writing—and most teachers of writing—emphasize making sure you have a clear expression of a main idea, or thesis, in your writing. But this recommendation only partially addresses the main issue. You as a writer also need to figure out the relationship between the thesis you're proposing and the audience you expect to read it. I call this the "TAR": Thesis-Audience Relationship. Your thesis won't "stick" without a carefully calibrated TAR.

Readers of letters to newspapers are probably as various as readers of newspapers themselves, but they're not casual newspaper readers, I suspect: they don't merely read the headlines and then skim the sports or local news. No. They seem to want to go a bit deeper—or perhaps they have a bit more time to spend with the paper than do most people.

As for the particular audience of *USA Today*, I would place them in the middle of the political spectrum. Some would certainly be opponents of the legally mandated "No Child Left Behind" testing-based curriculum and pedagogy; others would think that law was just fine. At the time the sample letter was published in late 2008, President George W. Bush was trying to institute reforms to that law, and these promised reforms were on the minds of the American populace, or at least on some people's radar screens. And the letter does respond to a previous letter, so it's not as if the writer is inventing an issue.

The miscalculation of TAR, however, and the reason the letter can't really "stick," at least not in its present form, is this: the audience for this letter is going to want not only a single, clear thesis—which this lacks—but they are also going to want evidence in support of that thesis, compelling reasons to believe that thesis.

For example, the writer could offer some evidence from her own experience in high school, where she might have excelled at math or proved to be an excellent taker of tests. Or she could look at schools in other cultures—or in U.S. cities with weak school systems—to offer a contrast. In short, the letter needs compelling and logically sound reasons for its assertions.

The letter drives us back to a single issue: what is the problem the writer wants to address? Is it the problem of our failing school systems? Is it the problem of falling behind the rest of the world in terms of, say, invention and discovery? Is it the problem of students becoming automatons taking test after test? Is it the problem of working parents not paying attention to their children at home, and expecting the schools to do everything?

In short, we need to have something in this letter to give the reader more direction. The possible candidates for thesis include the following:

1. It's the parents' job to teach creativity and make students want to learn.
2. Improving standardized test-taking skills will lead to world leadership in achievements.
3. Schools are doing a great job right now, preparing students to take tests.

One crucial feature of a thesis, at least in a letter to the editor, is that it be "argumentative" in nature: that is, it should not offer something that most readers would automatically agree with or concede. Instead, an argumentative thesis needs to be worthy of debate. It should stake out a position about which there is some controversy. Certainly all three statements succeed on this level. Perhaps this is why the letter was published.

But a pitfall of the argumentative thesis is this: it can't be too zany, too far-out, or too clearly irrational. If so, readers will dismiss it. This caveat would seem to suggest that thesis statements 2 and 3 will have to be abandoned. In 200 words, it will be well nigh impossible to prove either of those problematic assertions.

That leaves us with the first option.

Problems with this thesis, though, emerge from its wording and abstract conceptual basis: what do we mean by "creativity"? And what is it that parents need to do—as far as instilling that creativity, as far as that teaching goes—that differs from what's done in schools? These problems should form the basis for the remainder of the letter. Clearly the writer does not want to argue that creativity is taught either one place or the other. Nor does she want to suggest that "testing" is totally antithetical to creativity. My suggestion would be to develop the thesis by arguing that parental guidance should ideally complement schoolwork, which needs to combine the mastering of facts and principles (what has been called the "transmission model") with "creativity"—a term for which the writer needs to stipulate a definition. Finally, the letter should emphasize that both elements are necessary—and that both can be taught by the schools and by the parents.

A conclusion needs to move beyond the thesis and leave the reader with a new idea—the last one encountered by a reader, it tends to linger longest. Remember, though, that the conclusion is not a simple reassertion of the thesis, nor only a summing up of what's gone before. It's instead the final element of a chain of logic—the most powerful point that can only emerge after the essay's argument has been made.

The trouble with the sample letter is that in the end I don't know what it is getting at, what its main point is, or what plan of action it is actually proposing. Yes, the writer is advocating for more testing and more parental involvement at home, where parents should not necessarily provide a relaxing environment.

Oddly, the strongest writing, it seems to me, comes in the third paragraph, which says that "students are turning into dull, uncreative, test-taking machines." But in fact, that is the argument the writer is opposing. And her own position suffers because she's unable to characterize it with such vigor and lucidity.

Multiple Revisions: The Work of Writing

What follows is an experiment. Let's see if we can come up with a better sense of where this letter, this mini-essay, is going and how it should be revised. Often, changing the form of writing not only "improves" it, but makes manifest and apparent some concepts that had been either hidden or nonexistent. Poets will often do this, changing a poem, say, from free (unrhymed) verse into a rhymed and regular form, like a Spenserian sonnet or a villanelle, because doing so helps them to see what they really wanted to say.

One problem in the original letter is simply this: the paragraphs are too underdeveloped. I should point out that journalistic style dictates the use of short paragraphs, but this convention applies to reportage more than to editorial matter, which would include letters to the editor. The writing in these tends to be more "essayistic" in nature, and hence needs to follow the conventions of essays, one of which is that paragraphs need to be somewhat full (see Chapter 7). If they are not, the whole work seems to jump too swiftly from one topic to the next, without fully developing any single aspect of the argument.

So, just to see what happens, I have merged all eight paragraphs into one. In this run-together version, I've located two points that seem to me logical breakpoints for paragraphs.

REVISION I

Schools are getting blamed because they prepare students to take tests ("Schools teach for tests, instead of challenging students," Letters, Tuesday). Apparently, our schools aren't spending enough time inspiring kids creatively and academically. In fact, the students are turning into dull, uncreative, test-taking machines—all because the system is broken. ¶Yeah, right. I don't understand how the idea started, but it isn't the schools' job to teach creativity or foster a love of learning. That is the parents' responsibility. No, schools are doing exactly what they are supposed to. Schools should prepare students for standardized test-taking if we are ever to catch up with the rest of the world. ¶Then, at home, the parents should teach kids how to learn by providing books or promoting lively discussions. Children learn when they are surrounded by an atmosphere of learning. Home should be one such place. It's not just somewhere to relax at the end of a day. That can wait until after graduation.

Notice that merging the short paragraphs into one and then breaking that up these three units makes clearer how the letter contains three quite separate—but connected—elements of thought. Also, dividing up the original letter in this way, without even changing any other aspect of it, makes it seem to flow more smoothly, thus lending it a certain coherence.

When you write an argument, keep in mind that, as I suggest in Chapter 7, you should use a *topic sentence for each paragraph*. This topic sentence (i.e., the "controlling idea") essentially offers the main idea of the paragraph. It functions as a kind of mini-thesis of the paragraph that follows.

What's evident in the reformatted letter, though, is that the topic sentences don't quite work. The first paragraph seems fine, more or less summarizing the ideas of the letter to which the writer is objecting. But the second paragraph gets off-track. It starts by talking about how parents are supposed to take on some responsibility, but then it gets into how schools are doing just "what they are supposed to," and further goes off into a new direction when talking about how we can "catch up with the rest of the world."

Then, in the third paragraph, it's back to the parents and "an atmosphere of learning" at home. I would remove the "parents' responsibility" sentence in the second paragraph, since the rest of the paragraph is about the schools.

Schools are getting blamed because they prepare students to take tests ("Schools teach for tests, instead of challenging students," Letters, Tuesday). Apparently, our schools aren't spending enough time inspiring kids creatively and academically. In fact, the students are turning into dull, uncreative, test-taking machines—all because the system is broken.

Yeah, right. I don't understand how the idea started, but it isn't the schools' job to teach creativity or foster a love of learning. No, schools are doing exactly what they are supposed to. Schools should prepare students for standardized test-taking if we are ever to catch up with the rest of the world.

Then, at home, the parents should teach kids how to learn by providing books or promoting lively discussions. That is the parents' responsibility. Children learn when they are surrounded by an atmosphere of learning. Home should be one such place. It's not just somewhere to relax at the end of a day. That can wait until after graduation.

In short, then, each paragraph has to form a discrete—an identifiably separate—stage of the essay. Each needs to be complete, too, at least insofar as space allows. Sometimes people ask me how many sentences a paragraph should have, and I always point out that a paragraph can be any length. But in written essays, especially ones in the argument genre, the more successful essays tend to use paragraphs in the six- to nine-sentence range. (See the graph on page 131.) Although you can use any number that you want, keep in mind that you're striving for a full development of a single idea. If your paragraph has fewer than six sentences, ask yourself, "Could I say a bit more to explain what I mean?" If it has more than nine, ask this: "Should I break this paragraph anywhere? Is it really developing just a single idea?"

In the original letter, the paragraphs are all too short and underdeveloped. Even in the run-together and slightly modified version that I set up, the paragraphs seem a bit brief. In particular, the concluding paragraph seems to lack a logical connective or explanation. We need to know, really, why standardized testing will help the United States "catch up with the rest of the world."

But while the concluding paragraph seems brief, at least it is discrete from the others, offering as it does a surprising and interesting twist of the argument, a ΔT. It cries out for explanation and support, but that in itself suggests it's an intriguing idea.

I think that what the writer had in mind is this: if we have more standardized tests, then school will be much more rigorous. Students would be forced to read, to memorize, to reason—all so they can successfully complete the examinations, to be sure, but those examinations would give the impetus for a far more strenuous educational system. And this kind of set-up in the schools would force parents to provide a different kind of preparation and support at home. The parents could provide the "creativity-inspiring" environment, since the schools certainly would not. The writer is trying to separate out two elements of education: the testing culture and the culture in which testing is less important than providing an atmosphere in which one can think aloud, brainstorm, debate, and imagine: home.

The trouble is that the letter does not make this point strongly enough. In what's essentially an argumentative piece, the writer needs to take more seriously the opposite point of view, the "con" or counterargument. Why so? By looking at counterarguments, you as a writer increase your credibility as you refine your own ideas. In general, you want to show, then, how the counterargument is either irrelevant, not applicable in this situation, or somehow flawed. Alternatively, you could take some aspect of it into your own argument—that is, concede some ground.

In addition, con arguments lend complexity to your essay. One criticism that might be leveled against the letter is that it presents things in too simplistic a format. These are complex issues, ones that can't easily be solved by declaring standardized testing at every grade level the law of the land.

The writer has the counterarguments in her first paragraph, which is acceptable, though not perhaps ideal. And the way she refutes these is through a sarcastic "Yeah, right." Then she asserts her own, contrary idea. The letter would likely benefit by addressing these arguments more directly—and certainly it would benefit by eliminating the sarcasm. I would also delete the last sentence, "That can wait . . . ," which strikes a different tone from the rest of the letter, and introduces something that might be too strong a "con" argument (i.e., shouldn't home really be a place to relax?).

REVISION III

Schools are getting blamed because they prepare students to take tests ("Schools teach for tests, instead of challenging students," Letters, Tuesday). Apparently, our schools aren't spending enough time inspiring kids creatively and academically. In fact, the students are turning into dull, uncreative, test-taking machines—all because the system is broken.

I don't understand how the idea started, but it isn't the schools' job to teach creativity or foster a love of learning. No, schools are doing exactly what they are supposed to. Schools should prepare students for standardized test-taking if we are ever to catch up with the rest of the world.

Then, at home, the parents should teach kids how to learn by providing books or promoting lively discussions. That is the parents' responsibility. Children learn when they are surrounded by an atmosphere of learning. Home should be one such place. It's not just somewhere to relax at the end of a day.

Yet the letter still seems a bit incomplete; hence, here I would want to add a concluding paragraph that directly addressed the "con" argument about test-taking machines and came to some sort of new idea—an idea that could only be arrived at after those in the letter have been advanced.

I would add something like the following:

Standardized tests won't turn our students into "test-taking automata," provided that we use such tests with discretion and care, not as the sole teaching method, but as a facet of instruction. By doing so we will not only send the message to parents that they need to help their children learn how to think, but also that to do good work, one must master a body of knowledge and facts, for genuine creativity rests at once on imagination—and on a profound understanding of what's gone on before.

The paragraph I've added merely expresses the last stage in the thought process. But it's a necessary stage: a conclusion. It connects to the thesis but modifies it slightly; it's a stronger Δ-Thesis, or "second thesis."

At this point, too, the writer needs to look at the writing and make sure it accords with the style manual of whatever discipline she is working within. In letters to newspapers, someone else will do this for the writer. In fact, the letter seems in accord with the conventions of others that are published in *USA Today*. However, if you have to write a paper in MLA form, APA form, *Chicago Manual of Style* form, or one of many others, do make sure that you consult the appropriate handbooks or websites so that you conform to the current practices of the discipline in which you are writing.

This letter is relatively free of obvious errors. That said, I would nonetheless substitute "children" or "high school students" for "kids." I would (as I mentioned above) eliminate the sarcasm. Perhaps instead of saying, "Yeah, right," the author could say, "I strenuously disagree." I would also look hard at a few of the word choices and images, which seem to me a bit trite and tired:

... all because the system is broken ...
... foster a love of learning ...
... catch up with the rest of the world ...
... promoting lively discussions ...
... an atmosphere of learning ...

I think I've heard all of these particular locutions at least five thousand times.

REVISION IV

Schools are getting blamed because they prepare students to take tests ("Schools teach for tests, instead of challenging students," Letters, Tuesday). Apparently, our schools aren't spending enough time inspiring children creatively and academically. In fact, the students are turning into dull, uncreative, test-taking machines.

I don't understand how the idea started, but it isn't the schools' job to teach creativity or instill a love of learning. No, schools are doing exactly what they are supposed to. Schools should prepare students for standardized test-taking if we are ever to produce genuinely creative thinkers who can help solve the many pressing world problems.

Then, at home, the parents should teach their children how to learn by providing books or engaging in discussions about ideas, books, or culture. The parents, in fact, have a great responsibility. Children learn when they are surrounded by an environment in which intellectual risk-taking and challenge are encouraged. Home should be one such place. It's not just somewhere to relax at the end of a day.

Standardized tests won't turn our students into "test-taking automata," provided that we use such tests with discretion and care, not as the sole teaching method, but as a facet of instruction. By doing so we will not only send the message to parents that they need to help their children learn how to think, but also that to do good work, one must master a body of knowledge and facts, for genuine creativity rests at once on imagination—and on a profound understanding of what's gone on before.

Varied sentence lengths and patterns can heighten reader interest and provide surprise with vivid, eyeball-delighting, mind's-ear pleasing combinations. Yet striving for such combinations can sometimes introduce errors or ornate elaborations that confuse rather than delight. As your sentences grow more complex and lengthy, you need to be especially sure that your audience can follow them.

What more might the writer do with her letter, though? I suggest she combine some sentences with one another—making two or three into just one—and also introduce more variety throughout into her sentence structure. Here, then, is the final version of the letter/essay:

Schools are getting blamed because they prepare students only to take tests, a practice that is turning students into dull, uncreative, test-taking machines. ("Schools teach for tests, instead of challenging students," Letters, Tuesday).[1] Apparently, our schools aren't spending enough time inspiring children academically and creatively.[2] I don't understand how the idea started, but it isn't the schools' job to teach creativity or instill a love of learning. No, schools are doing exactly what they are supposed to. Schools should teach the fundamentals, but also prepare students for standardized test-taking if we are ever to produce the kinds of thinkers who can help solve the many pressing world problems.[3]

Then, at home, parents should teach their children how to learn. They should provide their children with interesting reading material and engage them in discussions about ideas, books, or culture. Because children learn best when they grow up in an environment that fosters and encourages intellectual risk-taking and challenge, parents, in fact, have a great responsibility.[4] True, home should be relaxing, but education should still be taking place there, and parents need to realize that their duty extends beyond simply providing food and shelter.[5]

Though it seems unlikely that standardized tests will turn our students into "test-taking automata,"[6] we still need to use such tests with discretion and care—not as the only method of instruction/evaluation, but as an epicenter, a cornerstone. By doing so, I'm suggesting, we will urge—even compel— parents to complement such a curriculum, provide support and intellectual stimulation at home, and help create an environment in which the many learned facts and ideas can be debated, socially weighed, and tested. In embracing such a strategy, we as a culture will be providing an important basis for competition in the twenty-first century and beyond, in a world that is globalized as well as digitalized, that's facing challenges we can now not even conceive of, and in which a

1. Similar to the original version, this opening must establish a context. It introduces a "problem" of sorts, which is good. It provides a point of departure, a "motive" for the entire piece that follows.

2. Revision: I have combined two sentences, and I've also made the first paragraph more fully developed.

3. I have changed some of the wording here, eliminating the idea of "catching up with the rest of the world." I also focus the paragraph on simply the issue of the schools and what they should be doing. Note also that I have changed the tone by omitting the sarcastic "Yeah, right." My revision includes the idea that schools teach more than test-taking skills, too.

4. Revision: note how I have changed the structure of the sentence here, so that not all are subject-verb-object.

5. Revision: last sentence of paragraph focuses on what parents need to do.

6. Revision: this whole paragraph directly addresses the "con" argument that originally was in opening.

solid understanding of what's gone before—of the very things that standardized tests test for—will serve as a strong foundation for rational, informed, inventive decision making.[7]

7. Revision: this last sentence tries to capture some of the complexity of the causal link between "standardized test-taking" and catching "up with the rest of the world."

Now, you might argue that these are my ideas in the last paragraph, not of the writer of the letter to the newspaper. But in fact, all of them are implicit in the original letter. The paragraphs I have added merely express and open up the last stage in the thought process. But it's a necessary stage: a conclusion. Is the argument finally an "imaginative" one, though? It seems to suggest that standardized tests are the ultimate good, the final boss, as it were. It implies students all live in a home with an actively involved family. It connects debate, reading, and intellectual challenge with success on the world stage. It fails to deal with the enormous influence of peers, not to mention of social media. There are places this letter might go, in short, but in its final version, we have a place to start from, and the writer deserves praise for the position she staked out in a wide-circulation national newspaper.

12 Figures and Fallacies, or Being Forceful but Not Cheating at Argument

How you present your ideas is in many ways just as important as those ideas themselves: your argument can be strengthened or weakened by how your express and explain it. But on the other hand, you don't want your argument to be empty, just prettily expressed but content-less—all "rhetoric" and no substance. You don't want to use language so striking that it conceals the ideas you want to convey. In short, you need to strive for a balance between being impressively forceful and being rigorously logical; between saying things poetically and saying things plainly. Sometimes pretty works, sometimes plain. Keep the reader a bit off guard, never knowing what to expect and regularly surprised by both your ideas and your manner of expression.

Figures of Speech

Rarely taught in today's schools and universities, except perhaps in specialized courses in rhetoric, figures of speech—names for the ways in which writers arrange sentences—are useful to know, if for no other reason than that they allow you to craft more complex and exciting prose. Hence these figures of speech might improve your effectiveness at communicating your ideas.

Some might consider these figures to be rhetorical "tricks" or sleights of hand. True, they can be misused. But at the same time, using them can help you think of new ways to phrase your ideas, and that exercise alone might prove valuable in helping you rethink what you're writing. Then, too, you need to be conscious of how the most effective prose typically contains certain focused areas of intensity, where the writer is working hard to convey a point of some importance. When you compose, you need to bear in mind that all your prose should not be at the same level, for if it is, it will be flat—lacking in excitement—no matter how carefully honed. Employing figures of speech, where appropriate, will make your prose both more interesting and more various, allowing you to highlight important areas and shade in significant details in subtle but useful ways.

In addition, it's good to be aware of these figures of speech so that you can identify them in speech or prose you encounter. They are often used to manipulate readers, to persuade them rhetorically—without the use of logic—so you need to be wary of them as well. Writing has to be more than just figures of speech. It must have a logical, reasoned basis—specifically, identifiable elements that form the basis of a solid argument. If used to excess, the figures can make readers or listeners fail to notice what you're saying, which should not be your goal, at least not here. Like most things, figures of speech can be overused or misused. But they can also be used effectively and honestly.

Though some rhetoric textbooks will mention figures of speech, the most comprehensive survey is Richard A. Lanham's *A Handlist of Rhetorical Terms*, which you should refer to for more examples or description. Here are a few of the most useful figures; some of these you have certainly encountered and can easily recognize. Others might seem a little alien to you.

1. **Alliteration.** Repetition of initial consonant sounds in order to call attention to an expression. This can also involve repetition of some vowel sounds (so it can have an element of assonance). The great baseball player Ted Williams was called, for example, the "Splendid Splinter."

2. **Anaphora.** Using the same word or group of words at the beginning of multiple clauses: "It was the best of times, it was the worst of times, it was the age of wisdom, it was the age of foolishness, it was the epoch of belief, it was the epoch

of incredulity, it was the season of Light, it was the season of Darkness, it was the spring of hope, it was the winter of despair, we had everything before us, we had nothing before us, we were all going direct to Heaven, we were all going direct the other way ..." (Charles Dickens, the opening lines of *A Tale of Two Cities*).

3. **Anastrophe.** Atypical arrangement of word order: "Backward run the sentences till reels the mind" (famous parody of *Time* magazine's style). Yoda, in *Star Wars*, typically uses this figure: "Trust you must."

4. **Antanagoge.** Conceding a negative feature of a situation or argument but offering a positive (yet relevant) one to more than compensate. Lanham's example comes from Alexander Pope: "A mighty maze, but not without a plan" (Pope's description of the universe and nature).

5. **Antimetabole.** Repeating the idea of a sentence or phrase, but inverting its components in the second half of the expression. For example, "The dragon was fierce, its breath flame-filled, or was its breath fierce and the dragon flame-filled?" "Rappaccini's daughter was innocent, though her lover was poisoned, but her lover was innocent, and it was she who was poisoned." (This is in reference to "Rappaccini's Daughter," a short story by Nathaniel Hawthorne.)

6. **Antistrophe.** Using the same word at the end of multiple, successive clauses. (See example for **Anaphora.**)

7. **Asyndeton.** Omission of "and" or "or" when writing out a list: "She was lively, intelligent, noble." (See also **Polysyndeton.**)

8. **Climax.** Arrangement of items in order of ascending importance. For example, "The man was admired, lauded, and finally knighted." "The animals were taught to obey simple commands, to convey their feelings to one another, and, eventually, to speak." Sometimes the order of climax might seem counterintuitive, and this in itself is surprising and effective. For example, a headline in the sports section of the *New York Times* proclaims,

For Giants,
Poor Start,

Poor Finish,
Poor Season

This is an effective ordering of information.

9. **Epizeuxis.** Repeating words one right after another. "He cried, cried for all that he had lost and all that he had won." A familiar line from politics: "We are shocked, shocked, at this indiscretion."

10. **Hypallage.** Lanham defines this as "[a]wkward or humorous changing of agreement or application of words, as with Bottom playing Pyramus: 'I see a voice. Now will I to the chink / To spy an I can hear my Thisby's face'" (86). What does this linguistic distortion convey? Is Shakespeare trying to call attention to the artifice of the "play within the play," and perhaps to the artifice of all drama as well? Or is he just using the synesthetic confusion as a way to show how wacky or maybe love-struck the character of Bottom is? Another example: "We have long held in this country the Byronic ideal that human nature is essentially good or graceful, that behind the sheath of skin is a little globe of glow to be harnessed for creative uses" (Slater 44). It can also refer to a modified expression of some kind: "Winning isn't everything, it's the lonely thing." "Early to bed, early to rise, makes a man healthy, wealthy, and despised." "Now that the genome project is completed, we're in the DNAge" (Justin Johnson, Princeton University freshman).

11. **Hyperbole.** Extreme and obvious exaggeration: "If all the Earthy Mass were rambd in Sacks / And saddled on an Emmet small, / Its load were light unto those packs / Which Sins do bring on all" (lines 41–44 of "An Extasy of Joy let in by this Reply returnd in Admiration" [section 17 of "Gods Determinations touching his Elect," in *The Poems of Edward Taylor*]). (Note than an "emmet" is an ant.)

12. **Metaphor/Simile.** A comparison, implied or stated, between two or more things, but one that isn't so common as to have entered common parlance (in which case it would be trite): "An ogre is like an onion" (*Shrek*). "With minimal overhang front and rear, the [BMW] is as compact and hard as bunched

biceps" (Dan Niel, writing for the *New York Times*). "Ships at a distance have every man's wish on board" (opening sentence of Zora Neale Hurston's *Their Eyes Were Watching God*).

13. **Oxymoron.** The pairing of opposites: "burning ice," "calm fury."

14. **Polyptoton.** Repetition of a form of a word that is not exactly the same as the word itself. "The idea of a revolving door revolved in his head." "Be kind, act kindly, reward kindness—and you'll be treated in kind." "Don't be concerned about the goods you can acquire; worry more about the good that you can do."

15. **Polysyndeton.** Inclusion of the conjunction between each element: "She was lively and intelligent and noble."

What practical application might these figures have? Do they transform one's writing—or are they only polysyllabic Greek terms that fill up rhetoric textbooks? Most of my examples are from literature, too: does one need to be a poet to use them? One exercise that always proves interesting and fruitful seems at first glance a little mechanical, but bear with me: take a short piece of your own writing—something you are not too pleased with—and, keeping the same "content" or basic idea, reword it using figures of speech. Try for ten figures in a paragraph. I know that sounds like a lot, but several might be applied to one sentence alone.

Here's a paragraph that doesn't exactly soar (it's from a college paper I wrote about medical malpractice):

> If the number of malpractice suits goes up, as indeed it ought to, costs would also go up. But with the general trend toward socialization of medicine, this should not be a problem. A more important development of increased malpractice litigation would be the arising of a new form of doctor. These "new" doctors would be less dependent on their own opinion alone and would seek out experts. Numerous and various tests would be conducted on each patient to determine exactly the nature of the disease. Only by elaborate testing techniques can the extent of an illness in a person be determined.

Admittedly pedestrian prose, it's nonetheless generally "correct"; it does make a point, though perhaps rather too circuitously. It uses a "hinge-structure," with the third sentence working as the topic sentence ("A more important development ..."). While this might be better placed earlier on, I won't touch it just now, since I want only to import changes in expression, that is, figures of speech.

Now, it's not usually just random what figures you choose. You want to use the best ones. But here I will simply import the above figures to see whether that makes the piece come alive or sing a little, or at least show some signs of once having lived.

Up climb the costs of medicine, as the number of malpractice suits soars.[1] Yet soar they ought to, and our government, more and more socialized in places that matter, will both pay those big Washingtones and impose their authority to create a new, super-breed of medical doctors: less dependent on their own experience and opinions, these doctors will seek out other experts whose opinions count, will seek out all the current research, will seek out, in a word, the truth.[2] Medical tests—numerous, various, exhaustive, probative—would come to bear, and as an entirety, they would bear what?—the fruit of knowledge: namely, the exact nature of the disease.[3] Using a panoply of tests as their first-line armamentarium, then diagnosing and treating and finally cornering that foe, these new doctors will high-tech disease to distraction, will information-overload it to death, will show that knowledge is indeed power.[4] The power to heal.[5]

Notice how the meaning of the original has shifted somewhat, too, even though I attempted only to change the way that I expressed my ideas. Suddenly, the paragraph seems to be a clarion call for an entirely new kind of medicine, something only hinted at rather listlessly in the original. In the next rewrite, I would strive to tone down the "figures" a little, and strive to make the

1. Anastrophe, alliteration, metaphor
2. Anaphora, polyptoton
3. Asyndeton, metaphor, polyptoton
4. Polysyndeton, hypallage, climax
5. Epizeuxis

paragraph a little less apocalyptic in tone. After all, it's just arguing that an increase in malpractice suits might scare doctors into doing more testing and more careful diagnosis; I could easily revert to that particular emphasis, all the while maintaining some of the verbal punch of the rewrite:

Medical costs climb, and simultaneously, the number of malpractice suits soars. And soar they ought to, as more and more people suffer from poor practice and either hasty or ill-conceived medical treatments. Malpractice suits are really the only way for society to take a stand against medical charlatanism, against those doctors who hurt us in more than just our pocketbooks. We need to in some way create, to enable, a new country-wide healthcare system, one that seeks not just to make money, dispense drugs with impunity, and perform as many surgeries as are physically possible. No. Instead, we need doctors to order more and more of the right kind of tests, to act in a much more consultative way with their peers, and to evaluate cases with both more information and more caution. While disease is elusive, with our current scientific know-how and the power of networking, doctors should be able to arrive at superior diagnoses and effective treatments. That this will take more work and more time is certain; it might initially cost more money. But with more patients being treated successfully, with more healing of our citizens, that money will be more than made back; doctors who heal patients will in fact be healing our economy as well.

What is slightly sobering about this version, though, is that after I removed some of the verbal adornments, its weaknesses became highlighted. For example, is it arguing that the government should help settle malpractice claims? Is that a reasonable expectation? It also seems to imply that the whole consulting/testing protocol is something new. It isn't. Doctors have been doing this for years. So what then might characterize this "new kind of medicine," finally? Still more tests? Seems to me an unimaginative solution. The last sentence, which hints at affordable health care, seems OK, as it goes back to the initial idea about climbing costs. But it strikes me that this nine-sentence paragraph lacks coherence: it has too many issues in it, and probably should be broken into two or possibly three paragraphs: malpractice suit increases; medical costs/access problems; testing and the "new" medicine, one that would be more affordable, more reliable, and more available to a general population.

Susan Bell provides several good examples of how F. Scott Fitzgerald edited *The Great Gatsby*, an enterprise that consisted of doing just what I have done here. But he was really good at it. Bell suggests that "Fitzgerald was a prose techie who would not merely polish but power up a weak passage" (155). He did this through skillful manipulation of rhetorical devices.

For example, here is an early version of some musings by the novel's narrator, Nick Carraway, as he listens to his companions' idle prattle:

> I was thirty. Beside that realization, their importunities were dim and far away. Before me stretched the portentous menacing road of a new decade.

Note that Fitzgerald's prose does not completely lack ornament—he uses the (admittedly tired) "menacing road" metaphor to describe the next decade of life. But in his revision, he added quite a lot more:

> Thirty—the promise of a decade of loneliness, a thinning list of single men to know, a thinning briefcase of enthusiasm, thinning hair. (Qtd. by Bell 156–57)

Bell remarks about Fitzgerald, "He was driven to edit a sentence silly until it punched" (156), and punch this sentence, or sentence fragment, does. In the revision, Fitzgerald has abandoned standard syntax. No longer are there three full sentences but rather just one fragment. Specifically, what figures does Fitzgerald use? I see metaphor, anaphora, climax, metaphor, alliteration, asyndeton, and something very like hypallage—all in a twenty-three-word sentence fragment.

A City University of New York student of mine, Eddie F., objected to the revised version, however. He said, "I think the first version is more straightforward, more easy to understand.

I mean what is 'a thinning briefcase of enthusiasm,' anyway? I have no idea." I thought that was an interesting objection. What Fitzgerald did to his prose was to transform it into something very much like poetry, and reading poetry requires a certain willingness to engage metaphorical thinking. Hence the sentence Eddie F. does not like will impress and amaze only those people willing to engage in Fitzgerald's metaphorical mode of thought, who are willing to deal with prose that has a poetic quality. In fact, let's look at it as a poem:

> Thirty—
> the promise
> of a decade
> of loneliness,
> a thinning list
> of single men
> to know,
> a thinning briefcase
> of enthusiasm,
> thinning hair.

It works for me. Audience, as always, matters the most. When you say something, you have a nearly infinite way of expressing the idea; it's up to you to figure out what's most appropriate to convey your meaning, what form of language is best suited to your purpose, and how your intended audience will understand what you are attempting to get across. Obviously the final version of his idea means something quite different from Fitzgerald's first version. The lines are from a novel, *The Great Gatsby*, and are not simply attempting to convey information or argue for something. Quite the opposite—in these lines, Fitzgerald aspires to create art, to write something that goes beyond the quotidian. The takeaway here is this: style helps to create content. The way you say things isn't just an inflection on the meaning you're attempting to get across, but something intimately conjoined with that meaning. If you can express yourself as poetically, as lyrically, as Fitzgerald does here in his final version, you're very fortunate—but not everyone wants that, and not everyone will understand you.

Logical Fallacies: A Sampler

As a counterpoint to the figures, I want to present a few logical fallacies: ways of expression and reasoning that many writers employ in an effort to cloud the issue, distract the audience, shift the focus, or blend the trivial with the important. As popular as these might be, they do not, finally, meet scrupulous, scholarly standards. Using them constitutes cheating at argument. (And using figures of speech insofar as you are relying on them to carry the weight of your argument is also "cheating at argument.") As I suggested, you must consciously maintain a somewhat precarious (or at least difficult) balance—between being, on the one hand, forceful in expression, saying things in an interesting, engaging way—and on the other, being logical, honest, and fair.

Logical fallacies have inundated our lives, as you might already have discovered; they are especially rife during election years, and in advertising; hence many of my examples will come from either politics or Madison Avenue–based campaigns. I should also point out that there are degrees of fallaciousness; some of these examples are more egregious than others. Note too that fallacies often overlap—or a statement can contain two or more fallacies at the same time.

I provide the following list for a couple of reasons. First, you need to avoid using these fallacies in your own writing. They gravely weaken your argument. Some people might be persuaded by them, but they are not the people you want to persuade, as they either agree with you to begin with or are not looking very carefully at the details of your argument. Thus their agreement can't be really either full or sincere, since they don't know what you are getting at. In addition, by using these you engage in an activity that damages your powers of reason. They suggest defective logic, and if you are inadvertently employing such a mechanism, you should amp up your self-awareness; if you are using them to manipulate an audience into siding with you, that might be even worse.

Second, as you read and evaluate sources, as you go through your daily life bombarded—verbally, textually—with all sorts of arguments, you need to be able to sort through them. You want to distinguish the strong arguments from the weak ones, the credible claims from the obviously faulty ones. A knowledge of some of the basic fallacies will help you do this.

Here are the most commonly discussed and easily identifiable fallacies:

1. **Ad hominem.** Attacking a personality rather than a position. (But sometimes a personality is important: character and personality might be relevant to considerations of how well someone might perform in a position of public office, for example.)
   a. Donald Trump's ideas about tax reform can't be trusted: he's just too wealthy himself.
   b. How can we take seriously Hemingway's advice about life—he committed suicide!
   c. "Alas, 'Sex, Sex, and More Sex' seems to have been rushed into print to capitalize on [Sue] Johanson's newfound popularity; it's not easy to trust a sex guru who misspells the name of Dr. Ernst Gräfenberg (the first modern physician to describe the alleged G spot) and also Peyronie's disease" (Sohn).
2. **Ad populum.** Suggesting that because something is popular, it is therefore good, valuable, or justifiable in any way.
   a. Smoking can't be so bad—millions of people do it!
   b. An argument in the United States in 1850: Why, what's wrong with slavery? Thousands of people practice it, and it's the very basis of our economy—and has been for more than two hundred years!
3. **Circular argument.** Using some key term—or a slightly modified version of it—in both the premise and the conclusion, this is also known as *begging the question*.
   a. "Hawking, the British physicist, claimed to have solved the black hole information paradox. New simulations suggested that the matter and energy jets that spew out of some black holes are caused by their spin" (Hawking).
   b. Home ownership is to be valued because owning real estate almost always increases one's net worth.

c. Almost all cars today are engineered to go at least 100 mph, so speeding must be safe.

4. **Either-or.** Sometimes called the fallacy of suppressed alternatives or the "false dilemma"—usually a tactic meant to alarm the audience. To be a genuine false dilemma, a statement has to offer a pair of "contrary" alternatives—ones different from each other but not absolutely exhaustive of the possibilities. If a statement offers a pair of "contradictory" alternatives, then it is not a false dilemma but in fact an obvious statement that has a tautological ring to it. ("Either the Republicans or Democrats will control Congress in 2020.")

   a. "Psychoanalysis: Is It Science or Is It Toast?" (Merkin).

   b. "We are fast approaching a watershed moment in our social progress. Either we will move forward toward a much more cooperative and coordinated global community, or we will regress into a more and more tribalized, combative, and totalitarian existence. To continue to ignore climate change means putting at risk billions of people around the world. Ultimately, it means consigning our children to a future of chaos and disintegration" (Gelbspan).

   c. Either we buy that house or relegate ourselves to paying landlords for the rest of our lives.

   d. Men can be divided into two categories: boxers or briefs.

   e. If I don't get the plastic surgery, I'll be doomed to a lifetime of anonymity and blandness.

   f. After President Trump sent cruise missiles to bomb Syria in 2017, people asked, "Is he an isolationist or an interventionist?" (Both positions imply a coherent foreign policy, a consciously constructed identity.)

5. **Red herring or distraction.** A form of statement in which the purpose is to distract the audience or opponent from the issue at hand. One usually resorts to a red herring when one's own arguments are conspicuously weak. This kind of argument attempts to shift the ground rather subtly (or sometimes not-so-subtly).

   a. "Leaving aside the fact that the human race evolved as omnivores and that we most likely would never have acquired our highly proficient brains through vegetarianism, no soy product could ever replicate to any degree a perfectly barbequed steak. I was a vegetarian for many years, and I was never fooled by any of the faux meats. And anyway, if I'm going to eat vegetables, I'm not going to pretend they're meat" (Felaco).

b. It's true that Mr. Obama didn't get all the reforms he wanted. But he did bring vengeance on Osama bin Laden.

c. So what if the university exploits part-time adjunct faculty? They're such good teachers! And besides, they don't have to work if they don't want to.

6. **Faulty analogy.** Using a comparison between two sets of circumstances or things that offers no proof of a significant connection between the things compared.

a. "JUDGMENT: The *Indianapolis Star* reports that the Indiana Court of Appeals has dismissed a lawsuit demanding damages from a cell phone manufacturer because of a collision involving a woman talking on one of their cell phones. The judge's reasoning was that people regularly eat while driving and it would be unreasonable to sue the cook if they crash" (Black).

b. An essay is like a peanut butter and jelly sandwich. The bread's the introduction and conclusion—inside, though, is the good stuff.

c. "You say the law discriminates against people of color. One of my coworkers had an accident that turned his skin blue, and yet we still treated him like one of the guys."

7. **Emotive language.** Using terms that prejudge the issue in a certain way, so the argument is made through the terms themselves rather than through logic.

a. "Frankly, I don't care about Formula I [racing] as it abandons Europe to sack the pockets of a collection of dim bulb Far Eastern potentates. But the plight of major-league open-wheel racing in America does concern me as it plunges toward oblivion" (Yates).

b. The monstrous corporation, ever feeding its giant maw with the flesh of average citizens, needs not to be tamed or cut down in size, but exterminated, just as any enemy of society should be.

c. People who brazenly parade their near-naked flesh, while they're making a transparent pretense of sunbathing on our public beaches, should be fined and jailed.

8. **Hasty generalization.** Arriving at a fallacious conclusion about an issue after only a small or unrepresentative sampling has been examined. Another way of looking at this might be as extrapolation from incomplete data.

   a. What are students like here? Well, I've only been to the gym, but in general the students seem more interested in sports than in studying.

   b. It's been rainy every day since we moved here. I guess the sun never shines in Seattle.

   c. "Rod doesn't have time for people who criticize his taste for roadkill. 'I'm willing to take responsibility for what I eat, while the vegans and vegetarians preaching at me eat vegetables shipped in from other countries and trucked up from down South so they can get the food that's not in season. They are guilty of feeding the monster machines that are creating the roadkill'" (Wells).

   d. Every philosophy major I've met is a man with a beard—so it's clear that women can't be philosophers.

9. **Post hoc ergo propter hoc.** Suggesting that since one event comes before another, it must necessarily *cause* that event.

   a. I had Earl Grey instead of Orange Pekoe tea at breakfast and then got an A on my exam. I think Earl Grey tea must increase intelligence.

   b. I lost thirty pounds and suddenly seemed to have no friends. It seems that fat people must be popular.

   c. "We're all going to die. And we all eat food. Therefore, food must be the culprit" (Windolf).

10. **Straw person/straw man.** Misstating the opposing position, making it seem simplistic, easy to knock down (i.e., like a figure of straw).

    a. "No," the professor said, "we must start the debate about abortion by substituting the word 'murder' for 'abortion,' since that's what it is. Who of you will defend murder?"

b. By trying to increase the writing required for graduation, the college clearly wants to increase levels of student stress, and hence withdrawals from the university.

11. **Non sequitur.** Latin for "it does not follow," this type of fallacy does not really fit into any other category. Lanham defines it as follows: "A statement that bears no relationship to the context preceding."

   a. "At the Nashua senior center, a Mr. Kim, who looked well into his seventies, addressed the audience. After apologizing for his English, he said, 'To hell with Lipitor, a hundred and fifty dollars a month! I decided to hell with it. If I die, I die. I exercised. I lowered cholesterol level. Ran half marathon!'" (O'Rourke).

   b. That car should prove to be ideal transportation. After all, it's shaped like a box.

   c. "Liberal. Conservative. Democrat. Republican. Every opinion in the universe" (ad for iUniverse.com).

12. **Slippery slope.** Saying that taking one action will lead to another, more threatening or grave situation, but failing to provide a logical connection that could prove such a sequence of events will happen.

   a. "In 1972, a night watchman patrolling a hotel-office complex noticed that the basement garage door had been taped open and, attributing this to the carelessness of a maintenance worker earlier that day, peeled the tape off. When, on his next round, he found the door taped open again, he called the police. As a result, citizens of the United States do not enjoy the benefits (or suffer the aggravations) of national health insurance" (Miller).

   b. "More and more [politicians] are staking out the rhetorical terrain pioneered by U.S. Representative Tom Cole of Oklahoma last spring: 'If George Bush loses the election,' he said, 'Osama bin Laden wins the election. It's that simple'" (Mitchell).

   c. If we don't increase homeland security, it seems clear that in no time democracy will completely disappear, as each democratic state is toppled by terrorists.

d. The library budget was cut again. At this rate, in fifty years there will be no books.

One of my erstwhile colleagues contended that he would no longer teach fallacies because "fallacies are actually true." I think what he meant was that fallacies often succeed at persuading an audience to your position. My point here, though, is that even though they might persuade your audience, they do so in the wrong way. They don't use logic; they use tricks. They are dishonest. Any practical value that they have—such as persuasiveness—is lost because they do not assess the evidence or analyze a situation in a logical, sober, and disinterested manner. They elevate persuasion as the end to be gained at almost any cost, including that of truth. At the risk of committing a logical fallacy myself (faulty analogy), I feel I must point out that there are many forms of persuasion (torture, coercion, bribery), which we in a civilized society should not employ, and using deceitful verbal trickery, while by no means the same thing as waterboarding a person, inhabits the same general galaxy of iniquity.

13 The Argument of Style

Style actually functions as a significant part of your argument. While many people separate form from content, style from substance, this division seems artificial. Style, especially when distinctive, can itself make an argument quite separate from the logical points that you make within your writing. If you work on your style, the argument of style will buttress the logical argument itself.

What makes for a good—a distinctive, original, effective—writing style? What do we even mean by a "good" writing style? It seems to me that most often people define a good style through negative characteristics, that is, by declaring that good writing must avoid certain linguistic constructions, certain kinds of language, or even certain words. In fact, writing has all too often been taught as if the keyboard or blank page were a minefield filled with all manner of hidden explosive devices, any one of which could blow you and your work to smithereens.

I will mention here what kinds of things you ought to avoid, but I'd also like to make some positive suggestions about what tactics or rhetorical strategies you might consider emulating.

Style: Some Things to Avoid, Probably

What should you try to avoid? Writing situations vary, but in general, try to avoid indirect, extremely complex, circumlocutious writing. Robin MacPherson captures this notion quite nicely in his textbook *University English*: "First and foremost, lucidity, economy, and precision are overriding considerations: no matter how demanding the subject matter, a good writer of academic English is never verbose or deliberately obscure, and will always try to visualize the reader and go out to him, instead of expecting him somehow or other to construe [the] meaning" (5). In general, academic writing should be direct, forthright, and truthful, though I think you also need to be aware that in some nonacademic contexts (for example, in a letter giving bad news) a forthright directness might be abrasive, harsh, or insensitive. However, learning how to write clearly and directly will also sensitize you to levels of tone and nuances of implication, and help equip you with the ability to be indirect or circumlocutious when it's needed.

But I promised some prohibitions, some things to avoid in writing, some stylistic pratfalls. OK. What follows constitutes a partial list.

1. Avoid frequently using "to be" verbs (is, are, were, was, being, been, be), unless avoiding them makes your writing sound weird or awkward. Often you will find yourself using many "to be" verbs within a paragraph. Such a strategy leads to somewhat leaden, slow-moving, difficult-to-understand prose, and dull "there is/there are" structures. Try to avoid using "to be" verbs more than a few times per paragraph. (Note that I probably use too many "to be" verbs here, but what can I say? *Nolo contendere.*)

2. Avoid using many "Th-openers," sentences that begin with words such as *The, This, There, Then, Those, That, Thus.* (Starting with "Though" would be OK, however, as would starting with names that start with "Th-" or with words other than those on the list above.) You should probably try to avoid these because using one on top of the other tends to produce sentences with very similar structures, which can lull the reader into a state of mindless passivity: rarely your goal.

3. Avoid sentences that use multiple prepositional phrases, especially prepositional phrases linked one after another. Using more than two or three prepositions per sentence effectively clogs your prose. Try to keep preposition use to a minimum. When you edit an essay, you'll find that the softest, most vul-

nerable places are prepositional phrases. Instead of writing, "*In* this essay, I want to explore how the minds *of* doctors work when they try to listen *to* patients talk *about* problems *with* their health," try something like "This essay explores how doctors hear—or ignore—their patients' stories."

4. As much as possible, avoid using nouns that end in *-tion*, *-cion*, *-sion*, which tend to accompany prepositional phrases and muffle a sentence's impact. Often you will find yourself using a lot of these noun forms that have been created out of a verb. "Justify" becomes "justification"; "hierarchize" (which came from "hierarchy") becomes "hierarchization"; "familiarize" becomes "familiarization." I suggest that you not pile up these words (ironic that they're called "nominalizations"), for doing so deadens your sentences' impact.

5. Avoid trite expressions, jargon, catchphrases. What is trite, though? What is jargon? Ideally you need to have some inner monitor that registers when the language you use sounds like a cliché—is old, tired, hackneyed, lacking in originality, ho-hum, boring, flat, colloquial, or just plain blah. However, no one is born with such a monitor; you need to develop one. To do so, be as conscious as possible of what kinds of words you use when you write formal essays. Ask yourself after each sentence, Have I expressed this idea in an original way—or am I borrowing something that's not ultimately worthy of repetition? Can I say this in a fresher, more striking manner? Are there other words I might use? To catch trite (overused) language or clichés, think whether you have heard a given expression—or seen it in print—more than three or four times; if you have, then it is probably trite and should be avoided. Usually these expressions involve a comparison of some kind (*He runs like a deer*), or some metaphorical language use (*He salivated over the prospect of driving the Ferrari*). In general, try not to rely on phrases that others invented long ago, and that long ago lost their power and imaginativeness. When Henry David Thoreau talked about how people should "march to the beat of a different drummer," the expression had some force, but now it has been used so much, plastered so often on posters and declaimed in

so many advertisements, that its initial impact is lost. While I in general disapprove of ending a paragraph with a quotation, I will do so here because I think these words of Martin Amis have especial force: "To idealize: all writing is a campaign against cliché. Not just clichés of the pen but clichés of the mind and clichés of the heart. When I dispraise, I am usually quoting clichés. When I praise, I am usually quoting the opposed qualities of freshness, energy and reverberation of voice" (qtd. by Turner 10).

6. Avoid vulgar slang. Four-letter words and the like are generally not acceptable in formal writing, unless you are quoting from a work of literature that uses such language. (Many contemporary works now do, I note.) Using quotation marks around slang expressions, as in "This novel really 'sucks,'" is also inappropriate; the quotation marks do not justify the use of vulgar slang. In addition, it's fairly clear that formal writing does not exactly replicate speech, with its many pauses, redundancies, and self-interruptions—not to mention its frequent use of vernacular language. So even though something sounds right out loud, it may not necessarily be correct when put into writing. I suggest you keep a list of all the words that your professors tell you are slang, and try to avoid those words when you write papers. Sometimes, too, words will be understandable within a given context but make little sense outside that context. The following sentence, for example, seems senseless, until the context is made clear: "I'll have an everything with nothing." (Ordering lunch at a bagel shop.) You need to consider audience and situation.

7. Avoid extremely obscure language. Words like *erumpent*, *thigmotaxis*, *sterquilinous*, *anentiomorphous*, *floccinaucinihilip-ilification*, *thesaurization*, or the like, while interesting, usually hide your meaning. (Of course, if your audience is conversant with such vocabulary, then these words would not be off-limits.)

8. Avoid monotonous repetition, such as following the same sentence structure for almost every sentence, or using the same words over and over in the same paragraph. Typically,

English sentences are set up as subject-verb-object sequences, a pattern that rapidly becomes boring for the reader.

9. Avoid excessive embedding of clauses (hypotaxis) within sentences (see the example from Henry James, below).

10. Avoid highlighting, boldfacing, underlining, italicizing, or capitalizing for emphasis—make your prose itself clearly establish what needs emphasis and what does not. If you want to highlight something and you don't feel that your sentence structures do a good enough job, use only one highlighting device (e.g., italics). Mixing the kinds of highlighting serves more to confuse than to illuminate the reader. One student I had would always turn in handwritten work, and he would use capital letters, yellow highlighting, quotation marks, and underlining to represent various levels of emphasis in his paper. This practice I found very confusing.

11. Avoid emotive language, "emoticons," and typographical eccentricities. "It was {{{{{{{{{Sheila!}}}}}}}}." And there you are. ☺ Also, you probably should avoid exclamation points in expository prose. One reader of a book of mine said that one is allowed two exclamation points over the course of one's writing life. I know that we're living in an effusive era, but rein it in.

12. In general, avoid passive constructions. You need to know the difference between *active voice* and *passive voice*. In active voice, an agent acts. It performs something. You mention it. "The shopping cart hit John's car." In passive constructions the agent receives the action. "John's car was hit." By what? By whom? Very often no agent inhabits passive constructions, which can make those constructions a little dishonest, as if they were withholding information: "It was decided that you are to be fired"; "The car was evidently hit." Who decided? Who hit the car? Since the passive construction tends to conceal agency, I suggest that you use active voice, unless you must conceal agency. Sometimes, though, the passive conceals not only agency but meaning as well. One essay I read contains this sentence: "Clearly, opposition to the cynicism of the qualitative symptoms of the disease is apparent." I don't

believe there is any meaning here, or if there is, I welcome you to find it. Once a student asked me, "Is it always wrong to use the passive?" and I thought about this awhile. "Always" statements are vexed: I usually try to avoid categorical statements, especially about matters of style and usage. In fact some academic fields, particularly in the natural and social sciences, consider the passive voice more scholarly (see Chapter 2).

It is important to note that writing evolves and changes as people challenge these "rules." Perhaps in the future, emoticons and stickers will be part of the standard formal essay. And in the past, much more hypotaxis was acceptable, even encouraged. Consider, for example, a section of Henry James's "The New Novel," originally published in 1914, in which James discusses some of the novelists of his day:

> The act of squeezing out to the utmost the plump and more or less juicy orange of a particular acquainted state and letting this affirmation of energy, however directed or undirected, constitute for them the "treatment" of a theme—*that* is what we remark them as mainly engaged in, after remarking the example so strikingly, so originally set, even if an undue subjection to it be here and there repudiated. Nothing is further from our thought than to undervalue saturation and possession, the fact of the particular experience, the state and degree of acquaintance incurred, however such a consciousness may have been determined; for these things represent on the part of the novelist, as on the part of any painter of things seen, felt or imagined, just one half of his authority—the other half being represented of course by the application he is inspired to make of them. (189)

Henry James's later writings often employ a style that supplants or supersedes content and argument. Or rather, the style is the argument. Such writing, difficult to read, embodies many of the prohibitions mentioned above. I especially like his insertion of "of course." And while the paragraph clearly demonstrates James's genius, his uniqueness, it also showcases many of the kinds of things that you should avoid in your own writing.

Try to straightforwardly communicate your ideas to an audience. And be aware that while the audience might read your words more than once, most will not likely go back again and again trying to puzzle out your meaning. James's paragraph is an elaborate expression of admiration for what the "new novelists" were doing, but it takes a few readings to "squeeze out to the utmost the plump and more or less juicy orange" of that particular understanding from his paragraph. I'd say it means something like the following, but you are welcome to arrive at your own interpretation:

> New novelists wring the ultimate from a theme, and while this very squeezing may or may not be interesting, it's only half the battle—they also need to show how their obsessive examination of what they are writing about applies to some larger issue.

This somehow seems to me a lot less interesting than the original. But it's also a bit easier to understand. In a way, it goes back to Eddie F.'s point about Fitzgerald: do we want quick understanding (something that we in the digital age, in particular, seem to value a lot), or do we want to linger over words and admire the way that masterful writers put them together?

Crafting a Style

Let me offer a few suggestions for what you ought to think about when crafting an individual and lucid writing style. In general, you should strive to make your writing communicative yet interesting. It's really as simple as that. A reader should feel something akin to delight while reading, should want to read on, should in some way forget that he or she is reading, and easily engage the progression of ideas on the page. There should be a smoothness, maybe even a sense of poetry to the writing, but at the same time it needs to carry intellectual content. It needs to present the individuality of your insights and your experiences, even though the language it uses is a shared one. You need to make the language your own while also making it something others will find understandable—maybe even captivating.

Retaining the reader's interest, then, conveying ideas, and demonstrating an originality of expression—some people can do this with little difficulty, while others struggle with it for years. For those who don't come to it naturally, let me offer a few suggestions about what to strive for in crafting a writing style. Keep in mind that these are only suggestions, and that this brief list does not exhaust the possibilities.

1. *Variation.* You need to make sure that your sentences do not follow the same pattern all the time. Employ some figures of speech—but do so judiciously. Make some sentences "right-handed" (i.e., starting with the subject), and others "left-handed" (starting with a modifier or subordinating element). Make some sentences long, some short; others, in between. Mix it up. Use compound, complex, and simple sentences. The linguist John Herum suggested to me once that we should also vary levels of intensity in our prose. If, for example, we cut out of an essay all "to be" verbs, almost all prepositions and nominalizations, the whole piece will be at "the same level" of intensity—hence "flat," not really all that interesting. Perhaps it's best to strive for a "sine-wave" pattern of emphasis or impact (though a sine wave might be more regular than you really want), with some areas of the essay more powerfully, tightly, and forcefully phrased than others.

2. *Lucidity.* In "Why I Write" (1947) George Orwell wrote that "good prose is like a windowpane" (*Orwell Reader* 395): you should easily see through it to perceive the ideas of the author. You need to keep in mind that you're trying to convey something to an audience, and that the words should reveal rather than block that process. Often we will talk about writing that is "clear" or "lucid," and this is offered as a virtue: the argument and ideas are easily seen, as if through a windowpane of prose. When you start clouding, frosting, embellishing, or cracking the pane, you undermine your ability to convey an idea.

3. *Directness.* Get to your point. Say what you mean. Give clear examples, and try to be specific rather than general. Tangents

may sometimes be interesting, but you should probably avoid them when you can—or deal with them in notes.

4. *Musicality*. Can we teach ourselves the music of language? It seems to me we can. Read aloud what you have written. Does it have a musical quality? Does it have a balance, a rhythm, a poetry? Does it sing? Maybe it shouldn't sing. But it almost certainly should have something to it that respects the oral/aural component of language. Look again at the figures of speech and try to listen to the music of various examples. In a way, this overlaps with variation, but the variation should be done to interest and delight, not just for the sake of formal variety.

5. *Sense imagery*. You need to realize that, as you write, your appeal should be to many senses, not just to the reader's visual sense, for example. Consider how Vladimir Nabokov appeals to at least four senses—including the tactile sense of pain—in his description (from his novel *Pnin*) of a man's sensations after having his few remaining teeth extracted:

> A warm flow of pain was gradually replacing the ice and wood of the anesthetic in his thawing, still half-dead, abominably martyred mouth. After that, during a few days he was in mourning for an intimate part of himself. It surprised him to realize how fond he had been of his teeth. His tongue, a fat sleek seal, used to flop and slide so happily among the familiar rocks, checking the contours of a battered but still secure kingdom, plunging from cave to cove, climbing this jag, nuzzling that notch, finding a shred of seaweed in the same old cleft. (38)

What can one do here but stand back and clap?

6. *Cohesiveness*. Good writing flows, one sentence to the next, effortlessly, in a manner of speaking. You need to think about how to connect your sentences, how to make for these smooth transitional moves.

7. *Organization*. Good style has logic to it, a progression that the reader can follow.

8. *Verbiness*. Again, good writing typically uses active verbs, rather than passive ones, which I suggest above that you should

avoid. As I have mentioned several times, passive constructions are often used in scientific writing, in social science writing, and in textbooks (I use many here, you've no doubt noticed), but I recommend limiting their use as much as you can. Try to "verb" your reader through your sentences; don't put him or her to sleep by omitting the agent and hiding behind a passive voice.

9. *Grammaticality.* This is neither the last nor the least, but it's quite important just the same. Good writers give the impression that they know the "rules" very well—that they have no trouble with the fundamentals of usage. Your style should display a similar confidence.

10. *Surprise: breaking the rules.* Perhaps I shouldn't mention this here, but impressive stylists not only know the rules; they flout the rules on occasion, when they think it might be effective. Often they are correct—in that this strategy does surprise readers. I don't recommend doing this on a regular basis, but you might think about how to creatively modify the "norm"—making your modification with an eye toward bolstering your argument and achieving an original and striking expression of what you want to say. Note that Nabokov does this in the passage quoted above—the tongue as seal metaphor is clearly excessive—but using that metaphor makes vivid and unforgettable the experience described.

A Dozen Extraordinary Stylists

At this point, what follows will test these suggestions. Before drafting this chapter, I gathered twelve examples of what I consider "good writing." Many of these writers are among my favorites and have been for years. But I had never looked very closely at their writing; I merely enjoyed it, stood in awe of it.

Will these examples of good writing in fact do the very things that I suggest writers avoid? Will they follow the principles I'm recommending? Will they do things other than what I suggest? Finally, perhaps, I wonder whether good prose may inevitably be idiosyncratic, never answering or lock stepping to rules laid out in texts. What I suspect is that these examples are not necessarily ones that everyone should emulate, but that each has a decided individuality. Maybe their violation of the rules shows that writers can break any rules so long as doing so exhibits genius. Or maybe they won't break the "rules" that much after all. We'll see.

Academic writing always has to negotiate among warring imperatives: it should be lucid but at the same time complex; it must be engaging but not too informal; it ought to be innovative but not eccentric; informative but not fact-choked, rhetorically rich but not fallacious. Here are my examples. All are nonfiction; some are academic, others less so. And here begins the test: do these writers actually perform "prohibited" rhetorical/stylistic moves? And to what extent does their writing exemplify the virtues I have outlined?

William James, *The Varieties of Religious Experience*, 1899

The normal process of life contains moments as bad as any of those which insane melancholy is filled with, moments in which radical evil gets its innings and takes its solid turn.[1] The lunatic's visions of horror are all drawn from the material of daily fact. Our civilization is founded[2] on the shambles, and every individual existence goes out in a lonely spasm of hopeless agony.[3] If you protest, my friend, wait till you arrive there yourself![4] To believe in the carnivorous reptiles of geologic times is hard for our imagination—they seem too much like mere museum specimens. Yet there is no tooth in any one of those museum-skulls that did not daily through long years of the foretime hold fast to the body struggling in despair of some fated living victim.[5] Forms of horror just as dreadful to their victims, if on a smaller spatial scale, fill the world about us today. Here on our very

1. Note interesting use of colloquial and formal (here using a baseball metaphor to describe "radical evil").

2. Passive throughout does not seem to diminish James's impact one whit.

3. "Lonely spasm of hopeless agony": extraordinary turn of phrase, one that's frighteningly musical and unforgettable. When I once read this aloud to an audience of senior citizens, there was loud groaning at this line. James seemed as if to anticipate this, given his subsequent sentence.

4. Switches form of address to comment directly to audience. When read aloud, this comment beautifully anticipates how audience had reacted to previous line. (And this work was initially delivered as a lecture, I might add. Often reading a work aloud will stimulate in the writer a particularly nice turn of phrase.)

5. James treads on the edge of the sentimental here, but doesn't slide in.

6. Note use of multiple sense imagery: sight, sound, touch, even taste.

7. Use of specific examples—museum skulls, cat, mouse, crocodiles, etc.—gives his prose a strong foundation in an actual world, thus bringing his insights to a concrete level.

8. The day dragging its length recalls the length of crocodiles and pythons, tying the concepts together visuo-spatially.

9. Suddenly bringing back the "melancholiac" in the last line surprises the reader but recalls the topic sentence, which now seems invested with even greater weight.

10. Note the use of -tion word: OK here. So much for that prohibition.

hearths and in our gardens the infernal cat plays with the panting mouse, or holds the hot bird fluttering in her jaws.[6] Crocodiles and rattlesnakes and pythons are at this moment vessels of life as real as we are;[7] their loathsome existence fills every minute of every day that drags its length along;[8] and whenever they or other wild beasts clutch their living prey, the deadly horror which an agitated melancholiac[9] feels is the literally right reaction on the situation.[10] (152–53)

This book, a transcription of the Gifford Lectures, which James delivered in Scotland in 1899, stands out for the vigor of its style and the powerful freshness of its language. William's writings sharply contrast with those of his brother, Henry (see above, page 22). (William was called the "philosopher who wrote like a novelist," and Henry, "the novelist who wrote like a philosopher.") The passage I have quoted comes at the end of the chapter called "The Sick Soul."

W.E.B. Du Bois, "Abraham Lincoln" (1922)

11. Note asyndeton. Also, a rather striking list.

12. Du Bois now moves into a somewhat less formal register.

13. Very simple language, "big inside," but at the same time very evocative. What does this mean? A stark contrast to the ugliness of Lincoln that had been painted by the first few lines. Such a reversal is often effective.

14. Vivid metaphor—as if habit and convention were merely clothing.

Abraham Lincoln was a Southern poor white, of illegitimate birth, poorly educated and unusually ugly, awkward, ill-dressed.[11] He liked smutty stories and was a politician down to his toes.[12] Aristocrats—Jeff Davis, Seward and their ilk—despised him, and indeed he had little outwardly that compelled respect. But in that curious human way he was big inside.[13] He had reserves and depths and when habit and convention were torn away[14] there was something left to Lincoln—nothing to most of his contemners. There was something left, so that at the crisis he was big enough to be inconsistent—cruel, merciful; peace-loving, a fighter; despising Negroes and letting them fight and vote; protecting slavery and freeing slaves.[15] He was a man—a big, inconsistent, brave man. (1196)

Writing in the NAACP journal (*The Crisis*) that he himself founded and edited, Du Bois felt it was important to tell the truth about Lincoln, even though that truth was perhaps not what his readers genuinely wanted to hear. Several months later, he wrote an explanation of his piece on Lincoln, and he elaborated some on his position. He ends that editorial, "The scars and foibles and contradictions of the Great do not diminish but enhance the worth and meaning of their upward struggle: it was the bloody sweat that proved the human Christ divine; it was his true history and antecedents that proved Abraham Lincoln a Prince of Men" (1199).

Ruth Benedict, *Patterns of Culture*, 1934

In our generation extreme forms of ego-gratification are culturally supported in a similar fashion.[16] Arrogant and unbridled egoists as family men, as officers of the law and in business, have been again and again portrayed by novelists and dramatists, and they are familiar in every community. Like the behavior of the Puritan divines, their courses of action are often more asocial than those of the inmates of penitentiaries.[17] In terms of the suffering and frustration that they spread about them there is probably no comparison. There is very possibly at least as great a degree of mental warping.[18] Yet they are entrusted with positions of great influence and importance and are as a rule fathers of families.[19] Their impress both upon their own children and upon the structure of our society is indelible.[20] They are not described in our manuals of psychiatry because they are supported by every tenet of our civilization. They are[21] sure of themselves

15. Again, a creatively shaped and interesting list. Du Bois surprises the reader by pairing opposing attributes in an unexpected way.

16. Benedict uses passive voice here and in the following, but still her prose retains clarity and elegance.

17. A striking contrast—Puritan divines and convicts, along with the "egoists" who form the subject of the paragraph.

18. "Mental warping" is a good phrase.

19. Climax effectively used here.

20. "Impress ... indelible"—another strong metaphor.

21. Anaphora is effective. ("They are" is repeated.)

in real life in a way that is possible only to those who are oriented to the points of the compass laid down in their own culture.[22] Nevertheless a future psychiatry may well ransack our novels and letters and public records[23] for illumination upon a type of abnormality to which it would not otherwise give credence. In every society it is among this very group of the culturally encouraged and fortified that some of the most extreme types of human behavior[24] are fostered. (256)

Edward Kasner and James Newman, *Mathematics and the Imagination*, 1940

To grasp the meaning and importance of mathematics, to appreciate its beauty and its value, arithmetic must first be understood, for mostly, since its beginning, mathematics has been arithmetic in simple or elaborate attire.[25] Arithmetic has been the queen and the handmaiden of the sciences from the days of the astrologers of Chaldea and the high priests of Egypt to the present days of relativity, quanta, and the adding machine.[26] Historians may dispute the meaning of the ancient papyri, theologians may wrangle over the exegesis of Scripture, philosophers may debate over Pythagorean doctrine, but all will concede that the numbers in the papyri, in the Scriptures, and in the writings of Pythagoras are the same as the numbers of today.[27] As arithmetic, mathematics has helped man to cast horoscopes, to make calendars, to predict the risings of the Nile, to measure fields and the height of the Pyramids, to measure the speed of a stone as it fell from a tower in Pisa, the speed of an apple as it fell from a tree in Woolsthorpe,[28] to weigh the stars and the atoms, to mark the passage of time, to find the curvature of space.[29] And

22. They followed society's dictates and succeeded exceptionally well—and didn't ever think of any culture other than their own. The "points of the compass" metaphor is subtle and powerful, bringing to mind the personality of more than one American president, for example.

23. Interesting metaphor—a "future psychiatry" "ransacking" our culture for understanding. Note polysyndeton.

24. At first the vagueness of this might seem too indirect, but upon closer inspection "extreme types of human behavior" works well—has evocative power. What does she have in mind? One can only speculate, but leaving it unsaid makes the horror even greater. This passage seems relevant today, over eighty years after it was first written.

25. Nice use of metaphor: at first it seems trite, but applied to numbers it has an originality.

26. "Queen" and "handmaiden" are opposites. A form of oxymoron. The terms are somewhat ordinary, but the specificity of Chaldea, relativity, and the like, more than make up for it. "Adding machine" dates the piece, I might add.

27. Again, excellent use of examples set in elegant parallel form.

28. I like the specificity of "Woolsthorpe," Isaac Newton's hometown.

29. Effective use of asyndeton.

although mathematics is also the calculus, the theory of probability, the matrix algebra, the science of the infinite, it is still the art of counting.[30] (28)

George Orwell, "Politics and the English Language," 1946

The inflated style is itself a kind of euphemism. A mass of Latin words falls upon the facts like soft snow, blurring the outlines and covering up all the details.[31] The great enemy of clear language is insincerity.[32] When there is a gap between one's real and one's declared aims, one turns as it were instinctively to long words and exhausted idioms, like a cuttlefish squirting out ink[33] In our age there is no such thing as "keeping out of politics." All issues are political issues, and politics itself is a mass of lies, evasions, folly, hatred and schizophrenia.[34] When the general atmosphere is bad, language must suffer. I should expect to find—this is a guess which I have not sufficient knowledge to verify—that the German, Russian, and Italian languages have all deteriorated in the last ten or fifteen years, as a result of dictatorship.[35] (*Shooting an Elephant* 173–74)

Erving Goffman, *Stigma*, 1963

[I]n an important sense there is only one complete unblushing male[36] in America: a young, married, white, urban, northern, heterosexual Protestant father of college education, fully employed, of good complexion, weight, and height, and a recent record in sports.[37] Every American male tends to look out upon the world from this perspective, this constituting one sense in which one can speak of a common value system in America. Any male who fails to qualify in any of these ways is likely to view

30. Striking conclusion to the paragraph: it brings the whole idea back to the opening, but now that idea has become enriched and complicated.

31. First two sentences are vivid, as they move from the abstract ("inflated style"; "euphemism") to the actual. One can almost see the snow fall, blurring what it covers.

32. "Insincerity" is a surprising word here to use as the complement. It's impressive that Orwell brings issues of language use down to personal, intimate terms.

33. Again, a strong metaphor. The cuttlefish is repulsive and primitive, at least in this context. (Today's reader might have a greater affinity for it, though, as more and more ocean creatures become threatened or extinct. In fact cuttlefish are surprisingly intelligent.)

34. Obviously I am partial to stylists who use lists effectively, and Orwell is one such writer. Note use of climax.

35. A surprise ending, especially given the opening sentence. The paragraph has evolved in a quite unexpected way.

36. "Complete unblushing male" is an odd, yet captivating phrase, at once metaphorical and precise.

37. The last attribute lends a comic effect, because usually the most important feature appears last in a list (i.e., if we abide by the formula of climax). The list overall is extraordinary because almost no one reading it will have all these attributes, which might cause a blush.

38. List includes three adjectives all very close in meaning but subtly different and strategically ordered.

39. Interesting pairing of opposite attributes. "To pass" means to successfully pretend to be something one is not.

40. Goffman packs an enormous amount of information into this sentence. It rewards rereading. Note use of polyptoton.

41. Interesting use of shadow metaphor. Something that does not really exist can cast "some kind of shadow"—almost illogical, but effective perhaps for that very reason. The idea is that these values can have a real palpability despite not being "fully entrenched." Goffman evokes a kind of mystical, inexplicable element into his analysis.

42. Updike risks the trite here. This "swung mightily" recalls "Casey at the Bat." But like Ted Williams, Updike knows what he's doing. The clumsy appearing language replicates the clumsiness of Williams's first swing.

43. Polysyndeton effective. Mirrors swing of bat.

44. Alliterative and striking, "vast volume of air" calls to mind the largeness of Fenway, the potential expansiveness of all outdoor baseball parks.

45. This vivid metaphoric imagining conveys the author's awe at the same time that it describes the high, majestic arc of the ball. I like the choice of the Tappan Zee, too, since that slows the reader down, allowing you to grasp the bridginess of the Tappan Zee, rather than letting you glide over the name, as you might were it the

himself ... as unworthy, incomplete, and inferior;[38] at times he is likely to pass and at times he is likely to find himself being apologetic or aggressive[39] concerning known-about aspects of himself he knows are probably seen as undesirable.[40] The general identity-values of a society may be fully entrenched nowhere, and yet they can cast some kind of shadow on the encounters encountered everywhere in daily living.[41] (128–29)

John Updike, "Hub Fans Bid Kid Adieu," 1965

Fisher, after his unsettling wait, was low with the first pitch. He put the second one over, and Williams swung mightily[42] and missed. The crowd grunted, seeing that classic swing, so long and smooth and quick,[43] exposed. Fisher threw the third time, Williams swung again, and there it was. The ball climbed on a diagonal line into the vast volume of air[44] over center field. From my angle, behind third base, the ball seemed less an object in flight than the tip of a towering, motionless construct, like the Eiffel Tower or the Tappan Zee Bridge.[45] It was in the books while it was still in the sky. Brandt ran back to the deepest corner of the outfield grass, the ball descended beyond his reach and struck in the crotch where the bullpen met the wall, bounced chunkily,[46] and vanished.[47] (316)

Here is what Stanley Fish, the eminent literary critic, writes in 2011 about Updike's sentence, "It was in the books while it was still in the sky." His overall insightful analysis unfortunately misses an important point:

> The fulcrum of the sentence is "while"; on either side of it are two apparently very different kinds of observations. "It was in the books" is metaphorical. Updike imagines, correctly, that this moment will be memorialized in Cooperstown, New

York, and he confers that mythical status on the moment before it is completed, before the ball actually goes out of the park. It is "still in the sky," a phrase that has multiple meanings; the ball is still in the sky in the sense that it has not yet landed; it is still in the sky in the sense that its motion is arrested; and it is still in the sky in the sense that it is, and will remain forever, in the sky of the books, in the record of the game's highest, most soaring achievements. On the surface "in the book" [*sic*] and "in the sky" are in distinct registers, one referring to the monumentality the home run will acquire in history, the other describing the ball's actual physical arc; but the registers are finally, and indeed immediately (this sentences [*sic*] goes fast), the same: the physical act and its transformation into myth occur simultaneously; or rather, that is what Updike makes us feel as we glide through this deceptively simple sentence composed entirely of monosyllables. (9–10)

Brooklyn Bridge, say. Also the Tappan Zee doesn't have the same historic associations as the Brooklyn Bridge, at least not for me, and can be just an architectural construction, not so much a cultural one.

46. "In the books ... in the sky": syntactically parallel but stylistically contrasting and striking. It's a clever and effective use of zeugma, or linking, of two very distinct concepts ("in the books" and "in the sky"). People are usually taught to avoid zeugma. Here it works.
"Chunkily" is interesting, a strange usage I would label hypallage, though it might be used onomatopoetically here.

47. "Vanished"—as if by magic. A powerful ending.

Fish has got the sentence's effectiveness nailed down, but he seems to miss a crucial element of the actual hit itself. The ball was hit so hard—the crack of the bat, the exit velocity of the ball, the arc it took, are all things we have to imagine but can imagine quite clearly—that before it landed in the seats, people knew it was a home run. It was a "no doubter." "In the books" tells us that in his last at-bat at Fenway Park, Ted Williams, age forty-two, hit no ordinary home run. That understanding helps give the sentence its impact.

Bela Hap, "Structuralist Meta-Analysis," 1972

As a starting point of our present analysis, we only ascertain that the first sentence of the analysis in question comprises twenty-three words. Further quantitative research will point out that the number of words in the following (that is, the present) sentence is only twenty-two.[48] Our working hypothesis, or what Mukařovský called "semantic gesture," is that the number of words diminishes by one in consecutive sentences.

48. Clearly, this is a humorous piece, though its not announcing that fact immediately is a good stylistic maneuver.

49. The equation is hilarious, still seriocomic, but just the sort of thing that you'd find in literary theory of the last generation.

50. Notice how many "Th-openers" Hap (or his translator, Gyula Kodolanyi) uses. What is the effect of this?

51. By now, you've figured out the organizing "trick" to the passage, so Hap must conceive of a way to further surprise and amuse.

52. Now you are wondering: how silly will this get? Why do I read on? But read on you do.

53. Ending on one word is effective—it gives an added punch to the paragraph. Since the whole paragraph is absurd, though, the ending is ironic: it has rhetorical punch but lacks semantic content.

$$Sx = S\,(x{-}1){-}1^{49}$$

The correctness of our hypothesis should be first checked in this sentence: the number of words, as expected, is twenty. The present sentence, by necessity, consists of nineteen words, as it will be borne out by a careful examination. The task that remains is then to check through the methodical analysis of each further surmise, the hypothesis. In other words, the following sentences should be the verbal equivalents of the mathematical formula given above.[50] Examples for examination need to be brought in from a sufficiently wide-ranging field of utterances. The validity of the formula will of course greatly depend on the liberality of selection. This view was kept in mind when choosing the present sentence of fourteen words. As the investigation advanced, the validity of the formula tended to become evident. This sentence, consisting of twelve words, was found at an advanced stage.[51] Even more promising results came when we explored a new medium. Like the present statement, unquestionably made up of ten words. Then, not surprisingly, followed an evidence of nine words. The eight words here came almost as natural. Expectedly, there are seven in this one. One, two, three, four, five, six. One, two, three, four, five.[52] There are four here. This seems reasoning. Proved indeed. Undeniable.[53] (310)

It struck me that when a piece is "pure style" or is composed simply to exemplify some kind of stylistic theory—a situation that rarely arises—the results are quite remarkable, even humorous. The formula of the piece—reduction by one of the number of words in each sentence—is carried out precisely, and the work seems "conclusive." But at the same time, while formally perfect, it's essentially contentless, devoid of meaning. According to Bela Hap, what he wrote forms "part of a single work, called

Meta-Anthology; the common idea in the single parts of it is the endeavor to draw (perhaps somewhat ironical) conclusions from the philosophical condition of today, in which *thought is reduced to language*" (qtd. by Kostelanetz 464).

Wisława Szymborska, "A Tale Retold," 1989

Job, afflicted in body and possessions, curses his fate as a man. That is great poetry.[54] His friends come to him and, rending their mantles, probe Job's guiltiness before the Lord. Job cries out that he has been a righteous man. Job does not know wherefore the Lord has smitten him, Job does not want to speak with them. Job wants to speak with the Lord.[55] The Lord appears riding the chariot of a whirlwind. Unto that man, open to the very bone,[56] He praises His creation: the heavens, the seas, the earth and the beasts. And especially Behemoth, and in particular Leviathan, pride-inspiring monsters. That is great poetry.[57] Job listens—the Lord does not speak to the point, for the Lord does not wish to speak to the point. Hence Job makes haste to abase himself before the Lord. Now events follow swiftly. Job regains his asses and his camels, his oxen and his sheep, all increased twofold. The grinning skull begins to take on flesh.[58] And Job assents. Job resigns himself. Job does not want to spoil a masterwork.[59] (49)

54. The short sentence as the second one in the paragraph has a strong impact. Usually the second sentence of a paragraph is lengthier. And what makes "great poetry"? That is the question that this paragraph sets up in the reader's mind.

55. Note use of anaphora—effective.

56. An odd turn of phrase and striking metaphor.

57. Note how this repetition of the second sentence ties the paragraph together. And readers still wonder what "great poetry" entails. This is a version of erotesis.

58. Metaphor is painful and strange: why "grinning"?

59. Ironic yet logical ending, I would say, but a bit surprising just the same. The repeated use of anaphora again ties the paragraph together cohesively. "Masterwork" recalls the idea of "great poetry": terrible affliction is only part of a wondrous entirety, all of creation—the supreme "masterwork."

Charles Frazier, Introduction to the *Book of Job*, 1999

But his [God's] long speech offers hope for an alternative reading, one that proposes quite a different channel of communication than the one Job recommends. What God holds out for consideration is Creation, all that is the world, its bigness and smallness, its infinite detail, its differing statements of motif and

60. Good list here using asyndeton. Note also use of climax and oxymoron.

61. Use of appositive is also effective. At first it does not appear to be an appositive (i.e., a repetition of noun phrases), which makes it stand out even more.

62. Frazier makes some interesting contrasts: God is pleased with the eyes of a monster, as well as with water, examples which contrast the gigantic to the every-day. The "details about horse anatomy" that "worked out particu-larly well" has a humorous tone, I think, but it's effective to see the Book of Job in this light; doing so makes its message still more complex—an example, perhaps of "the ulti-mate unknowableness of my elegant design."

63. Note use of polysyndeton.

64. Last two sentences are short, strong, punchy: they contain and convey the authority that God has over Job, indeed, over all creation, Frazier seems to suggest.

65. Note the conver-sational opening: "good for the soul," "only once in a while."

66. A sentence fragment, effective here in that its frag-mentary nature not only calls attention to itself but also emphasizes the unusual modification: stringing together fourteen words connected with hyphens in order to make an adjective works surprisingly well.

67. This sentence with its "ideal/real" halves— the first half mention-ing the supposed benefits of tourism, and the second half noting the actuality of how it makes Wallace feel—mirrors Wallace's mixed feelings and discomfort.

theme, their complex variation and repetitions,[60] beauty and terror intermixed.[61] It is a construct so finely made that even its wild and violent and enormous elements—Leviathan is an example God offers with particular pleasure—contain in their details the smallest and most delicate elements, for the eyes of the monster are "like the eyelids of morning" (41:18). God is rightfully pleased with the concept and execution of water in its various forms, rain and dew and ice and frost. His pride is the understandable pride of the artist who has succeeded in creating a whole world. The details of horse anatomy, he feels, worked out particularly well:[62] "The glory of his nostrils is terrible" (39:20)....
Look at it all, God seems to be saying. Don't trouble me with reason; what you need to know is there in the arts and the mystery and the ultimate unknowableness of my elegant design.[63] Love it and fear it. Submit to it.[64] (xv–xvi)

David Foster Wallace, "Consider the Lobster," 2004

As I see it, it probably really is good for the soul to be a tourist, even if it's only once in a while.[65] Not good for the soul in a refreshing or enlivening way, though, but rather in a grim, steely-eyed, let's-look-honestly-at-the-facts-and-find-some-way-to-deal-with-them way.[66] My personal experience has not been that traveling around the country is broadening or relaxing, or that radical changes in place and context have a salutary effect, but rather that intranational tourism is radically constricting, and humbling in the hardest way—hostile to my fantasy of being a real individual, of living somehow outside and above it all.[67] (Coming up, is the part that my companions find especially unhappy and repellent, a sure way to spoil the fun of vacation travel:)[68] To be a mass tourist, for me, is to become a pure late-date American: alien, ignorant, greedy for something you cannot ever have, disappointed in a way you can never admit.[69] It is to spoil, by way of sheer ontology, the very unspoiledness you are there to experience.[70] It is to impose yourself on places that in all noneconomic ways would be better, realer without you. It is, in lines and gridlock and transaction after transaction,[71] to confront a dimension of yourself that is as inescapable as it is painful: As a tourist, you become economically significant but existentially loathsome, an insect on a dead thing.[72] (56n)

Wallace is writing hard here. The insect image brings us back to the essay itself, recalling one of its best sentences: "The point is that lobsters are basically giant sea-insects" (55), and the funny footnote to *it*, relating how in Maine, people invite others over for lobster by saying, "Come around on Sunday and we'll cook up some bugs" (55n). I should mention here that this whole 231-word passage is itself a footnote in an essay about the Maine Lobster Festival. The essay first appeared in *Gourmet*, perhaps an unusual venue for such a piece. (In the subsequent issue it emerges that the magazine received more letters to the editor about Wallace's piece than it had ever received about a single article.) Wallace examines how we as a nation deal with food, and with all the largely hidden from us information as to where it comes from. He traveled to Maine on assignment from the magazine; he was, essentially a paid tourist. Hence the footnote about tourism serves as a comment on the country and a reflection on self.

Keep in mind that style cannot totally displace or usurp the argument because then—well, then there would be no argument. (You've heard the phrase "empty rhetoric.") But style can scaffold, buttress, drive home argument in a forceful and memorable way, and that's the effect of Wallace's prose here. It's an imaginative style that complements an imaginative argument. Read the passage again, and you'll see: its homespun, aw-shucks

68. A total prohibition in most writing, announcing in a parenthesis a comment on what it is you are going to do. But it works erotically: it makes me eager to see what "repellent" comment he intends to make. It ends with a nonstandard punctuation, a colon inside a closed parenthesis, furthering the oppositional nature of his position. Or is this an emoticon?

69. Asyndeton and climax. The shift to the second person also has the effect of redirecting the emphasis: it's not just about Wallace and his experience, but about yours, too. "Cannot ever have" and "can never admit" are parallel enough to suggest epizeuxis.

70. "By way of sheer ontology" and "unspoiledness" push this sentence into hypallage, I think—and it's effective in its deformation of language.

71. Polysyndeton.

72. Climax. "An insect on a dead thing" powerfully juxtaposes abstract idea and vivid image.

opening and the cagey conversational parenthetical only serve to make more surprising and palpable the shock of the last image: tourist as maggot. Scary. But that's the point. Tourism is scary—scary for what it does to the places being visited, scary for what it does to the tourists themselves.

Wendy Rawlings, "Food and Worker Safety across the Globe: A Nervous and Incomplete Case Study" (2016)

Sign on the wall says, WORK HARD ON THE JOB TODAY OR WORK HARD TO FIND A JOB TOMORROW.[73] Words to the wise. Some workers don't even have their own rooms. Twenty people stuffed into a three-room apartment. Rodent problems. Bummer for those workers.[74] Things could be a lot worse, Lai tells himself. (Things will get a lot worse.)[75] And then the explosion. Super-downer. Or whatever Chinese phrase is the equivalent to "super downer."[76] One Friday evening in May, workers covered in sparkling aluminum dust stand there buffing iPad cases nonstop. Over there (difficult to ascertain exactly where worker Lai is, as all are wearing masks and earplugs, all have slight aluminum sparkle in hair even after showering), Lai buffs iPad case after iPad case. IPad 2 has been released in the United States just weeks ago, and so many cases needed![77] Important to polish as many iPad cases as possible. Get priorities straight. Buff buff buff. Sand sand sand.[78] Okay, so[79] giant explosion caused by dust and inadequate ventilation blows up factory. Poor skinny Lai taken to hospital, where beautiful nursing student girlfriend recognizes him[80] only by his legs because most of skin seared away.[81] Giant bummer for everyone involved when two days later Lai dies. (352)

For the most part, Rawlings relies on hypallage, and her use of "weird English" makes this paragraph (and the article it is

73. Prose seems a little odd here, what might be called "weird English," a term invented by Evelyn Nien-Ming Ch'ien. The hypallage Rawlings uses from the outset is to omit or oddly use articles.

74. More hypallage: three sentence fragments strung together. Rawlings will repeat this device later, to even better effect.

75. Like Wallace, Rawlings breaks the rule of "anticipating one's effect," but it works here.

76. Use of slang, and then a self-conscious maneuver in which Rawlings calls the reader's attention to this fact. Odd mixture of registers works well, making her point.

77. Again, the use of "weird English"; the verb is omitted from the last clause. This is a special type of hypallage, in which the language is written as if with a foreign accent.

78. The humorous tone makes the subsequent tragedy more agonizing.

79. Starting with "Okay, so" in some sense seems to trivialize the whole event, but in fact this rhetorical tactic only makes the point more powerful and the situation more poignant.

80. Contrast between "poor skinny Lai and "beautiful nursing student girlfriend" is very vivid and visual, made more so by the information that follows.

81. Strong accent here.

from) really come to life. It is interesting how very few figures of speech she employs in this piece, how pared down it seems, perhaps mirroring the pared down quality of life these Chinese workers must endure. It is indeed a "nervous and incomplete" prose form, and using it in this narrative is particularly effective.

What can I add after having looked at these examples? First, I'm surprised by how many of the figures of speech they employ. I hadn't thought these examples would be quite so formally ornate. In addition, I notice that metaphor stands out as being one very powerful tool, and virtually all of these writers use it exceptionally well. These writers also show impressive variation in the way that they use lists, often bringing together rather disparate items. Then too there's an attention to making the language of the writing, even its sound, replicate something of that writing's content. And finally, what I am not surprised about, really, is that very element of surprise: these writers all catch the reader off guard, using some surprising turn of phrase, metaphor, or linkage—or sometimes returning to the thought that started their paragraph, once it has been modified in a surprising way by the paragraph itself.

But most surprising is the way these authors do all sorts of things that I listed among "prohibitions." They use passive voice, "to be" verbs, prepositional phrases, even some slang and trite language. I don't think this means, however, that you should violate the rules with abandon, but rather, understand that certain moves you make can more than compensate for your breaking those rules. Or maybe I mean something larger, more amorphous: a good style doesn't consist of following rules or taking care not to violate prohibitions; it consists of finding an original, striking, and genuine voice—your own—and freeing that voice up through the power of language and idea.

V

Creativity and Originality in the Epoch of the Post-Original

14 Technology and Writing: On Being Imaginative Now

Inasmuch as I have been touting the value of imagination, of originality, of finding your own unique perspective, it should be fairly obvious where I stand with respect to plagiarism, that is, to presenting the ideas of others as your own. I abhor it. Yet at the same time, I'm living in a world that's connected to, overlapping with, your own. Thus I know that our culture (and not just the culture of the United States, I hasten to add) aids and abets and sometimes even rewards plagiaristic behavior. Copying something, so long as it's good, isn't seen as all that awful, apparently. And at the same time, our schools and universities have developed a quasi-love affair with convention, wanting students to adhere to already established forms. It's OK—it's often required—to imitate established forms, the message is. Many classes you take don't want from you any trace or whiff of originality, but encourage a parroting, a repeat-back-to-me pedagogy, which is somehow seen as tantamount to education.

In this chapter, I would like to examine the various forces at work that seem to compel an unoriginal point of view, manner of expression, or way to come up with ideas. I hope that if I show you the outlines of how you are being manipulated by our culture into being less than fully original, less than fully yourself, you might be able to develop strategies of resistance. I am for some reason reminded of a great line from *Star Trek: The Next Generation*, as uttered by a character called Seven of Nine, and played by Jeri Ryan: "Resistance is futile." I guess my thought is that she might be right; but in that futility, I also feel, our very humanity inheres, a humanity where people are not numbered but have names, a humanity in which being part of a larger collectivity is important, but not the only thing of importance.

During the 2016 presidential election campaign, a media brouhaha ensued over speculation that Melania Trump (the third wife of Donald J. Trump) had plagiarized two paragraphs of the speech that she delivered at the Republican National Convention. This borrowing, from a speech given years earlier by Michelle Obama, made for more headlines than the somewhat pedestrian seventy-five-minute speech delivered by Mr. Trump himself. "Was Melania Trump's Speech Plagiarized from Michele Obama?" read the headline in *USA Today*. People were not even sure. Melania admitted nothing and never apologized. No one was fired from the Trump team, although Melania's speechwriter resigned. In some ways, it was almost as if it had never happened.

When German *Wunderkind* author seventeen-year-old Helene Hegemann was accused of plagiarism, she produced an epigram. She said, "There is no such thing as originality, only authenticity" (Kulish A6). I find this troubling. And more troubling still is that Hegemann's publisher, when the allegations of plagiarism emerged, stood by its author and her novel *Axolotl Roadkill*, whose sales actually soared (alongside sales of Airen's *Strobo*, the book Hegemann was accused of taking material from). Even Nobel Prize winner Günter Grass got in on the action, vilifying Hegemann for her actions.

Reading about Ms. Trump and Ms. Hegemann, though, changed my thinking about plagiarism. We have indeed, as a culture, moved into a new phase, into what I am perhaps portentously calling The Epoch of the Post-Original. No longer does Western culture have a single, easily accessed response to plagiarism; we don't even all agree about what it consists of, and not surprisingly we don't give systematic, coordinated, unified messages about it. Even in our subculture of academia, it is little better: we give you mixed signals. It's the worst thing you can do, but it's not really a crime; it doesn't deeply tarnish one's "moral career" (to use a term from Erving Goffman's *Stigma*); and it in some ways seems to be something completely in accord with what's done all the time. It's also what's rewarded and seen as valuable. And most important, perhaps, a plagiarized work doesn't really exist as an autonomous entity: what Melania Trump's and Hegemann's situations make clear is that plagiarism is a collaboratively produced and agreed-upon event. Teachers work with you to limn out the edges of the plagiaristic; editors similarly work with authors to collectively define the extent and limits of legitimate borrowing. And the legitimacy of this collaborative venture varies from professor to professor, as it does from publisher to publisher, situation to situation.

Perhaps most fascinating to me as a college professor is the clash between relatively conservative institutions (such as the academy) and emergent technologies, such as the Internet. The poet Kenneth Goldsmith is insightful about the problem. He writes,

> In our cut-and-paste world, words, ideas, and artifacts are shared, remixed, spammed, swiped, attributed, misattributed, contextualized, recontextualized, and miscontextualized with the push of button. In a sense, our words, our stories, and our images are no longer ours, nor can we expect them to be. As part of the great sea of shared culture, they are phished, scooped, reblogged, retweeted, regrammed, and reposted *ad infinitum....*
>
> The internet is one big copying machine—trying to discern the true origin of anything in it is nearly impossible. We spend all day long immersed in this replicative environment, yet we still somehow demand our leaders to express untrammeled authenticity when we ourselves are amalgams of preexisting ideas and materials.

This clash takes place on many fronts, of course: what is the value, for example, of the "online university" course or degree? Who knows who did the work for such degrees? Should brick-and-mortar colleges be offering such courses and degrees? What do we make of the wide-scale digitization of media and the gradual diminishment of printed material? How do we as teachers handle those students who come to our classes equipped with handhelds that provide instant Internet access, not to mention instant access to their friends and their own handhelds elsewhere? And finally, what do we do about the proliferation of material so easily available to students, so easy to patch together into an academic "paper"? (The "patch-written" paper is in fact condoned by some scholars.) In short, how might we reenvision plagiarism?

What I'm calling for, then, is a new ethics within this Epoch of the Post-Original. This ethics needs to do more than simply reject the notion or the possibility of the "original," as Helene Hegemann does. This Post-Original Epoch Ethics must instead recognize that while almost all ideas have already been thought of, while almost all phrases have been spun and turned, while almost all ideas have to have drawn on others, and while almost all that's original is simply the remixing of data that's been taken into consciousness, we still can and must ascertain the provenance of our ideas and words, and credit that as much as we are able. The fact that we do not have full access to all antecedent, possibly formative, ideas should not limit us from searching the Internet and elsewhere to find them. In short, instead of giving up on being original, as Melania Trump and Helene Hegemann and many others apparently have done, we need more self-consciously to search for the limits of our originality, just as we search for the limits and sources of our consciousness.

The Plagiaristic U.S. Culture

Plagiarism is a somewhat more complex issue than simply the copying of words not one's own—or the presenting of ideas of someone else as one's own. In fact, to expand Goldsmith's position, I am arguing that we live in a plagiaristic culture. In this culture the act of plagiarism is consistent with many other culturally endorsed and mediated activities, is a perfectly understandable and even reasonable response on the part of students, and will continue on as a "problem" in educational venues for as long as we see it in the way we've been seeing it—as a terrible academic "crime" that suggests the perp is morally corrupt, should be ostracized from the community that academia forms, and whose act should be held up as an example of wickedness or failure. The fact is that we as a culture, and we in our subculture of academia, are too ambiguous about the issue. When we warn students or the public against plagiarism, there is something confused in our warnings, as if we were simply repeating what we'd been told to say but don't really know what it means or believe in it, like a child who repeats by rote the prayers he or she hears every week in church, many words of which remain foreign and unfamiliar after years of repetition.

And the punishment we levy, when the plagiarist is caught, is equally odd: if this is so bad an act, why is the punishment so light? In our culture, the worse the punishment, usually the worse the crime. Getting caught plagiarizing can be, on the one hand, about as bad as getting a "warning" rather than a ticket for speeding, or on the other hand can lead to public humiliation, as Melania Trump's did or as Joseph Biden's plagiarism did a few years ago. I note that Biden's might seem worse than Melania's, but finally it didn't prevent him from becoming vice president. And this in the case of a man who not only plagiarized the words of Neil Kinnock but seemed to plagiarize, according to Richard Posner in *The Little Book of Plagiarism*, Kinnock's life as well, since Biden claimed that the plagiarized anecdote he was relating just occurred to him that morning.

But the interesting thing about this, which Posner wisely notes, is that we don't really know if Kinnock wrote his own speech. He himself probably had a speechwriter. And many public figures (including Ms. Trump) also rely upon speech- and ghostwriters to do the work for them. In our culture at large there is no real value in simple originality. It seems that the value, or the profit, or the money, or the sales, do not match up on a one-to-one basis with originality. Instead these indicators of success seem to rest on something much more evanescent and difficult to pin down, something a bit mysterious. No one could have predicted the incredible success of the not-exactly-plagiarized but awfully familiar seeming *Avatar*. (In fact, there were predictions, shortly before its release, of its total failure, perhaps because its plot is derivative to the point of utter predictability.) Few could guess how much money is made by direct-to-DVD movies called "Mockbusters," which are based on successful big-screen releases (Raftery). And if we look at consumer goods, what's wrong with copying a product if it's already proven to be successful? Just look at Ford Motor Company's now practically ubiquitous Aston Martin–like front grille. In fact, part of the challenge of the market is figuring out to what extent one needs to copy the already successful, and to what extent one needs to modify that. Originality consists in capturing this balance rather than in coming up with a wholly new idea.

So, on the one hand, as champions of originality (i.e., denizens of some epoch that predates the Post-Original Epoch), we are not getting too much help from the society at large. But on the other hand, we're not exactly doing a lot of work to stake out a higher ground, either, by establishing ourselves as ethical exemplars. A battle that I've fought over the years and at many different colleges consists in trying to get students to come up with something new, exciting, vibrant, different, original, and imaginative. I may partially succeed in my own course, but then, when my students take other courses, they are told that they need simply to prove that they "understood" the material. One of my colleagues at another university said to me, "You want to hear what students think about this material? Brrrr." He mimed shivering. Unconvincingly. At another college, a colleague team teaching a course with me and fourteen other faculty said, during a session in which we were creating paper topics, "I really don't want to know what our students think of, say, Condorcet or Locke. I really don't care. I do care, though, if they understand this material. That's why I think we should just ask for a summary of what they have read." This recalls the "transmission model" of teaching, and the more we use it, the more confused and difficult are the notions of plagiarism and originality.

Of course we want you to take in the material of our classes. But at this point my position diverges from that of most faculty. I want you to take the course material and make it your own, become inward with it, recast and maybe reuse it in your own way, so that what you provide for us on exams or papers isn't simply our own ideas and those of the authors of the course texts, but instead those ideas with something new and interestingly original superadded. I want your original "take" on these ideas. I want the ideas to be grappled with and challenged and maybe even modified, not simply replicated. You must know the ideas quite well in order to do this successfully, I might add. If we don't ask for this kind of response, we are in fact encouraging plagiaristic behavior, and while one must "transmit" a large body of knowledge, and as a teacher one would like to know that that transmission has been successful, we need to craft our assignments so that we do more than merely measure that raw transmission, so that we in addition encourage you as students to look for ways to update, reorganize, recontextualize, and make this knowledge your own.

Worship of Convention and the Finished Product

The second way colleges enable and even silently condone plagiarism is through the near worship of convention. Certainly some conventions must be followed, for example, of spelling, sentence structure, and the like. (See the William James letter, pp. 29–30.) But starting in grammar school, students are presented with conventions that seem far less apodictic in nature, and that suck the creativity from their brains. Let me mention one I have harped about above: the five-paragraph essay. The first paragraph offers the subject, topic, and thesis, the latter of which has three points. In each of the following three paragraphs, one of the three points is developed. The final paragraph, falsely labeled the conclusion, sums up the paper and restates the thesis. It offers a "soft landing," some students tell me.

What precisely is the value of this? Why are schools programming you in such a manner? Is it any surprise that, having been forced into such a narrow and confining format, you might be tempted to opt out of creativity altogether? Again and again, in the literature about plagiarism, writers say that students plagiarize because professors are so persnickety about conventions, and when something's been published online or in print, at least those conventions will be OK. "[F]ear of punishment for mistakes and errors that are probably inevitable (and often unimportant) and the desperation it can prompt is what provokes much of the copying and 'plagiarism' that takes place in writing classes," UCLA professor Lise Buranen writes (73). If you feel that your lack of understanding conventions will produce a failing paper anyway, what's more do you risk by plagiarizing? You know that there's at least a chance you'll get away with it, while if you write in your own voice and at your own level of competence, the chance of passing is drastically reduced.

Connected with this glorification of the conventional, consider one more enabling process that our culture at large and academia share: a sanctification of "product." To present this, I will quote a section from Ben Franklin's *Autobiography*, which nicely captures our culture's attitude—namely, if something is good, it doesn't matter if it's lacking in originality—and I also want to look at a student's "take" on the situation. A minister that Franklin admired was shown to have borrowed much of the material he used in his sermons, a discovery which "gave many of our party disgust, who accordingly abandoned his cause, and occasion'd our more speedy discomfiture in the Synod. I stuck by him, however, as I rather approved his giving us good sermons compos'd by others, than bad ones of his own Manufacture" (1400). There is something pragmatic about Franklin's attitude, and it certainly accords with his unwillingness to patent his own inventions, like the Franklin stove or bifocals. Trouble is, the utopian society that Franklin in some sense pretended to inhabit simply did not and does not exist. And wouldn't the best option have been for the preacher to generate sermons "of his own Manufacture" which were also good ones? Franklin doesn't even consider the possibility.

A colleague, Rosalie Purvis, gives an even more striking example of the value of academic paper as "product." A student recently approached Professor Purvis and asked her if it would be acceptable for him to buy a term paper to hand in as his final assignment. Professor Purvis was unequivocal: "Absolutely not." But the student clarified his position. "No, you don't understand," he said. "I will buy this paper—totally legally, you see. People sell these all the time, and I will pay whatever it costs. It will be a totally legitimate transaction." "If you do this, you will fail the course," Professor Purvis explained to him, "and possibly also get expelled from the college." The student was befuddled and annoyed. He thought his professor simply wanted the product, the ten- to fifteen-page paper, as something valuable in and of itself. He didn't quite understand the idea that the paper was evidence of how much he understood the material of the course, or of how he synthesized the presented ideas, or of how he conducted research. No, it was just a thing, a product that for some reason teachers wanted (they "collected" them), and the better products got the better grades, reasonably enough.

It's a weird story, but as I reflect on it, I realize it's eerily similar to the emphasis on product that many professors also share today. We often convey the idea that we want things that are good but not necessarily all that original. By taking this particular line, we put on you an enormous amount of pressure (to produce), and with the further enabler of the Internet, which gives its users seemingly limitless verbiage on almost anything, you are often tempted to abandon your own designs and ideas in favor of ones that at least were good enough for someone to have put online. (It seems hardly necessary to add that of course students plagiarized before the advent of the Internet—it just wasn't quite so easy, though, back then, prior to the present epoch.)

Our Distinctive Enterprise

My suggestion here is that we need now more than ever to separate ourselves ethically from the culture at large; we have to define ourselves against rather than in concert with it, especially over the issue of originality and plagiarism. We need to take the stance that conventions may be important to know but still might be discussed, debated, even at times challenged; that understanding a body of knowledge is important but needs to take place within a context in which that knowledge is evaluated and personally understood rather than learned by rote; and that intellectual products are of secondary importance to the action, labor, and process of completing those products.

We want to discourage plagiarism in college, it seems to me, not simply because such behavior after or outside college might be seen as illegal and result in fines or prison sentences, nor simply because committing plagiarism is unethical and forms the basis for a flawed "moral career." It might not. But we must in the academy hold up a standard of ethics that is higher than that of the culture at large—a culture that, not incidentally, demands repetition of formulas, clings to convention, and worships (especially) the successful product, whether it's derivative, imitative—or not. When you self-consciously reject such values, you are also working against the society of uniformity in design and thought; against the Levittownization of our lives; against the "replica" Rolexes, the take-offs, the sequels, the "sons of"; against the herd instinct that forces us closer to creature status and further from our status as creators.

I know it's possible that your creative self might be stupefied or stultified from disuse. And I realize that "research papers" are to a large extent just a reorganization and representation of already existent material. Finally, I concede that plagiaristic behavior in some form or another has always taken place and been rewarded, from Shakespeare to *Avatar*, from Doris Kearns Goodwin to FDR, from batteries to ebooks to automobile designs. But there is a series of ways to legitimately draw on already expressed ideas, already received knowledge, and already successful notions—and while doing so to still retain a core contribution that's new, striking, and individual, something that is in fact not just original but imaginative.

In a word, we need to focus on helping you learn how to think—about issues that others have thought and written about, and that have ramified and been transformed and recontextualized since they were written about, but still press in on us with urgency from all sides. When we encourage you to be genuinely original, to resist being co-opted by a surrounding culture, to reach inside yourself and pull out the individuality of who it is you truly are, and then to place that self face to face with the larger ideas we present you with—when we do this, we offer you an education of some real value, an education that draws on the past, so can't be entirely original ("nothing new under the sun"), but that seeks to see it in the light of the present, which makes it far more authentic than anything Hegemann ever came up with. Goldsmith is not quite right in his assessment of the digital age situation: it's not only that the Internet is itself a huge copying machine, but many of us have become copying machines—the internet's robotic slaves. Resist. It is not futile.

15 Concluding a Manifesto: The Future of Writing

Our culture has become one in which intersubjectivity is writ large. This concept, explained by the historian Yuval Noah Harari, refers to how we as humans connect up to one another via shared subjective knowledge—narratives, beliefs, values, myths, ideals:

> Intersubjective entities depend upon communication among many humans rather than on the beliefs and feelings of individual humans.... Sapiens rule the world because only they can weave an intersubjective web of meaning: a web of laws, forces, entities and places that exist purely in their common imagination. (145, 150)

When we noodle around the Internet, posting comments here and there, reviewing a pair of shoes for Zappos.com or a new car at Edmunds.com, posting a blog about a product or a sports star or a public event or a new book, it seems to me an either-or illusion emerges: the audience can be everyone with access to the Internet—or it could be no one at all. Essentially, in our writing we seek out other humans; we try to make contact with these biological other "softwares" as they loom and linger behind the multiple millions of hardware connections spidered out across the globe. There's a certain wild connectedness, an incredible superfluity of "hits" and links, an algorithmically, astronomically, ever-expanding array of possibility, to be sure, but writing classes need to get across the idea of the humanity behind this dizzying, electronic neurality. People are at keyboards, reading what we all write. They are looking for ideas, ideas that they can use to help them refine their own, that they can use to help improve their lives, that they can re-use and refine to fit their own needs.

As you situate yourself on the brink of verbally entering and co-creating that world, you need to recognize that the written communication you are undertaking—using language to reach other souls out there—has tremendous potentiality and power. Your writing can actually change the world, and your reading of other writing can alert you to what it's like out there and what is necessary to change. Writing is ultimately equivalent to seeing the world through others' eyes, so that others can see the world through your eyes.

What's that world like, though? And how might language and writing affect it? In his rightly famous essay "Politics and the English Language" (see p. 235, above), George Orwell contends that "the present political chaos is connected with the decay of language" (*Orwell Reader* 366). I wonder how right he is, how prophetic his words have really been. My suspicion is that if everyone spoke and wrote completely lucid prose, or prose even better than that—say, on the superb level of Orwell's own—we would still be troubled with war, inhumanities, disease, poverty, environmental collapse, and famine. Or would we?

Of course Orwell does not contend that political chaos has caused decay of language, only that the two events are connected. Yet I think the two elements have more than just correlation; they together form an ever-downward-spiraling vortex. I believe, for example, that to use logical fallacies is to damage the public discourse, as it creates an atmosphere that diminishes freedom of thought. It adds to the overall mechanism in our culture that grants the fake news more value than the actual, that parades the viability of "alternative facts," and that demonstrates that what matters is putting things over on an audience, engineering cons, or lying to get what you want—even to be elected as president. As UCLA Professor Lauri M. Mattenson writes in a trenchant piece, "Teaching Student Writers to Be Warriors," "Unfortunately, [students] are learning that success means mastering the system rather than their own impulses; that they should seek money, not meaning; and that as long as they shut up and figure out what the teacher wants, they'll get their stamp of approval" (B10). And later, Mattenson distills the situation even further. She says that students have "become calculated, not motivated" (B10). It's as if we as a society—even in college classrooms—are endorsing the credo of the late Vince Lombardi, football coach and American icon, "Winning isn't everything, it's the only thing."

I strenuously disagree. Winning is not everything. What about Pyrrhic victory—the victory at incalculable cost and enormous loss: hardly worthwhile, is it? What about cheating? If you win a debate but argue unfairly, is this a good thing? If you win a game by cheating, is that good? What would Lombardi himself say? In a society in which winning is the only thing, one might think that cheating to win is acceptable. When did obsession with winning eclipse our interest in truth and honesty?

Even the arena that uses argument as a staple—namely, the law—is not solely interested in discovering the truth. Rather, it's interested in what a jury can be convinced of. Federal Appeals Court judge Jerome Frank captures this idea when he writes,

> [T]he lawyer aims at victory, at winning in the fight, not at aiding the court to discover the facts. He does not want the trial court to reach a sound educated guess, if it is likely to be contrary to his client's interests. Our present trial method is thus the equivalent of throwing pepper in the eyes of a surgeon when he is performing an operation. (736)

This description of our legal system suggests that Lombardi's doctrine is revered not only in high schools or on football fields, but also in that supposedly sacrosanct arena of justice—the courtroom. Frank's attack on our arbiters of the truth and justice does not stop there: he contends that, even worse than manipulating facts in the interest of winning, our system unfairly denies access to the facts to those who lack the funds for legal discovery. And remember, a trial, one would think, is intended to uncover "what really happened." When I taught in the prison system in Indiana, the standard inmate joke was that convicts could pay their way to a shorter sentence, and those behind bars were only the ones who lacked sufficient funds. Admittedly, none of this seems too surprising in the post–O. J. Simpson trial United States (remember him?), but I bring it up to remind you that if a society values winning above all else, then logic, reason, and careful argument are only tiny fingers in a dike whose entire structure is as susceptible to collapsing as were the Twin Towers.

Our own age, saddled as much as Orwell's with political chaos—what age has not been?—differs, perhaps, from that of seventy-five years ago in the following manner: too many people don't want to challenge the system and show where it is unfair, crazy, and flawed. They have become complacent, self-satisfied—fat and indolent with their own relative success. They don't want to confront existing assumptions. They don't want to challenge the president or the Supreme Court. Yes, that's the mantra: trust those in authority, especially in times of duress; let them make the decisions that will affect our lives. People don't want to do their own thinking, much less their own writing, about the issues of the day. People don't want to read material that will shake up their preconceived ideas—it's not too surprising that they don't habitually do a lot of research or thinking on their own.

Well, that's natural, isn't it? We have jobs to do; we have lives to live. What am I recommending here—that people spend huge amounts of time in libraries or hammering out manifestos like this one?

No. What I want to convey is that writing about things— books, art, ideas, relationships, houses, poems, politics, movies— represents an important first step. It seems a small step, but it really can be that "giant leap for mankind," in the words of Neil Armstrong, the man who first walked on the Moon. Writing can allow you to discover what you really feel about the world around you, and once you discover this, maybe you can work for change. Try it: go to a movie and then write up a review of it; send it to your local paper. Odds are it won't get published, but that isn't the important thing. Watch a speech on TV and then write a review of it for an op-ed page, as if you were a pundit.

What's important is that by writing the review, you will have discovered something about yourself, something that you didn't know before. At the same time, you will have discovered (or do I mean "uncovered," "excavated"?) details about the movie, the speech, that you had forgotten. In short, you will have made your experience more valuable because more complete, more understood, more articulated. And your reviews might get published at that.

Many people just don't have to write anymore, except in schools and colleges, experiences that are for most too brief. What happens when people don't write? They have others do their thinking for them. They have computers fix their sentences and correct their spelling. They accept written communications from companies or organizations and submit to the authority of that institutional rhetoric. They hire attorneys to write for them, attorneys who themselves often have to rely on associates or paralegals to do the actual composition. Writing is passed down and passed down, and the result is that people don't have to think for themselves, and society lurches along more and more mindlessly. Once I had a student (whose name I've slightly changed to protect his identity) submit his paper with his own name grievously misspelled. His name was, let's say, Don Wavely, yet his paper had on it "Don Waffle" "What's this?" I demanded in front of the class, perhaps a little peremptorily. "Didn't you write this? Don't you know how to spell your own name?" "Yes," he stammered. "It's just that the computer highlighted my name as a misspelling and suggested 'Waffle' instead. I automatically took its suggestion." Everyone laughed. They had been there.

"Automatically took its suggestion": is this the latter-day version of the Nuremberg Defense? ("Just following orders, sir. From my computer.") Computers, which when they first appeared seemed like a technology without much application to our daily routines (people stored recipes on them), now dominate our lives, especially our writerly lives. We're doing a lot of writing now that we used not to do—consider the omnipresence of email, texts, IM'ing, tweeting, for example—but the things that computers focus on differ from what we as humans focus on. I can't log in to my email unless, for example, I spell my password exactly right. It has to be in the right case too—all lower-case, for mine. If I put in my name into Google but misspell it Coiffi, I get nothing, except perhaps "Do you mean *coffee?*" The computer demands accuracy, repeatability ("What is your password? Retype your password"), simplicity. And if you as a computer user meet its demands, you are amply rewarded; you can get information from a website; you can compose an email; you can do on-line shopping. But these are relatively simple, not to say simplistic, goals. What has happened to the complex crafting of language?

I have subtitled this work a "manifesto" for various reasons. Primarily, it seems to me you are no longer so willing as you used to be to voice an opinion. At the same time that you shy away from argument, you are surrounded by disputatiousness and incivility, especially in the media and in the political arena. Perhaps that's *why* you have shied away from argument—you're sick of it. You want answers, to be sure, to various problems, just so long as they are not circuitous, windy, long answers. You want straightforward answers. This is reasonable enough. But when it comes to composing your own work, you also shy from "long answers"; you don't want to fight and struggle to defend a position. You don't want to be afflicted with what the critic David Bleich calls "chronic on-the-other-handism." It's much easier for you—and it's also often rewarded—to provide for your audience the already established, the somewhat derivative, the unassuming: to reproduce what's already out there. (And to keep it short.)

I'm encouraging you to break out of this attitude. We as a culture bolster it, I know, forcing you—and everyone else—into a position of being cowed by information, knowledge, words. Think of how the media intervenes, tells us what to think: after every speech, after every play in every professional sport, an "expert" is on hand to explain significance. After the acceptance speeches at the national conventions in August 2016, a team of pundits dissected what Mr. Trump and Ms. Clinton had to say and assessed the effectiveness of their words. This hardly encourages your freedom of thought. What happened to the days of yore—did these ever exist?—when people could just listen to a baseball game or political speech and make of it what they would? Of course, we might turn to the most articulate or the most informed among us to hear what she or he had to say, but at some point, each of us would play that very role.

And it is just that role—the amateur but revered thinker—that seems to be disappearing in our culture. Why think "outside the box" if the box thinks so very well for us and does so in color, to boot? Why imagine a solution if in fact eighteen thousand different solutions emerge at the right cue of a search engine? Why not change the inquiry so that one of those answers will work? Indeed, perhaps the writing class of the future will work on honing student "search phrase" skills, so that students can suck information from the Internet (or whatever it will be called) with greater efficiency and speed. Actually, this isn't an entirely bad thing, just so long as it doesn't usurp independent thought.

Perhaps, though, we can take a page or maybe a silicon chip out of the computer's book. Consider, for example, what's known as fuzzy logic. Can this help with writing, with creativity?

In a lecture at Bard College, computer science professor Sven Anderson laid out two important principles of what he called fuzzy logic:

1. An agent must sometimes act nonoptimally to explore his or her world.
2. Agents in fact develop representations and actions via experience.

To put these ideas into alignment with some ideas about writing, it seems to me that the second suggests that while writing (i.e., going through the experience of setting out your thesis, laying out the evidence for it and against it, etc.), you need to leave yourself open to modifying your ideas, developing them via the experience of writing. (Think of the blueprint or road map thesis in relation to this.)

Anderson's first idea, about agents acting "nonoptimally," has even more relevance, since indeed, as you do your writing, you'll be best off if you explore stuff that might not first off seem directly relevant, if you go down some apparent blind alleys, if you write in tangential relation to or around an issue rather than necessarily directly to it. This might involve taking the other side, inventing a new persona to deal with the issues at hand, possibly even embracing areas of your subject that seem most hostile to your sensibilities, full of sharp spikes and thorns, in a manner of speaking. Using some equivalent to fuzzy logic allows you to handle material that you can't immediately classify; it forces you to engage a broader range of possible examples. Mathematician Deborah J. Bennett gets at the same idea: "Fuzzification," she writes, "takes into account the imprecision of data, the vagueness of language, and the uncertainty inherent in systems. Where two-valued Boolean logic is sufficient for worlds with two states such as true and false, fuzzy logic allows us to deal with shades of gray" (173). In fact, the argumentative paper's structure itself replicates how fuzzy logic works: as writers of argument, we live, we thrive, in that gray zone.

But fuzzy logic really applies not only to writing but to the creative process as well. I mean, how is it that people come up with new ideas? How is it that that "aha!" experience works for some so often, so regularly, while for others that experience is a rarity? When Thomas McMahon writes (in *Ira Foxglove*) about how ideas just seem to come to him automatically, without any conscious effort (see p. 154), is he describing only the experience of the creative genius, or does what he writes apply (at least potentially) to everyone? It seems to me that our culture has deposited in us all a certain residue, but that residue has begun to crowd out our individual selves. Or to use a different metaphor, culture speaks through us, as if we were loudspeakers, and now we've all been reduced to bookshelf-sized units or to tinier, earbud speakers.

Can we provide an output that really exceeds, goes beyond what was "programmed in" by culture and education? John Stuart Mill suggests that we are getting more and more trapped by culture (and this was in 1859—what would he think today?):

The circumstances which surround different classes and individuals, and shape their characters, are daily becoming more assimilated. Formerly, different ranks, different neighborhoods, different trades and professions lived in what might be called different worlds; at present, to a great degree, in the same. Comparatively speaking, they now read the same things, listen to the same things, see the same things, go to the same places, have their hopes and fears directed to the same objects, have the same rights and liberties, and the same means of asserting them.... Every extension of education promotes it, because education brings people under common influences and gives them access to the general stock of facts and sentiments. Improvements in the means of communication promote it, by bringing inhabitants of distant places into personal contact.... The increase of commerce and manufactures promotes it, by diffusing more widely the advantages of easy circumstances.... [T]here ceases to be any social support for nonconformity—any substantive power in society which, itself opposed to the ascendancy of numbers, is interested in taking under its protection opinions and tendencies at variance with those of the public. (70–71)

Mill's got his finger not only on the touchpad but on the pulse of what's going on today. No one wants to be different, nonconformist. And the way this plays out in writing is that no one wants to take the unusual path, the not-obviously-optimal solution.

Maybe we need to go beyond the idea of fuzzy logic, of making inferences based on incomplete data, or of doing stuff that is not immediately or obviously relevant to the task. That's the fuzzy logic of computer programs, of refrigerators. We need what I'm going to call a "fuzzy subjectivity." We need not just to write around an issue, not just to dig a hole in a new place rather than dig the same hole deeper (*pace* Edward deBono); no, we need to reimagine the shovel, the hole, the act of digging, even the self. We have to see creativity as involved with reimagining who we are, leaving our subjective self behind, inhabiting not just other personalities but other races, other species. Hence the act of imagining isn't just one of digging a hole yourself but of say, gyring and gimbling in a wabe, of finding the most apt slithy tove, of total self-Jabberwockification. I don't yet know what any of that means, but maybe I'll figure it out as I go along.

If there were a formula for exceeding or escaping our cultural programming, then that would not be exceeding our cultural programming. Just bending down, grasping your legs and looking through them behind you at an upside down world—as the Transcendentalist writer Henry David Thoreau supposedly suggested we do—is not quite enough: we need also to use different eyes, and something other than the usual parts of our brain.

I don't think the battle must be lost. There is a lot of "headroom" still left for most of us, and I hope to have suggested some positive ways to tap into it. First, you need to allow yourself the opportunity to be creative. Think of that nine-dot grid in Figure 2, and then think, just for fun, of five ways other than those I mentioned earlier to solve the problem. The key to thinking outside the box is just this: there is no "outside" and no "inside"—it's all just thinking; as I mentioned earlier, the box itself is an artificial (and trite) construct. And what is "the" box? In what sense is the deictic "the" meant? Are inside and outside in real opposition? Think about this: could you think both inside and outside simultaneously? Isn't the whole model just a little too three-dimensional in a multidimensional universe? Don't be afraid to pursue paths that seem to lead nowhere. Go down them; explore them; look for interesting flora and fauna along the way. Maybe you'll meet something odd too—an iguana, a dodo, a tapir, a tapir that talks, an android dodo from the future. Lots of things emerge, not only serendipitously, but because taking the odd path is in itself a creative act.

Yet you can't allow yourself to be seduced by your own ideas, your own cleverness or creativity: question what you're doing, what you've written, what turns of argument you have taken. Don Quixote makes a flimsy helmet for himself early in Cervantes's novel, and then he goes after it with his sword to see whether it can stand the rigors of combat. He destroys it utterly. He rebuilds it, but the second version he decides not to test, assuming that it will work just fine. To offer ideas to an audience without at least subjecting them to your own toughest testing strikes me as equally deluded. My second suggestion, then, is that you very seriously consider what kinds of objections will be raised against your ideas, what sorts of counterexamples might be brought to bear, what ways you will have to accommodate these wrinkles, modify your own position, backtrack, or defend yourself—remember Mill's "75 percent rule." I know these are all challenging, potentially exhausting things to put yourself through, but what creative endeavor is not?

And that creativity applies to research, too. My third suggestion is that you don't want just to accumulate small mountains of data, piles of books, printouts, photocopies. No. You want to make some sense of it all. You do this by having some angle on the issue before you do research, or by discovering an angle early in your investigation. Don't worry about material that you don't use: as I said earlier, waste is as necessary to the research/writing process as it is to life. And what you think might be wasted could turn out to be useful at some other point. In your research, you need to direct your inquiry, looking not just for material or evidence, but for issues that arouse some controversy, some points of fracture, some fault lines. You protest, "But how can I—a college freshman, a first-year graduate student, an average person—challenge existing research, research by experts in the field?" and my response is that as you do research, you will discover that there are many angles and points of view; scholars ("experts") challenge and undermine and argue with one another all the time. Ralph Waldo Emerson looks at this very issue in his 1837 "The American Scholar." Here is what he suggests: "Meek young men grow up in libraries, believing it their duty to accept the views, which Cicero, which Locke, which Bacon, have given, forgetting that Cicero, Locke, and Bacon were only young men in libraries when they wrote these books" (57). There really is something wonderfully democratic (or maybe I mean meritocratic) about scholarship, for as you do research, you become a scholar too. As you discover what it is that others are arguing about, you join the ongoing debate and perhaps open up a new area for research.

At the same time, you need to be honest in your research, honest with how you present the opposition, honest in the language that you use. As the economics writer and editor Peter J. Dougherty remarks in an article about globalization studies, "flimsy arguments can have disastrous worldly consequences, but ... sound and innovative ideas can yield untold benefits." You might think that your ideas don't matter, that no one is listening, or that the impact you create will be negligible, a tree falling in a forest on an uninhabited planet. Think again. To vary Henry Adams's dictum about teachers, a *writer* never knows when his or her influence will stop—or even start. Mark Edmundson remarks sagely: "Words are potent. Ten years after the fact, people often can't remember a grievous pain.... But a decade on, they'll remember every word and tonal twist of a painful insult" (12). No, words have tremendous power, and the Jim B.'s of the world, who think that "wordsmithing" should be left to minor functionaries (see Chapter 2), might consider not just the impact of powerful written documents but the anguished anfractuosities of everyday discourse.

A fourth suggestion: you need to keep your audience in mind, but you also need to balance your sensitivity to them against the freedom to tell them something they do not know beforehand. This is a version of "speaking truth to power." If you intend to disagree with the audience's opinion, or with "received opinion," that's fine—you can respect that view and show in what ways it is not adequate or true. But too often it seems to me people say or write only what they think others will want to hear; they offer, that is, only a confirmation of the audience's perceived values and ideas. How does that kind of activity advance knowledge, complicate thought about an issue, solve ongoing problems? If your audience does not want to be challenged, not even a little, here's my suggestion: find a new audience. If the unchallengeable audience is your college professor, drop the course. If it's your parents, don't engage them in debate. If it's your friends, run with a new crowd. If it's your boss, get another job. I know this might be hard. Think of my suggestion as tough writing instructor love.

And finally, I make an appeal here for some attentiveness to language, to its style, its music, its beauty. Probably half of my impulse in writing this book was to find a vehicle by which

I could quote from authors such as James, Nabokov, Goffman, Updike, and Wallace. As I wrote, I found that what links most of these writers' work can be distilled into a single word: surprise. They surprise me. Their writing, even when I encounter it for the seventeenth time, catches me up short, makes me catch my breath. Their works do not follow predictable verbal circuits; they spark insights that I could not have foretold. Think of these great writers, and try to offer a similar level of surprise.

And that, perhaps, is what heartens me, what makes me think that writing, argument, and "style" are not obsolete notions, dying icons worshiped only by fuddy-duddies who still read books. Rather, many years after having been composed, the words and the works they're from still breathe, still give off the pungent aroma of well-wrought things that required labor to make, and still send their idea-infused tendrils into our modern brains. And they link us, if briefly, to the genius of inventiveness, the weird unknowability of language well used, the vision of which will always be the human condition—to live in an instantly dissolving present informed by a not-well-enough-understood past and to face a projected but ultimately unpredictable future. In a metaphysical sense, it's as if the near infinity of all past space-time has suddenly pinched in to a single point—a vanishing point, a present at which you now sit—and on the other side of this point looms an equally vast, or maybe even vaster, expanse of space-time: a projected future. Your writing can capture that present and solidify it, freeze-frame it, imbue it with meaning for time immemorial. And if your writing says something new, you can change that future, can make it worth living in and into. You can make it yours.

A Instructors' Guide: How to Use This Book in Class

Students need to purchase, rent, or borrow the text. They will need to have a personal copy, at least for the duration of the semester. Some students will want to use the first edition, which was widely pirated and is available online for free. I would discourage this, for a number of reasons. But the initial struggle, I have discovered, is about the purchase of any text. Many students don't think they need a text to teach them how to write; they have written papers before and are sure that they "know the drill." You need to disabuse them of this notion.

Once they have bought the text, they will need to read it. This involves some work, especially since the vocabulary is at times off-putting. Some teachers assign the entire book, while others assign only key chapters, such as the ones on "thesis," "development," and "style." It seems to me that some students like this but others are annoyed that they had to pay for a whole book when they were only assigned 20 percent of it to read. Hence I would suggest you just have students read the whole text.

Chapters 1–5 and 7 should be read prior to having a paper come due.

Chapters 8–11 should be read after a paper has been written and graded, and preferably prior to having students do rewrites of their papers.

Chapter 6 needs to precede the writing of a research paper.

Chapters 12–13 should come about two-thirds the way through the time you allot to this text, and Chapters 14 and 15 should ideally be read toward the end of the unit.

How long you should spend on this varies from class to class, and of course from college to college. It seems to me that it might be compressed into no shorter a time period than seven or eight weeks, since you want to assign students some papers to complete and you want to get them to do some research. At the end of the eighth week, you might have the research paper come due. If you meet twice a week, then, a chapter should be assigned for each class period.

What to do, actually, with this text in class also will be quite interestingly various, depending on the instructor and the class. In general, I want to run a "student-centered classroom." This involves engaging students and having them speak and write during class.

In general, what I try to get out in classes is the following. In each chapter, I try to present or elicit ...

- the main idea(s)
- any controversial ideas or points of confusion (references, words)
- places where you as the instructor disagree
- some sense of how what's being suggested jibes with students' prior education
- connection to the requirements of your course
- connection of ideas in text to the larger surrounding culture
- interesting texts quoted in part or in full
- connection between imaginative argument and other texts in the course

To get at this material, you can use discussion, some streamwriting, and other pedagogies.

Conducting Discussions in the Student-Centered Classroom

The Imaginative Argument is not tightly tied to a specific pedagogy, but it does ask students to generate their own, imaginative ideas. It's not really a text for a "transmission model" classroom, or one that uses (for example) multiple-choice exams. It's a book that argues for the independence of spirit and confident individualism that inventing an argument nurtures, and for the sense of communality and generosity needed to send that new idea out into the world.

As you probably know, there is always a certain risk involved when you enter a "student-centered" classroom. The risk is this: you never know what's going to happen. What is going on in the outside world? What's affecting your students' lives, work, mood, and willingness to cooperate? Some variables also concern the physical environment you're in, that is, your classroom. Will the heat or air conditioner be operative? Will the classroom be too hot or too cold? Too noisy? Will there be rats, mice, spiders, or other distracting/repulsive vermin in the room? What about that huge bumblebee that took everyone's eyes off of you as you tried to elucidate a particularly important point? And to break the problem down still further, each student has his or her own life situation to deal with and live through. In your class of twenty-five, you are engaging twenty-five very distinct brains, and each three-pound universe, as it takes in what's going on in your class, incorporates, encompasses, or groks in an individual, unforeseeable way.

Your butterflies, then, are justified. Keep in mind, too, that your students—at least some of them, and a majority of them if you are in fact doing your job well—will have butterflies, too. They will be nervous because they're in public and could potentially be put on the spot, could embarrass themselves. Even though one of your goals as a teacher is not to embarrass them but to engage them and get them to respond, still, on a regular basis, students will be intimidated or inadvertently humiliated by what you do, say, or ask of them. So we have a nervous-making situation for the teacher, who must be speaking in public—something most Americans supposedly fear more than death itself—surrounded by twenty-five or thirty or more students who also stand on the brink of this potentially terrifying enterprise. It's as if you're not on the edge of a single precipice, but as you turn around and look about you, you notice other voids yawning as well. You are as if on a single tower, standing alone, surrounded by a large abyss, and the tower you're standing on isn't ivory, either.

The Four Modes of Discussion

I see discussion—one of the primary pedagogical methods that this text should encourage—as involving at least four major modes of discourse. First, you can engage students in conversation, casual talk about their other classes, the weather, how they are feeling at a given point in the semester, what they think about this or that news item. Second, you can check to see if they have been listening or doing the reading. I call this second activity a "catechism," since you might ask questions for which there are specific and correct answers. Third, you can work with students on difficult issues, and try to help them solve these. This activity resembles the catechism in that there is usually a correct answer, but it's one that needs to be arrived at through various acts of ratiocination and also through an understanding of contextual or external material. I call this activity "problem solving." Finally, you can offer to your students questions that don't have answers but that tend to cause people to develop strong emotional responses. I call these provocations. These are the heart, of course, of the "imaginative argument."

The conversational aspect of a class is not hard to master or invoke. Students like to talk, and they often have very interesting things to say, so engaging them in conversation is usually rewarding and fun. But of course conversation is only the beginning. You will want to move on to the other levels of discussion, but do remember that you can lapse into conversational mode every now and then. This gives students a bit of relief from the pressure of "performing" or of being engaged with a serious, oftentimes difficult topic. They don't fear getting the wrong answer during conversation, though sometimes material emerges such that a "values clarification" moment might ensue. Overall, though, conversation represents a relatively risk-free zone.

Less risk-free is the second mode of discussion I mention above: the "catechism." Here, there are absolutely wrong and clearly correct answers—and it's a mode most students and teachers are quite familiar with. It's fine to slip into this for brief periods—for it's here where you can "check" to see if students have done the reading, and it's here where students who have done the reading but haven't really reflected on it very deeply really have an opportunity to speak up. They might be able, for example, to tell you the names of all the characters from *The Great Gatsby*, but they might be befuddled by a question such as "How is Daisy a quintessential all-American girl?" The catechism should not go on for long, though. A professor asking questions and fishing for particular answers all too quickly becomes a tiresome and straining master of ceremonies. It is surprising to me, I confess, how many teachers rely on this mode alone, and believe in fact that what they're doing is conducting a discussion. They're not. They're just conducting a catechism. It's not entirely without value, but you want to move on from there.

Another mode I urge teachers to employ is what I call problem solving. You need, in engaging this particular type of discourse, to try to figure out what puzzles or difficulties the students themselves face—what questions might arise in their minds. (See Ken Bain's work on this idea.) That is, look for material about an issue or in a text that you see as important but is likely to be missed by your students. And you, someone who has more experience and education that they have, can help illuminate some of these difficult aspects of issues or texts. There is, as with the "catechistic" discussion, a correct answer, or one that more or less accords with your own answer or that of other scholars, but it's not an obvious or simple answer, and you need to work through with your students how you arrived at it.

For example, to take a well-known poem, Robert Frost's "The Road Not Taken," you might ask students why the speaker emphasizes that the "two roads" the traveler chooses between are "really about the same." You might want to point out that the speaker's twice-repeated emphasis on the roads' similarity seems to stand in sharp contrast to the ending lines, "and I—/ I took the one less traveled by / And that has made all the difference" (lines 18–20). Critical opinion on this poem has, in the last couple of decades, suggested that this disjunction lies at the heart of understanding the poem.

But it's still tricky for students to figure out. You need to offer some guidance in this "problem solving" mode, as well as allow for some latitude of interpretation. Remember that this isn't really a catechism, this mode; it's a way of communally puzzling out texts and issues, and while scholars might agree on a certain interpretation, and that might have resonance and persuasive power for you, you might have to do some work to convince students of its value.

Finally, you want to ask questions that I call "provocations." These are questions that I myself find personally perplexing and really very difficult to answer: they are questions that might be answered with an "imaginative argument." An example of this type of question might be, to stick with Frost's poem, "OK, if the poem's speaker is ultimately not a 'reliable narrator,' and the poem is about how people tend to mythologize their own past, how do you account for its incredible popularity as a poem about 'making the hard choices' or taking the difficult path in life and finding great rewards from doing so?" Or, to make it more provocative still, "When the words say one thing but millions of readers believe another, what finally does the poem 'mean'?" Some students will say it means what critics say it means; others will contend that the poem has moved into public understanding in such a significant way that its message is the somewhat trite uplift of choosing the harder but ultimately better way.

Now, I don't know the answers to these questions—they are not nearly so pat as to have answers—but I have a general idea of where I might go to find an answer. They are usually unanswerable—sometimes even unaskable—and always real questions. They are what might be called the "let's-get-to-the-underlying-issue" kind of question. I think this is the type of question you want to infect your students with, for in fact one goal of your class should not be just transferring knowledge to them, giving them some of what you learned in order to get your college degrees, but teaching them how to pose questions like those you employ in your discussion. If you can get students to ask polarizing questions of this sort, then, to a large degree, you've succeeded, since you are providing them with a small model of the way of thought behind the argumentative academic essay.

The Value of Discussion

Too often, it seems to me, college education is about providing just pat answers, correct choices on multiple-choice tests, or bald reformulations of what the professor him- or herself said in lecture. The class needs to work together, asking real questions, and arriving—where? I'm not sure, but at a level of interrogation that probes as it stirs reflection, that answers, to an extent, by asking. What are some of these questions? How do you come up with an "unaskable" question? If it's not askable, how can you ask it? Well, I'm not sure. Perhaps we should discuss it.

You as a discussion leader want to keep the discussion going, but you want it to have a direction. That's really your major goal once a group has been ignited, or at any rate begins to talk. You want to keep it moving. But it has to move productively. You need to create a special kind of atmosphere in the class—one that helps establish a community, which is supportive of multiple voices, but which compels students to perform at a high level—to think and say good things.

Your job as leader or facilitator of discussion is to keep it going, to find out things, to give everyone a space. When someone makes a comment, then, you want to pick up on that comment, not just say, "Good point" or "Uh-huh" or "What do the rest of you think?" or "Anybody? Anybody?" perhaps unconsciously replicating the famous economics teacher played by Ben Stein in *Ferris Bueller's Day Off*.

What you want to do, then, is ask for elaboration of a student's remark. Ask him or her to give examples from the text. Or you could dispute the claim, playing a pleasant devil's advocate, as in "Convince me. I'm willing to be convinced, but I don't quite see what you are getting at." Or you could mention some evidence that would seem to contradict the point being made: "You claim that Jordan Baker is a good person in *The Great Gatsby*, and that Nick jilts her. But isn't it true that she cheated as a golf pro, and isn't it also true that she is a bad driver? And bad drivers, in the novel, can be deadly, no?" Another response would be to enlarge on a student's comment, especially if you think it's on the right track. This is far better than saying simply, "Good point." In your responses to your students you don't want to shut down conversation or judge it, and you especially don't want to remind students that you are judging them as they speak. You are, I know, but you need to put that activity in brackets for the duration of the discussion, because your goal is to draw them out, to create a space in which opinions and ideas can be expressed and developed, and to even find out some new things for yourself.

You will notice that some student responses will be better than others. These you need to highlight, repeat, rephrase, come back to. Weaker responses should be listened to as well, but honestly dealt with, I think, either by you or the class. Try to get your class, though, to imitate you in terms of how to disagree politely. Some responses will be flat-out weird, though, and here you need to ask for clarification. Once in a seminar on Transcendentalism that I was taking, another student said, in response to a photo of Thoreau that the professor had shared with us, "Well, it seems clear that Thoreau was simply not sitting in his own dish." The professor, who often responded to the student, Boulos, by saying, "What do the rest of you think?" here took up my classmate: " 'Not sitting in his own dish'? And what does that mean?" Boulos, who was from Lebanon, explained the idiomatic expression for us, which meant that Thoreau was not happy, though the expression has an additional flavoring, one might say, or implication, that now escapes me.

But as a student I should have pressed Boulos to explain other comments he made. One thing that a professor needs to encourage and develop in a class is getting students talk to one another rather than making them filter all their comments through the overriding intelligence of the person at the front of the class. If all the students must get approval from you as the teacher, then this isn't really much of a discussion at all, but a sort of competition for the teacher's approval.

Reticent students, who often try to slip through classes and say as little as possible, I try to draw out. "What do you think, Cedric?" you might ask. This occasionally draws student wrath, I note. Once a student said when I called on him, "If I have something to say, I'll raise my hand. If I don't raise my hand, please do not call on me, as I have no response." Whoa. I said, "OK, but I'm asking you for a spontaneous reflection here—just kind of trying to draw you into the conversation. I'd like to hear what you have to say." The student did respond, but from that point on, I have included on my syllabus, "I will call on you in class. Be prepared to answer questions on the material."

And as far as how to pattern the discussion, I won't offer a fixed template. I'd recommend starting with pre-conversation ("business"), moving into an actual conversation, and mixing some catechistic elements in every so often. The more challenging discussion modes such as problem solving and provocation should probably not be invoked during the first five minutes, but as I said before, you can cycle from one mode to another. Provocation for a whole period's discussion is too intense, perhaps, so you need to mix it up. And, too, you can occasionally break off discussion and present a mini-lecture, say of three or four minutes. Or you could have the students break into groups to discuss and then in the re-formed full class present their group's ideas to the whole audience. Variety of discussion and variety of modes of discussion make for a lively, effective class, but you need to decide when to change modes and when to pursue one in favor of the other. Try to be sensitive to your students' wishes, try to figure out their inclinations, and try to gauge their level of involvement with a particular issue, text, or idea. Try to figure out where the class itself wants to go. Though sometimes difficult to ascertain, this is worth the effort.

Anxieties/Problems of Class Discussion

Some suggestions. Don't worry about "coverage" of all the material. You won't be able to cover as much as you'd like, so forget that metaphor. Instead, allow students' own interests and focuses to help create the shape of the discussion. If students want to go in one direction, then don't force the conversation back to where you want it, at least not right away: explore a bit. You can gradually bring it around or even discover in a new direction a better way to go than you had initially planned. Don't be afraid of briefly going "off topic," especially since very off-topic discussions can be legitimately cut off at any point with, "Well, getting back to the text," or something similar, and sometimes it's good to have such discussions since ideas and perspectives and quiet students will emerge.

I advocate a device-free classroom. It's not that I am indulging my Luddite self but, rather, that I want to create a community of people interacting with one another, face-to-face, without the distraction of electronic digital media. This policy I'd recommend announcing the first class period, and students should be urged to drop the class if they cannot go for the class time without checking their messages. Keep in mind that many people, students among them, are addicted to their devices and feel terribly uncomfortable not being able to constantly monitor them. Hence you might institute a five-minute "device break." It's up to you. Some teachers penalize the whole class (the "*Full Metal Jacket* treatment," my colleague Daniel Hengel calls it) if a student's phone rings or is consulted. (Hengel withholds "bonus questions" on quizzes when a device goes off or is consulted, or when a student yawns or sighs or drifts off. Another colleague, Matt Eatough, simply counts a student absent if he or she consults a device during class time.)

Running a discussion like this has an element of intensity that many students find a bit exhausting—so it's usually best to break the discussion at various points in order to dilate on a topic of interest, to consult the Internet for some information, or to write a key term or reference on the board. But be prepared: students will fight the discussion format as you go into and out of it. They are not used to this, for the most part. Some students, I've noticed, pack a meal with them, and they have no hesitation about tucking in right there in class. I discourage this. I tell my students, "Remember, this is not a spectator sport, to which you bring your soda, hotdogs, and cell phones. You're not in the stands. You're on the field; you actually have to play. You don't see Nolan Arenado munching a hot dog on third base, do you?" This idea has to be reinforced again and again, probably because most students are used to classes in which they sit and passively absorb information or passively be passive.

Sometimes, of course, the discussion will die down. No one will be saying anything at all. That's OK. This is called "dead air," and I urge people not to be worried about it. Sometimes you need time to consider a statement, an idea, a passage from the text. You might not have an instantaneous response, so hold off. Modeling this behavior for your students can be useful, too, as it shows how sometimes the slower response is better; how reaction can quickly or easily devolve into knee-jerk reaction, and how a considered, thoughtful response can often bring the conversation to a whole new level.

A useful variant of discussion is the student-led discussion. I've seen this wonderfully used in a class taught by Hengel. Students are asked to bring in three or four "discussion-type questions" as well as to write a brief response to the literature being assigned. The questions are of the "provocation" type I describe above, or at least of the problem-solving kind. The teacher forms a circle and then sits outside it. He or she is not part of the discussion, at least not ergonomically speaking. He or she tries to keep his/her mouth shut after naming a student as discussion leader. Dead air occasionally prevails but not often. And students take the initiative. Like many effective pedagogies, this one puts pressure on the students to make the class effective.

This pedagogy resembles that of Don Finkel, whose book *Teaching with Your Mouth Shut* advocates for some classes in which the teacher says absolutely nothing at all. The class, warned ahead of time that this would take place, simply has to go it alone, with the teacher sitting in their midst, mutely listening. This dead air really forces students into coming up with something like a discussion on their own.

Miscellaneous Suggestions: Teacher Energy, Confronting the Pantheon

Overall, the most important factor in terms of keeping a discussion going is your own energy. Students respond very positively to displays of energy in the classroom. A blasé, nonchalant, detached persona, an ironically distanced or robotic attitude, seems to squelch chat and to generate an endemic listlessness. But if you display emotional energy, that will infect your students and can be, in a manner of speaking, relatively easily converted into intellectual energy.

Finally, you need to understand, I think, that to an extent you as a teacher represent not just yourself or your discipline or institution, but a much larger cultural icon. Your presence and person reverberate in each student's mind down that long corridor of remembered teachers, K–12 and beyond. Thus when students see you, they see arrayed behind you some thirty or forty other teachers, different for each student. As you speak in your own voice, you at the same time form part of that group chorus. Even though you won't know what these other teachers were like or what impact they had on each student, you need to be aware that your students' history with previous teachers makes it impossible for them to have a tabula rasa conception of you. You've been to an extent predetermined. In joining each student's individual pantheon of teachers, you will have a different position, a position that's likely to shift over the course of the semester, as you get to know the class and assign grades to various assignments. But in general, I feel compelled to add, that group of teachers has represented authority, some sort of intellectual standard, and an external-to-family group of adults that knows how your students think. You happily, or at least willingly, join that group. But you need to remember that, in joining it, you will be compared, contrasted, judged, and even understood against and in relation to the other members of it. The irony is that who these people are, you'll never know.

Reanimating Pedagogies: Group Work, Workshops, Student Presentations

The pedagogies I deal with here tend to shift the teaching/performance focus. The teacher, in what I'm terming "reanimating" pedagogies, is no longer at the center of the classroom or necessarily its focal point. Instead, she or he hands over the teaching to the students themselves. As they take over this duty, they come to terms with the material in a new, different way—an imaginative way. They internalize it because they have to express and convey it to others. Such a shift is not new or revolutionary, I realize, but it's still used only rarely in writing classrooms.

There will be some resistance. It often takes the following form: "I [my parents, the federal government, the state of x] paid a lot of money for me to attend classes taught by people like you, Professor, people with many college degrees and books in print.... I didn't pay money—my good money—to listen to someone from Hoboken blather on about why *The Great Gatsby* is a flawed vision of the American Dream. I mean, c'mon!" Another form I recently encountered involves complaints from students that the teacher is lazy: "All she has us do every day is write and talk about what we've written," a student recently complained to me about a colleague. "She's not doing her job! She assigned essays for us to read and should talk about them!" The subtext of this is as follows: "She should tell us what these texts mean."

Well, OK. Superficially, these objections seem fair enough. The students are paying for knowledge, wisdom, information, insight, experience—for the very things that the professor represents and often has—for those things that in fact define a professor. So my response to such objections is, initially, acknowledgment of a relatively reasonable point of view. And the quality of many oral reports, group presentations, or student-led discussions often reinforces the strength of my hypothetical students' objections. I have very often found myself observing a class and struggling to retain interest (or consciousness) during one of these slightly avant-garde pedagogical experiments. I've also found myself drilling my fingernails into my bloodied palms as students presented material that was ill-informed, confusing, or wrong—usually with the aid of PowerPoint. There are dangers inherent in such pedagogies.

Just the same, even when these techniques don't quite work out, they often provide for students a release from the usual lecture or possibly pressure-inducing discussion, or even a bit of "fun," a break from class, a move toward just hanging out and talking. They improve the atmosphere of the classroom, making it a friendlier, less intimidating place. I know that's faint praise.

Yet such techniques often do effectively get across some material, can get students grappling with ideas, debating possibilities, and situating themselves in a new relationship with their own way of handling ideas, specifically in the position of having to formulate and express their own ideas with an eye toward presenting them to an audience.

This very activity—formulating ideas—constitutes the center of *The Imaginative Argument* and of the writing course, perhaps more so than it does in other college courses. That is to say, crafting an argument is more than merely imagining an audience. It requires the invention of ideas. Thus while the transmission model of instruction certainly has to be engaged sporadically, interfiliating it with more student-centered pedagogies leads to greater student independence of thought yet keeps as a touchstone a professor-generated model of how to think critically. An audience, for example, might be heterogeneous; some audience members or segments might disagree. Additional perspectives need to be anticipated and addressed. Ideas must stem from some problem that has an urgency the audience finds believable; perhaps other obvious or already-existing solutions to the problem should be acknowledged. In short, putting the student in the role of presenter forces him or her to think of the discourse situation in a sophisticated way. No longer is the student just trying to prove that he or she has read the text or listened to the lecture. Now that student has to come up with something genuinely insightful.

When students complain about having to listen to this person or that, I tell them the following: actually, your fellow students often come up with valuable insights into the material. They should not be trapped by ad hominem dismissals of their peers—dismissals which don't ultimately differ in kind from dismissals of the course and its instructor because that course is "only a general education distribution requirement," or worse, dismissal of all courses offered at a given institution because it's not, say, in the Ivy League.

To the dissenting student, too, I have a second response, namely that it's up to her or him, at least partially, to make another student's report more responsible or informed, to challenge its inconsistencies or inaccuracies, to engage the presenter in debate, realizing all along that every dissenter is potentially subject to the same level of challenge that the presenter her- or himself faces. In short, students need to be reminded that in a relatively small class they are themselves largely responsible for the level of discourse being employed and for the type of community created.

Finally, though, it seems to me that the underlying objection—the crux of most student and faculty resistance to student centered or student led classrooms—stems from our joint situatedness in the Epoch of the Post-Original. When students lead a class, they often feel the (wonderful) compulsion to be original, to do more than merely repeat what they have heard, to not merely parrot the professor's ideas or rehash a summary of text material. They have to come up with something—gasp!—new: something their own. Using such pedagogies as much as forces students against the grain, forces them to do something that they were not only rarely taught to do, but maybe (in other classes) prevented from or punished for doing. Thus the teacher here isn't simply conveying information but instead engineering a widespread behavior modification. Sometimes students will recognize this and express gratitude. At other times, they will resist. Mightily. I mention this here because other faculty also might see the techniques and methods I advocate as a cop-out or a refusal to take responsibility for conveying what we as professors should convey: The Truth. As you know, I don't believe in the "The."

"A schoolboy can read *Hamlet* and can detect secrets of the highest concernment as yet unpublished therein"

Emerson, writing this comment in "Experience," was onto something in 1844, I think; yet his lesson no longer has much currency. It should. It seems to me that students, and the general population as well, to an extent, have been brainwashed into the following belief: what they say or think does not matter. Only the proclamations of important people (like professors) have any value. Oh, we have slogans such as "Every opinion counts" or "If you see something, say something," which imply that the individual can make a difference and has decided responsibility. But in fact the days of "marching to a different drummer" or of posters proclaiming "Question Authority!" have receded into the past.

I am reminded of a memorable TV episode of *My Favorite Martian* in which the Bill Bixby character, Tim O'Hara (an average U.S. white male middle-class human), assisted by Ray Walston's eponymous "Uncle Martin" character, a Martian with preternatural abilities, can paint extraordinary imitations of Leonardo, Matisse, Van Gogh, and the like. From across a room crowded with art critics and enthusiasts, Uncle Martin surreptitiously directs Tim's paintbrush. (He can make things move by pointing to them.) An onlooking audience is awed and amazed—at least until someone asks for a painting not in imitation of another artist, but in an original style. Tim looks over at Uncle Martin, who shrugs and then gestures in a way to say, "Go for it; you're on your own!" Then Tim starts creating on his own, and he's entirely talentless. So his short-lived fame dissipates. That was in the 1960s. Today, I think the same character's lack of originality would not matter—people would simply latch on to his ability to reproduce beautiful simulacra. After all, the summer I write this has witnessed not one or two but four Hollywood blockbuster movies based on comic books. We are in a culture that adores the simulacrum, the mash-up, the prequel and sequel, the "son of"—even if it's not the son of Leonardo.

So maybe my sensibility emerges from the 1960s, during which era originality had more value than did imitation, and people did things for the value of doing them, not simply for the value of having done them. This is a new concept for many, I know, that I'm setting out here, namely the importance of the experience within the classroom itself, not its instrumental value as a way toward students' completing a course or achieving some predetermined "learning outcomes" (though these do have value). I want to stress the intangibles that emerge in the classroom, the moment-by-moment sense of understanding and community that the classroom represents. It's a crucible in which amazing things can happen: enlightenment can dawn, for example. My sympathies more clearly align with those of Geoffrey

Sirc, who argues that the writing class should be an intense experience, and less with those of agencies, offices, and administrative boards that want to assess precisely what it is that each student has learned in each class. I see formal education as a complex and oftentimes metric-resistant process of intellectual and social accruing. We often teach and convey attitudes, abilities, and facilities that we are unaware we're conveying, that are impossible to accurately measure, but that are, finally, useful for students, insofar as they increase the students' ability to be independent thinkers, collegial team workers, and co-creators within the unique intellectual community of the classroom itself.

Varying Classroom Dynamics: Group Work

The late novelist David Foster Wallace once remarked to me—we were both teaching in the same university consortium, and kind of grousing about Southern California in general—that what he found most depressing about the Los Angeles area was that the weather was the same every day. Classrooms with the same weather patterns day after day also tend to be depressing; they tend toward something like weatherlessness, an ideal clime for those who don't want to feel, or think, or bring awareness to the surface. You as the teacher should employ various techniques, styles, and pedagogies—should even change the seating configuration of your classroom if possible—to keep students a bit off balance, a little uncertain of what the next class will bring. You do this not out of perversity, but out of a desire to involve all the students, and to involve them in various ways, where, for example, some students who play minor roles in one type of ergonomic structure might play the principals in another.

One way to significantly vary a classroom dynamic is through the use of group work. What might be a hostile, threatening, ominous environment if the class were left in one large group often transforms instantaneously into a much sunnier and more productive place when the students are put into groups. Early one semester a colleague asked me how my class was going, what we were doing, and I told him we had done group work that day. "Oh, so it's come to that point in the semester, has it?" he asked, chortling, as if to suggest a certain pedagogical desperation on my part. It wasn't mean-spirited, I want to emphasize, but a moment in which we both realized that sometimes classes taught in traditional ways cause ennui or succumb to an entropic flattening out of energy. Fair enough. These things do happen, and group work does seem to combat them.

What happens in group work is sometimes ... nothing at all. Students just chat and come up with something on the spur of the moment when asked to present. But oddly enough, just as often, it's something rather special and amazing. The key is that group work disrupts the usual dynamic of the classroom. Suddenly it's not just that students are "performing for" or responding to a teacher; suddenly it's not just an undifferentiated "us" and "the professor'"; no, the arrangement has changed in a major way. Now it's just a group of three or four, and if they have been given an accomplishable and interesting task, that group sets out to do it in a way that differs from how they responded in the class as an entirety.

What happens is that each student has the opportunity to take on the role of the teacher. Each student, when this technique is done well, teaches his or her peers, goes in some way beyond himself or herself in assuming understanding of material and in modeling how one ought to respond. The mini-class formed by each group establishes a wholly new personality and then applies that personality to the course material. That's why group work can be so valuable.

But group work is still quite difficult to organize well, and requires as much if not more energy than lecturing or leading a discussion. It should probably be familiar to most readers, so I won't dwell on it at length. I simply want to highlight some techniques for organizing it, techniques that make it an effective use of classroom time.

Groups can range in size from pairs to half the class. I prefer to split the difference, and usually put students into groups of three or four. Fours are probably better than threes; fours make up real groups, rather than just troikas. This effectively creates a number of mini-classes, which I think function better than twos or threes, which fail ("bad chemistry") if the students don't like one another, or if two of them are emotionally involved in some significant outside-of-classroom relationship. Groups of more than four students allow some people to disappear. Many students make it a practice, over their college years, to disappear in their classes, to blend into the Formica-work. Grouping students foils such willful self-zombification.

What should their presentations be like? My suggestion is to keep these informal in nature, done seated among other group members (rather than standing in front of a class). I usually urge groups to choose a "note taker" and a "spokesperson," so that groups will be prepared to present something once everyone finishes with the group work. And despite the existence of a single spokesperson per group, I urge non-spokesperson group members to speak up if they feel the impulse to add something of value. This presentation aspect is usually much facilitated by your having assigned to groups a very specific task—usually an open-ended discussion question—to which the group can provide a least a provisional "answer."

One example of a very specific task emerged from a workshop led by Thomas Bartscherer, at Bard College. Leading a group of fifty or so teachers in a multiple-day workshop, Bartscherer asked us to compose an essay for the next day. It was to be a "stab at a draft" of an essay, one that asked some important questions of the texts and that made something of an attempt to answer them. We were supposed to limit ourselves to 500 words and not to take more than an hour to write the assignment.

The next day, he put us in groups of three or four, and asked us to work with our essays. His instructions were nicely specific. He said we needed to appoint a "timer" who would be very strict. Then we needed to read aloud our essays to one another. Twice. After that, the people listening would offer responses, ones that the timer would closely monitor and make sure were no longer than three minutes per person. But the best thing about this exercise was the constraints regarding responses. We were supposed to cover three areas: first, what is the main point of the essay being read? Second, what interesting language jumps out at the listener? And finally, how might this essay be either continued or improved? All these questions, again, had to be answered in under three minutes per listener. The exercise made for an intense sharing of ideas, and we were busy every second of the forty or so minutes that had been allotted.

Oral Reports and Draft Workshops

This brings me to another "talking" pedagogy used often in writing classes: the "oral report." Again, this provides a valuable variation from the teacher speaking and the class listening or discussing. However, I find that student presentations often lack pizzazz or vitality—lack a point, even. Students seem not to realize that they are supposed to be making a point. They read from notes or a text, or (worse) use PowerPoint and simply read a presentation screen by screen. It seems that students are no better prepared, on balance, to give oral reports, than they are to write formal essays. I think that you as a teacher need to work, perhaps individually with the students, to explain how an oral report is most effectively delivered, how to speak in an organized fashion but extemporaneously and engagingly, how to make eye contact with an audience, and the like.

It might be best for students to start by posing the problem or asking the question they intend to explore. They need to make it clear why this is an interesting, important, or pressing question. Then they should provide their "solution" or "answer." This, the essence of their presentation, should be delivered within the first two or three minutes. The remaining time, I suggest, should be devoted to asking questions that they encountered along the way to developing their idea, and offering answers to these. Finally, the conclusion should extend the opening point. This pattern, as you probably noted, closely mirrors that of the argumentative academic essay; it reinforces that conventionalized but I think very useful pattern of inquiry. It varies, somewhat, from the typical "tell the audience something, tell it to them again, and then tell them what you told them," but it still includes sufficient redundancy to be comprehensible for listeners.

Another kind of presentation pattern emerges in the "draft workshop" class, a class in which all students are required to talk about and comment on two or three students' draft essays. I usually schedule as many of these per semester as papers are due (usually three to five), and I try to make sure that each student in the class, at least once, has his or her paper the subject of a "draft workshop." These workshops involve circulating a draft of a student essay ahead of time and then discussing it in class, trying to locate its strengths and weaknesses, as well as suggesting ways to improve it in a final version.

I use a method taught me in creative writing courses I took from Peter Michelson, a poet who taught at my undergraduate institution, Northwestern University. Here is what I am calling "The Michelson Technique":

1. At the start of the term, every student signs up for a draft workshop day. Note that to cover five or six student essays in this draft workshop format, two or three class days are required, assuming a class size of twenty to twenty-five students and a ninety-minute class.
2. Prior to the draft workshop, the students whose papers will be discussed need to email their drafts to the rest of the class (or they need to distribute these in photocopy form the class prior to the draft workshop).
3. The class should be organized in a circle. The workshop proceeds by having the student whose paper is under discussion present his or her thesis. (In fact, the whole introduction might be presented—the student's choice.) Then, that presenter must *remain silent* while each and every member of the class offers a critique. Sometimes I set a time limit of one or two minutes for each critique or specify that students make exactly three suggestions.
4. The person whose paper is under scrutiny ("on the block," the students say) *may not talk* during his or her classmates' comments. Hence it is important that the commenting students not ask direct questions. There should be no back-and-forth dialogue between the author and those offering critiques. If the student responds, his or her winning, charming,

or hostile and aggressive personality will inflect subsequent responses to just the paper itself. These responses won't be so helpful, since such responses will be to the writer plus the paper or maybe in lieu of the paper. But we want as much as possible to look at the paper in isolation.

These responses to the draft should be "constructive" in nature and substantive rather than merely suggestions for copyediting (though some sentence-level corrections do come up). In terms of defining "constructive," I use some of the same ideas that I use when trying to describe the proper tone for teachers to take when evaluating student essays: one must be supportive of the student but at the same time honest in one's appraisal of the work. For example, you might have students look at just a few aspects of the student paper under discussion:

a. The thesis—is it there?
b. Is it an argument?
c. Is support/development offered? How convincing is that?
d. Are counterarguments engaged? Are important ones being ignored?
e. Is there a Δ-Thesis?
f. Are the fundamentals of paragraph development/cohesion/coherence etc. respected?
g. Is the form correct?

These criteria follow the main ideas of *The Imaginative Argument*, reinforcing them and bringing them to bear on real-world examples.

5. I urge students to try to add at least one new idea when they offer the critique, though admittedly this task is increasingly more difficult as more and more students take their turn speaking.

6. After the critiques, the author may respond—to questions raised, to doubts, to problems he or she encountered during the composition of the essay. She or he may ask questions to the whole group.

7. The class then moves on to the next draft. Again, over the course of the semester, the goal is for all students to have one paper "draft-workshopped."

I know this is a difficult process for the student whose paper in "on the block." I've been on the block myself. But it's a useful process, in that usually as a group the class offers quite valuable suggestions. And generally students are kind and do offer constructive suggestions—especially since they know they themselves will inevitably be on the receiving end of commentary. By critiquing others' papers and listening to multiple student responses, students get a fuller sense of what is being required of them, of what works and what does not, and of how academic writing, with its own conventionalized and particular format, has a special value: in fact, the academic argument exists as a kind of discourse that functions in ways that the draft workshop makes less and less alien.

During this process, the teacher can take on several roles. She or he can remain entirely silent, simply calling on one student after another, moderating the discussion by cutting off the over-lengthy comment or softening a too harsh attack. Alternatively, the teacher him- or herself may offer a response, along with everyone else. This has a democratizing effect, but it also allows the teacher to reinforce various ideas and principles. If the students are attentive, they infer a kind of "oral grading" of a paper, and they get a better sense of what it is they are being required to do. Another teacherly role would be to record the essence of "valuable" comments and to reiterate these as a sort of summary prior to the author's "reply."

Other Patterns, Other Genres

A final suggestion I'd like to offer here as a way to vary your "weather pattern" is to ask students to express their ideas in a different genre altogether. For example, having students act out a short story or a poem (usually in groups) can be very enlightening, can make them come to terms with the material in new and sometimes profound ways. The caveat here is that students can't be given too much time to rehearse. When dealing with a nonfictional work, too, they might attempt to construe a scene or confrontation between opposing forces or ideas. Again, these should be completed during the class in which they are assigned.

Another, perhaps even more challenging genre—and one that, when students engage it, will probably bring a small tempest to your classroom—is requiring students to illustrate or draw in response to texts. Get students to produce, on the spot, a "non-alphabetic text." In a recent workshop I attended, run by Cindy Parrish, our group was given four or five blank graphic novel pages. One page had three equal-sized panels or boxes horizontally arrayed on the page, one atop the other. Another had six panels, another just one. We were then provided with the written version of a scene from *Romeo and Juliet* and asked to draw that scene on one of the provided pages. Cindy acknowledged that most of us were not likely to be artists, but she enjoined us to make the best of it, using stick figures, caption bubbles, and thought balloons to graphically convey our idea of the scene.

Students, many of them familiar with graphic novels, might have an easier time with this than the roomful of professors had: one of the professors grumbled, in fact, midway through, "This is the assignment from hell!" And while no one had that much artistic ability, the results I saw were impressive, as they conveyed understandable and often creative interpretations of the scene. Such an exercise reinforces the value of process over product, too—in trying to come up with a product, an illustrated work of art, however successful or unsuccessful, each participant had to reimagine the text, to see it in a way he or she had never seen it before. That process was valuable in and of itself. Perhaps the ideal follow-up on this would be for people to present their illustrations (perhaps using a document camera of some kind). In Parrish's workshop, we just laid out the illustrated pages on the floor and walked around the room to look at them.

If one assigns this kind of exercise, one must be courageous enough to try to respond in an open, nonjudgmental way to the wide range of possible responses inevitably produced. For a negative example, when my sixth grade teacher asked my class to draw a political cartoon based on "current events," my twin brother, Grant, took the opportunity to make a strong statement about segregation. It was 1963, and my brother's cartoon simply showed two men shaking hands. One was labeled George Wallace; the other, unlabeled, had a shock of black hair and a black toothbrush moustache. Both men wore swastika armbands. When our teacher received this, she held it up to the class as an example of "a lack of patriotism," "disrespect," and "awful exaggeration." She was, in short, outraged, and said that a pro-segregationist differed from a genocidal monster. My brother held his ground. "I didn't say they were the same," he said. And I think that most of the class must have realized at the time, too, that to have sparked such passionate ire from our teacher, this must have been a very good political cartoon indeed. The assignment was in some sense proven effective by my brother's response to it. The teacher's failure was in not recognizing this fact.

The Value of Such Pedagogies

All of these pedagogies place the onus of instruction, in some real sense, on the student. And by interspersing these with more "traditional" lectures, discussions, and in-class writing, their effect resonates. It is true that these pedagogies do not directly teach the genre of academic writing, do not show students how to develop an argument, use evidence, or even punctuate a sentence. Instead, they work on modifying and enriching the way students think and respond. They compel students to consider the material in meaningful-to-them ways. The class then becomes less a venue for teachers to present their ideas and interpretations, and more one in which students strive to make the material their own, to understand the material in the same way that one must understand something in order to teach it; and to do a public presentation that requires students to adjust and shape their own notions into ones understandable to and tailored for a specific audience.

Naturally, you will develop your own methods and exercises that you will use to run your classes. I'd recommend that you develop in-class "talking" practices that feed into the way of thought that informs sound critical writing, a way of working that requires student independence, that gets students thinking about and addressing an actual audience, and that gets students to assume a perhaps-new-to-them role, a role in which they get to take charge of the material in an authoritative, teacherly way. Empowering students in this manner—even if only temporarily empowering them—reconfigures the college classroom into a space where ideas can be exchanged among equals.

Using Streamwriting in Class

What follows is a description of how streamwriting might be used in a writing class, how I have seen it misused, and what I see as its primary value. It seems to me that it's too often dismissed as a "touchy-feely" kind of pedagogy, one that's detached from any real intellectual purpose, and one that's associated with production of an often inchoate if intermittently torrential flow of random ideas. The label it has gained, "expressivist writing," neatly sums up what its detractors don't like: it's writing that does little more than express feelings, and what emerges from practicing it, like expressionistic painting in some way, resembles a raw evocation of feeling, like that embodied, say, by Edvard Munch's *The Scream*. Streamwriting (or Peter Elbow's "freewriting," or some variation of these) has often been confused, I think, with raw emoting, with uncontrolled outpourings, and with writing that really has very little to do with the kind of writing usually taught in or required by college-level courses.

There is certainly some truth to these allegations, but I want to argue here that while streamwriting is indeed useful for generating lots of words, it also fulfills other non-invention-related functions. Specifically, when used in the writing class, it helps students uncover ideas that they didn't know they had. In addition, it creates a sense of community—a sense of shared purpose. As it creates that community, it also establishes for student writing an actual audience, complete with its own built-in diversity of experience and response. And finally, it helps students get some sense of what kinds of questions are interesting, worthwhile, and important to ask. It models for them the interrogative mode and approach so necessary in academic writing.

Yet at the same time, streamwriting, as I have seen it used in dozens of classes I've observed or attended over the last few decades, has the potential to be a truly classroom-deadening pedagogy. If used in a certain way, it reinforces a dynamic in which the loquacious, confident, assertive students dominate (as they always tend to do), and it eats up class time in a way that most students will perceive as quite simply wasteful and counterproductive—one that reinforces individual and class-wide poor habits. And, sad to say, I more often see streamwriting used in this way than as a technique generating ideas, creating community, or empowering otherwise silent voices within a classroom.

It's true that using streamwriting as a common, repeated feature of a writing course has many advantages, but as I've observed it over the last few decades, its use carries great risks as well. You risk losing your class's seriousness of purpose. You risk giving students the impression that free-flow, stream-of-consciousness transcription of what's in their brain's forefront equates with the sequential, thoughtful, argumentative essays they should probably produce at some point or points. You risk turning the class into an encounter group, where everyone is so in touch with his or her feelings that sober analysis and reflection are all but impossible. You risk confusing spontaneity with real creativity.

Just the same, I maintain that such risks are worth taking. Such risks, while clear and apparent dangers, can easily be guarded against, and your class's overall level of discourse easily elevated, by following a few relatively straightforward guidelines. In general, these guidelines strive to give every student equal time, to inculcate/support/shore up/make evident/dramatize the value of the written word, to validate the class itself, and to give students a genuine gift: their own ideas. Perhaps these ideas will be somewhat unformed, nascent, poorly or tentatively worded, inevitably incomplete. But in providing students the opportunity to streamwrite, by giving them that space, that time, and that audience, you vouchsafe them an entrance to a world that many of them had previously never known.

Streamwriting: A Description of the Method

Before I go on, I need to distinguish streamwriting as an individual practice—that is, something one might do alone in one's office, or riding a subway, or writing in any favorite locale—from streamwriting as a pedagogical practice. These two are not the same, though since the pedagogy is based on the individual action, I ask you to review Chapter 10, which outlines this use.

Using streamwriting in a writing class has rules of a sort that are perhaps a bit more fixed than most practitioners would like to believe. It's not just a matter of getting students to write without stopping to go back or pausing to think. It also involves figuring out what to do in order to get students to write something that's somehow valuable, that is, worthwhile to have written. The goal in most writing classes is not just producing verbiage of any sort, but rather writing something at once good and consonant with a relatively fixed conventional framework, that of the academic argument in the humanities or social sciences, most typically. Hence, streamwriting, while something that certainly might be used in order for students to develop and discover new ideas, also has to be connected to the admittedly more challenging enterprise of writing an academic essay.

The stream in which the student simply writes without cease, and on anything that comes to her or his mind, that is, the "secret spring," should, I suggest, be used at the beginning of a class period. It only takes about five minutes, and, I've discovered, has the salutary effect of calming everyone down, of clearing away the anxiety and hubbub of whatever preceded the class proper. It is important to start with this secret spring, too, because the ideas, anxieties, and pressures informing it inevitably would find their way into any prompt-driven streamwrite anyhow, and would probably detract from its effectiveness. At the same time, starting with a secret spring allows students to get into the—is it a rhythm? a habit? a method? a routine?—of transforming something that's in their heads into written words on a page. That's what writing is, to an extent. But starting with something sometimes called a "low-stakes" writing task allows students time to warm up, to establish various cerebral-sensory-motor pathways that facilitate that transfer of ideas from head to page.

The teacher, or facilitator, or leader, should also do the writing. This is a shared endeavor, finally.

From the secret spring, it's a simple move to what I call a streamwrite done to a "rainmaker"—a "wellspring" of sorts. Here, the teacher needs to provide a prompt or rainmaker, a way to get students thinking in a certain way. I don't believe that enough attention has been paid to the kinds of things that teachers or facilitators do to invent prompts, but it's clear that they draw on something quite sophisticated and special when inventing questions to get students writing. A quick test of this is to ask a student, early in the semester, to provide a rainmaker. Almost always, it doesn't work. This happens, I think, because in fact a large part of the challenge, as I've suggested above, resides in the asking of the "right" kind of questions, and students need to be taught this—or untaught how to ask the wrong kind of questions. Later in the semester, students start to get the idea, and they can often provide prompts of considerable value.

The guideline for rainmaker-creation is fairly simple. You have assigned some reading material, and you know the stage and direction of the course's arc. You have a good idea of where you are, what texts have been read and assimilated, and what kinds of responses students had and will have. Hence, you are in the perfect position to come up with a rainmaker, using the guideline that it needs to be something that you yourself are willing— nay, even eager—to write to for at least the next five minutes, and then publicly share your thoughts about. It should be something that interests you. And again, you write along with the class. You don't sit, by contrast, reading the *New York Times*, your feet propped up on the desk in front of you. (I've seen this on multiple occasions.)

Be sure to alert your students to the need to write legibly, as they will have to read aloud what they've written. And many students are not used to writing things out in longhand, much less reading them out loud just minutes later.

When your students reach the four-minute-thirty-second mark, or thereabouts (I actually never time these myself, unlike the scientist with the stopwatch; rather, I just write along with the group and bring them to a close when I feel as though I'm running out of prose myself), you might announce to them, "Try now to find an endpoint to your thoughts." And in twenty or so more seconds, "Just finish the sentence you're on." And finally, "OK, now put your pens down and look up, please" or, "If you're really onto something, maybe you can come back to it later. Make a mental note to do so."

(Another aside: using streamwriting, you have the opportunity to treat your students like fellow writers—they can come back to their private work later; what they write has some power, some insight, some value. You are trying to share with them some of the attractions of being a writer, and to help them reinvent a self: a writerly self. This is part of what I see as a defamiliarization that only takes place in the best classes.)

Students have set down their pens. Or they have stopped typing on their laptops. (Again, I try to get them to handwrite in a notebook, since the laptop sets up a barricade between students and the rest of the class and also gives students the option to multitask between your class and various websites.)

Now students—and you—share, that is, read aloud, their work. The whole group goes oceanic, I offer, a term in some ways so ridiculous that no one laughs. There are a couple of key elements here: first, you should not allow disclaimers, as in, "Oh, this is really stupid; it's not what I meant at all but I'll read it," or "I couldn't come up with anything any good," or "This really sucks but here goes." Why no disclaimers? It's as basic as this: you gave the students and yourself just five or four or six minutes—so of course what you have come up with, what they have come up with, is somewhat imperfect. That's a *donée*. Yet also, why prejudge it? Why allow students to decide that what they have produced is no good? Indeed, if you allow this to happen, too, when students read what they have, they will hurry through it, reading it as if it were something poor and not worth reading or sharing. And if everyone or almost everyone offers a disclaimer, then everyone might wonder, "What are we doing here, reading stuff that we all admit is of low value?" or, "Maybe we should be reading aloud really insightful stuff that's been published by professionals?"

That brings me to the issue of reading aloud. After producing their streamwrites, students now share them. All students should be given a space to share what they have written. Everyone should read. And they can read in any sequence you as teacher would like. They might simply go around the circle. Or you might call on people. Or you might randomly ask people to read, whenever they feel that the time is right, Quaker meeting style. I've witnessed a facilitator wait for as long as two minutes until a student volunteered to read a streamwrite. The facilitator had his eyes closed, as he calmly, quietly waited. There were close to seventy high school students in the room. The pressure was almost unbearable. You as the facilitator should read as well, though neither as the first person to read nor the last. I try to read usually at about the half to three-fourths mark.

Notice how many times, if you will, I used the word "read" in that last paragraph. Eight times, to be exact. The idea is that everyone has completed a piece of writing. It's a script. It's not a list of talking points. It's not something that you are asking people to summarize or use as the basis for a new, oral, extemporaneous response. You just want them to read what they have written, and you need to give every student a chance to do so. Therefore, even the shyest student has some time to read—that person doesn't have to fight for time or space—and not only that, like everyone else, the shy student has a script. So just as you have to rein in the voluble students, and ask them simply to read what they have written, so you have to open up space for chronically timid under-responders, vouchsafe them a few moments during which it is their voice that predominates. Often this is a unique, life-changing, first-time experience for them, and it sometimes will modify that shy student's in-class role so that, from then on, he or she will voluntarily start participating in activities and discussions.

As might be expected, students do not like to read their own writing, verbatim. Sometimes they are unable to make out the scrawl that is their handwriting. Sometimes they are simply too timid. On several occasions, students have said, "Oh, please, don't make me read—what I have here is ... too *personal*." Well, OK, I say. But that only works once. If, every time that students streamwrite, the same student writes something that is "too personal," then maybe that student has to be counseled—or be called for bluffing. On some occasions, too, if time is running out, the facilitator might say, "Bracket off some material to read—this might be the entire piece you've written, or it could be as short as a phrase or even a word." I prefer not to do this, but it's a possibility. At other times, only a few people will have time to read—but the caveat here is that it shouldn't always be the same few people reading when time is short.

Try to make your students good readers, too. Have them read their work with some care, some expressiveness, some feeling. It seems to me that the worst and most frequent mistake is reading too quickly. You as the facilitator will have to get students to read so that others can understand and appreciate what's been read.

In addition, you will need to teach the other students how to listen. They need to listen. They need to be attentive. They are not supposed to interrupt the reader, though once she or he has finished, it is perfectly legitimate to ask for a sentence or portion to be reread. If the reader had come up with an especially good insight or turn of phrase, I make it my policy to ask for that to be reread. I also suggest that students write down material that they like. They keep it in collection bottles. Listeners grab interesting, exciting, refreshing, intellectual thirst-quenching bits—in this case, of prose—as they hear it read aloud. They can keep a list of what they have captured, and in class, now and then, I'll ask people to read from some of the prose they've bottled.

Often what a student reads will spark some controversy and discussion. I encourage this, though I know that sometimes it can have the effect of squeezing out time that other students need to do their own reading. But in general, if students want to take issue with something that's been read, or if they have questions or comments about it, I go with it. Keeping pressure on the discussion, too, is the weight of the still-unread streamwrites.

Problems with the Pedagogy

Now, some problems do emerge because this pedagogy takes a great deal of time. A teacher must be careful to plan out these streamwrites so that all the students have a chance to read and, at the same time, such that it doesn't end up that everyone has read and there is simply not quite enough time for another streamwrite, nor really enough material for discussion. And in classes of more than twenty students, you might need to have every other person read, or maybe use very short streamwrites. In a large lecture class you'll just call on students or volunteer people yourself.

A larger problem, though, can develop if students come away with the impression that what they have done in class, in a streamwrite, is equivalent to what they might do in a formal essay. While often students will use portions of streamwrites in their formal essays, they need at the same time to understand that the streamwrite differs quite radically from the academic essay, and that they need to hone their editing skills at the same time as they work on their "expressivist" ones.

Finally, do keep in mind that as students get used to this format, as they find it more and more comfortable, more and more a venue in which they can transfer their thoughts and feelings to the page, they will write material that verges on the highly "personal." So you as a teacher must be aware that a prompt that might seem innocuous could have the effect of generating a deeply disturbed response. For example, using a William Stafford epigraph to "Postscript," a poem by Naomi Shihab Nye, "Think of something you said. Now think of what you wish you had said," can have devastating results. Some students inevitably end up crying and distressed when I use this prompt. An equally probing but less moisture-producing prompt is one that I've borrowed from a recent National Public Radio series, "This I Believe." I give some examples of actual responses that were aired on NPR, and then I ask students to write their own "This I Believe" response. Although these may not be prompts that connect closely to the theme or subject matter of your course, they nonetheless fulfill the very useful function of helping to establish a community. And of course, if you write to them yourself, you'll find that the self-revelation you undertake brings you closer to your class and maybe also to its concerns.

The whole process of writing and sharing is most valuable, though, as a way for students to see how students respond to their peers' thoughts, words, and experience. It gives an immediate, unrehearsed, and authentic response to writing, and this response from an audience—not just the audience of one that is the teacher—shows students that what they write can make an impact. It also shows them how sometimes it can make an impact where they as the authors least expect it. And it shows them how prose can come to life—or not—right before their eyes. No longer is writing a mechanical process of simply fulfilling the requirements for a given course. Instead, writing is something that can tell them what their neighbors are thinking, something that can help them make connections they never before had even considered, and something, too, that can allow them to impress on others their own ideas.

I believe that college students are not, generally speaking, asked to be especially "creative" or imaginative/original thinkers. Most of their work involves proving that they have received the transmission of ideas from lectures and texts. In addition, our students do not seem to be stretching themselves verbally: they are not experimenting, playing around with language—at least not in their college courses. (Maybe they are, though, in personal writing such as blogs or texts or tweets. But we rarely see these.) Instead, the language of their college writing is typically just communicative, often chock-full of fundamental errors, slang, misusages, jargon, repetitions, broken or strange sentence constructions, and miscellaneous mixtures of form. It's also usually boring.

College writing, for most students, is also boring for them, something that must be done in order to get the degree, to get the job, the spouse and 2.5 children, the house in the country with the two cars and the pool and the big chocolate Lab that slobbers on you when you come home at night.

Writing, then, for its own sake, has only minimal value. Writing in college, it seems to me, has been relentlessly instrumentalist for several generations now. Writing as a path to new ideas, as a way to know oneself, as a way to generate fluency and to play around with words in the process, has been relegated to a dustbin, or perhaps to an icon of a trash can on most people's cerebral equivalent of a desktop. Look, we're busy people. We can't be involved in frivolous stuff. We have things to do, places to go, messages to send and answer.

I'm suggesting here that we need to back up, that we need to consider this world we've in some real sense (as college teachers) co-created, and think again. What is it we want our students to do? What do we want them to be? And as we consider their relationship to language, to writing, even to thinking, we need to consider ways that our own pedagogical choices reverberate down long, as-yet-unseen corridors of a future world that we, if we're lucky, will not only inhabit, but will want to inhabit as well.

New Terms

Most of my experience with this pedagogy comes from my many years teaching in Bard College's innovative "Language and Thinking" Program. The program, initially started by Peter Elbow, has become adept at using Elbow's freewriting in complex and interesting ways. I have altered the terminology used at Bard (and by Elbow), however. It is possible that you are familiar with some of these terms, so in what follows I will discuss four or five useful classroom practices and mention their original names along with my new nomenclature. But it's the practice that's ultimately the most important thing, not the terms.

"Loop writing," the Elbovian term for taking some aspect of one's freewritten work and freewriting on it, has always struck me as confusing. I propose instead "meandering," including "Meander One" and "Meander Two." (I give examples of these in Chapter 10.) These terms imply a branching off from but still a connection to the original writing stream. Using these terms might ameliorate the problem of students' forgetting the original freewrite while doing "loop writings" based on it.

Another typical prompt requires someone to read aloud a text—a poem, short story, or essay, perhaps—while the others in the group listen and write. Reading aloud is in general a useful practice, but in this particular pedagogy, students write what is called "movies of the mind," or the thoughts that pass through their minds as the poem or work is being read aloud. Writers attempt to capture the exact thoughts that the words of the read-aloud work seem to be sparking. I suggest renaming this "mind-streaming," which at once connects up with the "movies of the mind" name but also emphasizes how the writing reproduces the stream of thought inspired by the material that that mind is taking in.

Several other terms I also propose modifying. For example, what's called "dialectical notebooks" (or sometimes "dialogical notebooks") seems to me a term too suffused with ideology. The practice is valuable, however: it involves streamwriting to a rain-maker, then exchanging notebooks with one's neighbor, who streamwrites in response. Calling this process "dialectical," it seems to me, urges strong disagreement, of the thesis-antithesis-synthesis variety (though it need not, of course); but it strikes me that many of the comments one makes on a neighbor's stream-write are positive ones, or ones that spark another direction to be explored. They are not really antitheses. Perhaps this is why "dialogical" is preferable to "dialectical," because the "notebooks" are in dialogue. (Mikhail Bakhtin's use of "dialogical," however, complicates the issue—it's in some ways an ideal fit, but perhaps is too specialized for most students to feel comfortable with.) At any rate, I propose using a new term to describe what is basically the same activity, namely "coalescing streamwrites." I like the image it provides of streamwrites coming together, coalescing, and the cooperative nature of this event.

I'd also substitute for the "freewrite" of "what's lurking," which might be usefully employed when appraising and engaging the ideas of other students or participants, a streamwriting notion that continues the natural flow metaphor: "aquifer discovery." Instead of asking "What's lurking?" one might ask, "What aquifers feed into this?" Like an aquifer, which is an underground spring feeding rivers or lakes, many hidden ideas underlie a text, a commentary, a point of view, or a perspective. What are these? I find "lurking" a bit too sinister: for some reason, I always recall what my linguistics teacher proposed in a class I took in graduate school. Gene Kintgen said, "The sentence 'I was lurking' doesn't make sense. One never views oneself as lurking."

Another substitution of terms involves a very good exercise called "believing and doubting." This exercise involves having a participant put forth a thesis or an assertion about a text, an issue, an idea, and then asking the rest of the group to offer "beliefs" (support for it) and "doubts" (problems with it). The great utility of such a practice is that it gets people into a somewhat argumentative—one might say dialogical—frame of mind, and it reveals the value of statements that can be doubted as well as believed. The problem I have with this terminology, however, stems from the words "belief" and "doubt." It seems to me that "belief" is perhaps not the right term: we can agree with a proposition, find it convincing or persuasive. But that's not really the same as "belief." Beliefs are often things one cannot be talked out of. They are not always logical. And the term "doubt" also bothers me—it seems for some reason too contrived an activity —a pretending, a role-playing of sorts, which doesn't really belong in the same category as "belief."

Instead, I propose to continue the water imagery: when someone writes something that is persuasive, productive of insight, powerfully vivid, I suggest that that's a "white-water rapids." And if, by contrast, a piece of writing seems to have missed the point, seems to have gone off course or offers little intellectual momentum, I think it's "run aground." "White-water rapids" and "runnings aground" don't have the smoothness of "believing and doubting," but I think better capture the ways people respond to discursive prose—as in, here is where this writing is really active, turbulent, productive of something maybe new and exciting; or by contrast, here is where it's hit dry land and has to be towed back on course. And getting back on course, back on the water again, is itself a valuable activity, akin to responsibly and creatively answering the strongest of "con" arguments.

Finally, an interesting Bard College freewrite is named "exploding poem," but I want to recruit the exercise to my own pedagogy: I'm calling this "geysers and waterspouts." Here is the exercise: read aloud, in class, a poem or a short piece of prose—ideally, a work that is somewhat challenging, perhaps even difficult to understand. Then have students read it aloud again, slowly, giving them time to note a reaction or association or question to the line or image that's read. A third reading proceeds as follows:

1. A reader reads aloud, slowly, pausing at the end of each line;
2. If someone has a response to a line, that person should read the same line aloud again and then read his or her response to it. This repeats for however many people have responses to a given line;
3. When all the responses are finished for a given line, the reader resumes reading the text.

Ideally, this would be followed by a rainmaker such as "How has your understanding of the poem changed after having heard your classmates' various geysers and waterspouts in response to it?" This would be an example of a "reflecting pool," a piece of writing in which the students think back on their own thought processes and evaluate how they have been modified by the experience of writing, of listening to others, and to writing again.

Writing Prompts for Papers

Here are some prompts that you might use for formal papers students would complete outside class. They require some research and will take multiple steps for students to complete.

1. Take one of the assigned texts and look for a book review of it, one written at about the same time the book appeared. Next, look for a scholarly article about the book. Compare and contrast the two pieces, showing in what way the review and article differ, and how that difference can be connected to the idea of a different conception of audience.
2. Look for a contemporary review of a book similar (same theme, genre, author) to one of those from the reading list so far. Using it as your starting point, try to develop a similar evaluation of the book on the reading list, using criteria similar to

those advanced by the reviewer, but in your paper strive for a more balanced approach than that offered by the review.

3. Many works of fiction are "thesis" stories. They present an idea or thesis, are arguing for a particular position. Write a paper in which you argue that *a subsidiary or correlative thesis* underlies the book's main thesis. (The main thesis of the book is typically more or less evident, even obvious, but looking for underlying assumptions or theses is ultimately a much more difficult and rewarding task.)

4. Many "thesis" novels are ones that could be accused of propagandizing rather than functioning as "art." Using one or more of the works on the reading list, explore the differences between art and propaganda.

5. Earlier on, I used the concept of the "writing production device"—the mechanism you use to generate prose (see Chapter 3). Describe your WPD: How does it work? What kinds of unusual features might it have—or how do you think the way you go about writing differs from how most people do, or from how I describe it here?

6. One of the sections of this book went through thirty drafts. Literally. Is this a good idea, do you think? What do you think is the ideal relationship of drafting to a finished version of a piece of writing? Can a piece of writing be rewritten too many times? At what point does it not behoove you to rewrite any more, presuming of course that you still have time before a deadline?

7. Do a "newrite," then "streamwrite" about it, maybe including a meander or two, and turn that work into an argumentative paper about one of the works on the reading list. Include all the prewriting with the final version.

8. Use one of the suggested methods of coming up with ideas (aporia, disjunction, etc.) in order to generate a paper about one of the course texts.

9. As I mentioned in Chapter 4, the humorist Dave Barry once suggested that the best way to write papers in college writing courses was to make the most outlandish comparisons possible. Try inventing such an outrageous thesis and then attempt to modify it, through the course of revision and rewriting,

into a reasonable but argumentative thesis. Start, that is, with the zany, self-consciously out-there idea, and mold it into something of analytic value.

10. Take one of the texts that seriously challenges some deeply held personal belief—for example, one involving religion, the family, morality, or the like. Generate a paper around a thesis showing how this text's challenge to your personal belief has some validity, how it should not be dismissed, and how it might have advanced your belief structure in a significant way, even though it did not force you to entirely abandon that belief. Make sure, though, that you still focus on *analyzing* the text—revealing something important about it.

11. Play around with a sphere/disc metaphor with regard to thesis: how is a ΔT really like a sphere? What attributes are "sphere-like" and make for a good conclusion?

12. Taking a work of nonfiction that is relevant to the course (or is one of the course texts), analyze and evaluate its structure. Develop an argument as to why the author chose the structure she or he did, and show in what way that structure either is successful or could be improved.

13. Again, using nonfiction works that are on the reading list, look at two argumentative essays and isolate their thesis statements and conclusions. In what way or ways do the conclusions of the two pieces represent an evolution over their respective thesis statements? Which thesis-conclusion relationship seems to you superior? Why?

14. Take one of the writers' passages in Chapter 13 and do a detailed stylistic analysis of it. Why is it effective? Could it be better? What "virtues" of style does it possess (as enumerated earlier in the chapter)? What faults does it have? What new ways does it allow for us to talk about style, or what new virtues can you infer from it?

In-Class Writing: Sentence Combining Assignment

When students study writing, they often develop a fear of using any kind of elaborate sentence structure. They end up writing essays in sentences as simple as the following: "My puppy is cute. He has a long tail. He wags this a lot. He also has a sweet and warm pink tongue. He licks me all over my face. I love my puppy a lot." While all these sentences are correct, and while the paragraph that contains them also has details and some sense of development, this writing can hardly be considered college-level work. What's needed is complexity as well as correctness. It is important that you write correct prose, but it seems to me every bit as important that you develop an individual and distinctive prose style, one that reflects the patterns and complications of your thought process. And to make matters even more challenging, at the same time that your prose is complex and correct, it must also be lucid.

Write a brief story based on the simple sentences that are provided below. Try to put in paragraph breaks where appropriate. And strive for lucidity as well as accuracy. Use more complex sentences than the ones provided, though you may (if you like) retain some of the simple sentences. This is basically a simple story, so the narrative structure should be simple. However, the challenge is to make the story interesting and much more complex on the sentence level, putting the sentences in paragraphs, including revisions, and the like. Try to use a variety of ways to connect the sentences too (subordination, coordination, etc.). Make sure that you capture all the ideas the sentences present. For example, you might combine the first six sentences in this way: "It was comfortable and dark in the Queenston house, even though the sound of cars and trucks passing on the street that was so close to the house occasionally broke the stillness." There are lots of ways to combine them, preserving the details; feel free to use your own imagination and inventiveness as you combine the sentences. I have made this example kind of wacky, since I'm hoping that will unleash some creative juices.

The Glymphiad, or The Frfrlungenlied

1. The Queenston house was dark.
2. It was very comfortable there.
3. There was an occasional sound.
4. The sound was of trucks or cars.

5. These cars passed on the street.
6. A street ran very close to the house.
7. No noise came from the wormhole.
8. The wormhole was in the house.
9. The wormhole led to Bim sub-two.
10. Bim sub-two is a planet.
11. Bim sub-two is very far away.
12. G'Narth is Supreme.
13. G'Narth is a Philosopher.
14. G'Narth is the Leader of Bim sub-two.
15. G'Narth is very jolly.
16. G'Narth is basically dinosauric in origin.
17. G'Narth is interested in the Queenston house.
18. Asleep in the house are Frfrnrfr and Glymphyr.
19. Also asleep is Biinken.
20. Biinken is a deer.
21. Actually he is not a deer.
22. He is an android replica.
23. Jathy and Frak snore softly.
24. Their snores hardly disturb the air.
25. In the household there are others.
26. There are the dinos.
27. The dinos are pets.
28. They frolic.
29. Now they too are asleep.
30. Suddenly a sound rips the air.
31. The sound is loud.
32. It is piercing.
33. It is confined to the house.
34. It is a flying saucer.
35. Flying saucers often visit the Queenston house.
36. Aliens come out of the saucer.
37. They are not very chatty.
38. They shoot all the entities and people.
39. Their ray guns are set on stun.
40. Biinken does not get stunned.
41. Androids cannot be stunned.
42. Biinken pretends to be a stuffed animal, though.

43. The aliens drag all the stunned entities aboard their saucer.
44. It is cold in the saucer.
45. The aliens do not feel the cold.
46. Biinken is left behind.
47. The saucer takes off.
48. Biinken thinks quickly.
49. Biinken goes into the wormhole.
50. He goes through it to Bim sub-two.
51. Biinken finds G'Narth.
52. G'Narth is tall.
53. G'Narth is benevolent.
54. G'Narth is especially interested in the story.
55. G'Narth wants to help.
56. G'Narth goes to Earth via the wormhole.
57. G'Narth brings the Bim sub-two scientists with him.
58. The scientists are middle-aged.
59. The scientists are very advanced over Earth scientists.
60. The scientists bring instruments with them.
61. The instruments are very sensitive.
62. The instruments can record energy residues.
63. Energy residues are all over the Queenston house.
64. These residues tell the scientists information.
65. The information pertains to the abduction.
66. Evidently a very powerful technology was behind the abduction.
67. The Bim sub-two scientists are scared.
68. G'Narth is not scared.
69. Biinken is not scared.
70. Androids do not feel fear.
71. Biinken experiences a simulacrum of fear.
72. The Bim sub-two scientists can say where the saucer is.
73. They cannot say exactly where it is.
74. They can give a rough radius of where it might be.
75. This radius is large.
76. This radius is not insurmountable.
77. They need a plan.
78. Once they locate the saucer, they need to decide.
79. They need to decide how to capture it.

80. They cannot destroy it because of its Earth occupants.
81. It would be best to make contact with the alien abductors.
82. Suffice it to say that they locate the saucer.
83. They make contact with the abductors.
84. The abductors are not evil.
85. They are not good.
86. The abductors are only seeking information.
87. The abductors want the contents of the brains of the abductees.
88. The Bim sub-two scientists offer an exchange of information.
89. They offer this instead of the contents of the brains.
90. The alternative is that the abductors can be reduced to Z-particles.
91. Z-particles are types of weakons.
92. Z-particles are very small indeed.
93. The aliens return their abductees.
94. The group is returned to the Queenston house.
95. Everyone is OK.
96. Glymphyr has taken something.
97. What he has taken is a key piece of technology.
98. This piece of technology is very significant.
99. This piece of technology allows Glymphyr to monitor the whereabouts of the aliens.
100. It indicates that they are on a return path.

B Sample Essays

I include here three sample papers, one by Justin Ramon, one by Lydia Morgan, and one by Frank Salvatore Cioffi (my late uncle). Ramon and Cioffi wrote these papers as first-year college students; Morgan was in her third year. In footnotes, I append comments.

Ramon's paper responds to a writing exercise that appears in this volume, page 311–14. The "sentence combining" exercise requires writers to generate long-ish, complex sentences, but it often tends toward the unimaginative. People just copy what's on the page, dutifully combining sentences using any of a variety of means, more or less replicating the "content" of the listed sentences. Justin Ramon avoids this problem by looking a little beyond just the basic sentences as they are laid out in numbered form, and the result is both humorous and frightening.

Lydia Morgan wrote in response to the following prompt: "Explore the idea of 'language class.' Does this actually exist? What are the classes? How do they relate to social class? Can one change one's 'language class' any more easily than one's social class? If, alternatively, you don't believe 'language class' exists, explain why you think this" (Cioffi, *One Day in the Life*, 312). Morgan's paper effectively uses sources to help her explore an argumentative and imaginative thesis.

Frank Salvatore Cioffi's paper was one he wrote as an entrance essay for admission to Oxford University. While I do not know the original prompt, what we have seems to be an attempt to characterize the human condition. Admission essays tend toward such challenges, and I think my late uncle, writing this at age twenty-one or twenty-two, came up with a splendid answer. He later became a philosopher with many books and articles to his credit.

Justin Ramon

Professor Cioffi

English 2150

15 October 2015

The Glymphiad

It was a dark night, and outside of the Queenston house the occasional sound of a car passing on a nearby rode[1] broke the silence. The air was calm, the mood peaceful. The Queenston house looked quiet, warm, and cozy. Nothing seemed out of the ordinary. But this was no ordinary house! Little did anyone driving by know that inside the Queenston house lay a wormhole which led to a mysterious far away land! A distant planet named Bim sub-two.

A large planet, shrouded in mystery, Bim sub-two was ruled with an iron fist by its supreme overlord, the philosopher lizard king G'narth. Having ruled Bim sub-two for aeons, G'narth was both ancient,[2] and wise. A master manipulator, the always smiling G'narth used a cheerful demeanor to conceal his malevolent scheming. Over the centuries G'narth had become knowledgeable in the ways of travel through space and time and had used this knowledge to subjugate

---

[Note: this is a response to the sentence combining exercise in Appendix A.]

1. "Road" is the word needed here.　　2. I would omit this comma.

many planets in many different realms. He used wormholes to visit the furthest reaches of the galaxy, and had his eyes set on one particularly distant region that contained immeasurable riches. The closest wormhole to this intergalactic goldmine lead[3] directly into the Queenston house.

Back at the house its inhabitants were all passed out from a night of heavy drinking. Jathy and Frak threw the party, and at one point during the evening's festivities they were so inebriated they couldn't even pronounce the names of their two best friends correctly and proceeded to call them Frfrnrfr and Glmphyr while laughing hysterically.[4] Throughout the night all were entertained by Jathy's brand new robot deer Biinken, who was equipped with the newest state of the art artificial intelligence, and beer can holders.[5] Their pet monitor lizards who[6] they lovingly referred to as "The dinos,"[7] joined the fun as well after they escaped from their cage when Frak stumbled and crashed into it, spilling alcohol all over them. They spent the rest of the evening romping around the house until they too fell asleep, seemingly drunk themselves. After all the fun was had, only the soft sound of Jathy and Frak's snoring could be heard at the Queenston house.

---

3. "Led" is the word we want.

4. This is a funny explanation of all the odd names in the original.

5. Note the addition of details that support the original idea Justin is developing.

6. "Whom."

7. Omit comma.

Then all of a sudden a thunderous, pulsating sound ripped through the house, waking everyone!

The sound was deafening, yet confined to the house. Bright lights beamed down from what appeared to be an alien spaceship![8] They had been watching for quite some time, but now, illuminating the darkness with a fluorescent glow, they finally revealed themselves. Tiny green spacemen with beady eyes and disproportionately large rear ends[9] hopped out and rounded up everyone in the house. Jathy, in shock, was barely able to muster the words "who are you little green men and why are your butts so bi ...," but before she could finish her sentence the eensy-weensy green spacemen zapped her and everyone in the house with their stun rays, swiftly incapacitating them all. The little green alien midgets then promptly stripped them naked and beamed them all into the spaceship where, much to the hostages' dismay, the temperature happened to be below zero. The aliens felt right at home though since that temperature was considered balmy on their home planet. Thinking they got everyone, the aliens set their destination and warped into the night sky. They didn't get everyone though: they forgot about Biinken!

8. No exclamation points, perhaps, are needed here.

9. Another interesting added detail.

Shaking off the space dust and wiping the green goo off his little robot deer snout, Biinken knew he needed to think fast if he planned on saving his new family. Using his advanced geographic information system, and state of the art mapping technology, he quickly determined that the pulsating four dimensional black orb in the basement was in fact a wormhole leading to a massive exoplanet twenty-three million lightyears away! "You only live once," Biinken processed[10] to himself, and he dived in head first immediately popping out on the other side, falling into a pit surrounded by creepy lizard imps who began gnawing on his little robot deer hoofs while chanting incoherently. Suddenly the sound of a loud horn caused the lizard imps to scurry away. A party of G'narth's royal guard and top scientists had arrived to take Biinken to speak with the supreme ruler face to face.

When Biinken arrived at G'narth's royal chamber he was quite simply shocked at how tall G'narth was. G'narth stood 50 feet tall! Biinken yelled up at G'narth that he was pleased to meet him and was comforted by G'narth's pleasant demeanor. He told G'narth of his family's abduction and was assured that everything would be done to rescue them safely.

---

10. This is a great inclusion, using "processed" instead of "thought."

Always smiling, G'narth then turned to his scientists and told them that the time had come, that they should ready their devices, for they would be accompanying him to Earth.

Arriving at the Queenston house with G'narth and his crew of aging reptoid Bim sub-two scientists, Biinken showed them the scene of the abduction. The scientists proceeded to scan the house for energy residues with their technologically advanced electron spectrometers. They didn't actually need to use this advanced machinery as the miniature green space beings left huge globs of green goo all over the place. The scientists analyzed the goo and gave each other a worried look. They then explained to G'narth that these pint-sized green aliens were on the brink of discovering an unheralded energy source of dangerous origin that could challenge his supremacy of the galaxy. This signaled Biinken's mechanical fear receptors and he started shaking. G'narth let out a mighty roar of laughter and reminded Biinken that robots can't feel fear, to which Biinken responded "oh yeah," and immediately composed himself. G'narth then turned to his scientists and told them that if they ever doubted his divine power again he would reduce them to Z-particles. He also told them that same fate awaited them if they failed to locate the spaceship. The scientists hurriedly unsheathed their galactic homing devices and got to work.

After tinkering about with their devices for a while, the scientists informed G'narth that they located the general region that the spaceship was in but couldn't pinpoint its location, to which G'narth callously replied, "Z-particles," prompting the scientists to continue searching feverishly until they found the spaceship's exact whereabouts. The scientists then meticulously devised a plan to ensnare the spaceship without injuring its Earth occupants by using electro-magnetic shockwaves. G'narth was pleased.

Using a special portal, Biinken, G'narth, and the scientists warped to the alien spaceship and trapped it inside waves of electro-magnetic force. G'narth summoned the itsy-bitsy green spacemen and asked them why they felt it necessary to abduct the innocent earthlings. They explained to G'narth that he misunderstood their intentions, that they took no pleasure in the earthlings' suffering, and that their collection of human brains was for research purposes only. G'narth sighed and insisted that the humans be released immediately in exchange for valuable technology from the Bim sub-two scientists. He told them the alternative was that they would be reduced to Z-particles. The micro-sized green space dwarfs then asked G'narth what Z-particles were. G'narth then aimed a phaser at his least favorite scientist and zapped him into a steaming pile of saurian ash, to which the aliens responded with nervous laughter, assuring G'narth that the exchange of information was more than a fair trade. Jathy, Frak, Glymphyr, and Frfrnrfr were then all handed over and returned safely to the Queenston house.

G'narth, delighted at the prospect of this new planet, bid the earthlings farewell and returned to Bim sub-two. While at the Queenston house Biinken was overjoyed to have his loving, and still very inebriated, family back, safe and sound, Jathy and Frak decided that they all should celebrate their safe return with more beers, when suddenly the group noticed a vibrating red glow coming from Glymphyr's pants. "Oh that just happens sometimes when I get excited," Glymphyr nervously proclaimed, but no one was buying it. Glymphyr, a kleptomaniac, then confessed to pickpocketing one of the aliens as they were leaving the ship. Shaking their heads in disbelief, they forced Glymphyr to hand over what turned out to be a large tracking device which then started to beep. Biinken scanned the device and started to shake as the beeping got louder. "The aliens are coming back! Quick, to the wormhole!" he shouted, leading everyone to the basement and head first into the wormhole.

Plopping out on the other side, they were relieved to see G'narth there to greet them. But much to their horror, G'narth ordered his royal guard to slap collars around their necks, locking them in cages. G'narth broke out into a sinister laugh and declared that the earthlings would be his new pets, he would call them "The dinos." Biinken tried to protest but was zapped into a burning heap of scrap metal. Terrified, Jathy, Frak, Gylmphyr, and Frfrnrfr then watched helplessly as G'narth led his legions through the wormhole to conquer Earth.[11]

11. The reversal, or peripeteia, here, is shocking. Justin has really made the assignment "his own," almost going so far as to reverse the ending (though the original has an ambiguous, possibly sinister, ending, I should note).

Lydia Morgan

Professor Cioffi

English 3001

8 December 2015

The Ethics of Language Exposure:

The Way We Talk to Our Babies

A recent ad campaign on the New York subway featured a poster depicting a smiling baby in a bathtub reaching towards a yellow rubber duck in the hands of the man (presumably her father) facing her. The ad copy reads, "Talk to your baby. Anytime. Anywhere. Their brain depends on it. Talking, reading, and singing build your baby's brain." Putting aside the politics of non-gendered pronoun use for babies,[1] this ad is part of a campaign from the New York City Department of Health that aims to increase awareness among New Yorkers about the developmental benefits of early language use around infants.[2] While for some parents and caretakers this may seem like an intuitive part of childrearing, in fact research from a 1995 article by Betty Hart and Todd R. Risley called "The Early Catastrophe: The 30 Million Word Gap by Age 3" indicates otherwise. Hart and Risley studied "how

---

[Note: The prompt for the following paper is as follows: "Explore the idea of 'Language Class.' Does such a class system exist? Can one change one's language class? Or do you think this concept is not applicable to today's society?"]

1. I think the issue is that the pronoun is plural, not just nongendered. And since the antecedent for "Their brain" is singular, using a plural pronoun is a slightly risky choice. However, I believe that it will be the norm within the next lustrum.

2. I would break the paragraph here.

parents of different socioeconomic backgrounds talked to their babies" and discovered that the amount of language use around infants showed a strong correlation to the income and educational status of their parents (Rosenberg). Tina Rosenberg cited this research in a 2013 *New York Times* article: "Children whose families were on welfare heard about 600 words per hour. Working-class children heard 1,200 words per hour, and children from professional families heard 2,100 words. By age 3, a poor child would have heard 30 million fewer words in his home environment than a child from a professional family." And this discrepancy is not without detriment. Rosenberg reports further, "The greater the number of words children heard from their parents or caregivers before they were 3, the higher their IQ and the better they did in school." The socioeconomic learning gap between poor children and wealthy children may then be correlated to a type of language use introduced far before any concerns of gendered pronouns or subtly biased standardized testing come into the picture. If one of the greatest determining factors of a child's future learning success is the amount and level of language that the child hears in the first three years of life, the ethics of the problem become far more problematic. That a child can be so deeply impacted and formed by language before he or she even has the capacity to use that language indicates that the ethics of this issue lie not in language use, but merely in the form and volume of language exposure.[3]

If an infant's early exposure to language is as formative as Hart and Risley argue that it is, then the problematic issue arises of how to close the language gap between children of different socioeconomic statuses. According to Hart and Risley's research, directives such as, "Put that down," or, "Eat your apple," are common to all parents but more likely to comprise the extent of talking from parents to their children in families on welfare (Rosenberg). Middle and upper class parents, however, use language towards and around their children in more extensive ways. The form of the language to which the child is exposed in the early developmental years appears to be relevant. The upbeat stream-of-consciousness chatter of mothers pushing strollers along a Park Slope sidewalk—"Look at the doggy! What a sweet little doggy. Maybe the doggy is going to the park. There is grass in the

3. These last couple of sentences are the thesis. Well expressed.

park. The grass is green. We are going to the park! What should we do at the park?"[4]—serves as a prime example. From this drivel, found either amusing or annoying depending on the listener, the child derives exceedingly great benefit. The child's experience, before he or she can do so for himself or herself, is interpreted by the surrounding adults.

In their conclusion, Hart and Risley explain, "Behaviorally, infancy is a unique time of helplessness when nearly all of children's experience is mediated by adults in one-to-one interactions permeated with affect. Once children become independent and can speak for themselves, they gain access to more opportunities for experience" (9). Until the child gains that independence, however, adult caregivers mediate her experiences.[5]

The quality and content of the words the child is exposed to are not excluded from the equation. In the Hart and Risley research, children in professional homes heard on average a ratio of 6:1 affirmative statements to prohibitions per hour, while in working class families the ratio was 2:1, and in welfare families the ratio of affirmatives to discouragements dropped to 1:2 per hour. The researchers were able to extrapolate from

4. This seems to me a cleverly composed piece of invented, overheard language.

5. Paragraph seems underdeveloped. Maybe a con argument would have fit here?

this data that "By the age of 4, the average child in a welfare family might have had 144,000 fewer encouragements and 84,000 more discouragements of his or her behavior than the average child in a working class family" (8).[6] The compound impact of language exposure by volume and by content seems to be a major contributing factor in the future success of the child, developmentally and otherwise. This is before the child even has a choice of what type of language to use or an innate understanding of the type of code-switching that different audiences require. If the quantity and quality of words heard by lower class children are so far below those heard by upper class children, the gap between the two groups seems doomed to an ever-widening chasm. The ethics of this problem, how-ever, cannot fall to the infant, who in the early years is an audience to language but not a user of it. The burden of ethical developmental language falls to the caretakers of the children.

Researcher Meredith Rowe offers a compelling answer.[7] Rowe posits that lower class women (usually the primary caregivers) are "simply unaware that it [is] important to talk more to their babies" (Rosenberg). If this is the case, then perhaps the issue of language class is not a foreign one here.[8]

6. These are astonishing figures; Lydia has captured the essence of the study she quotes from.

7. Not sure what this is an answer to.

8. I question this word choice; it's not wrong, but in context it adds confusion about whether we are talking about non-English-speaking families.

In order to facilitate socioeconomic mobility, language class must have a malleable, transformative aspect. And that aspect is being lost on poor families whose children start out behind on their language use before they even begin using it. If this is the case, the responsibility lies with those professional, middle, and working class families who are aware of the importance of talking to babies to educate the lower class of families who are unaware. The subway ad campaign is one step in this right direction. Mass public transportation in New York City, a common and affordable means of transit for many low-income residents, offers a visible platform from which to tout this public service announcement. But is it enough?[9]

Works Cited

Hart, Betty, and Todd R. Risley. "The Early Catastrophe: The 30 Million Word Gap by Age 3." *American Educator*, Spring 2003, 4–9. American Federation of Teachers, aft.org/sites/default/files/periodicals/The EarlyCatastrophe.pdf. Accessed 30 Nov. 2015.

Rosenberg, Tina. "The Power of Talking to Your Baby." *New York Times*, 10 Apr. 2013, opinionator.blogs.nytimes.com/2013/04/10/the-power -of-talking-to-your-baby/?_r=0. Accessed 30 Nov. 2015.

"Talk to Your Baby." *NYC Health*. City of New York, n.d., www.nyc.gov /talktoyourbaby. Accessed 30 Nov. 2015.

9. I think the conclusion needs to be elaborated a little bit more. We need a Δ-Thesis, I think, maybe something like this: we must cast a wider net than just a subway ad campaign to get people talking to their children—and talking in the right way. Until we come up with something, though, language class divisions will persist, as will social class divisions.

Frank Salvatore Cioffi

Ruskin College

20 January 1950

Resignation: An Antidote to Infantilism

Though a secularized belief in the doctrine of original sin is an indispensable psychological ingredient of any worldview which seeks stability, religious forms of this belief open to the charge of superfluity.[1] As Freud remarks, "When the faithful find themselves reduced in the end to speaking of God's inscrutable decree, they thereby avow that all that is left to them in their sufferings is unconditional submission as a last remaining consolation and source of happiness. And if a man is willing to come to this, he could probably have arrived there by a shorter road."[2]

Even so, religious beliefs have this merit, that they are generally innocuous to society.[3] They at least dissuade their adherents from turning the world upside down in a hopeless quest.

One indication of the inadequacy of secular faiths[4] is the predilection for illusions displayed by the ostensibly emancipated. General semantics, Reichian Analysis, Conditioned

---

[Note: This essay was written when Cioffi was twenty-one or twenty-two years old, in 1950, a first-year student at Ruskin College. It anticipates many of his philosophical preoccupations of the next six decades.]

1. It seems to me that this opening sentence could be expressed somewhat more simply.

2. From *Civilization and Its Discontents*. We need a reference. Combine this paragraph with the next two.

3. Many people would vehemently disagree and cite the many atrocities that have been committed in the name of religions.

4. An interesting concept, "secular faiths," but one in need of definition.

Reflex Therapy, Dianetics (and among social panaceas, Marxism, Nationalism, and political Anti-Semitism): the words change, but the tune remains the same.

In spite of their sensationalism, some of the abovementioned doctrines have accomplished a limited amount of good. Each, however, has as an implicit premise the same pernicious fallacy. The belief that man has it within his power to make himself happy.[5] Our need must be indeed intense when even millstones are mistaken for lifebelts;[6] for any doctrine which makes such a claim must be ultimately detrimental. "Not contemplating what kindles desire keeps the heart unconfused."[7]

These panaceas fall into two groups: those which preach individual perfectibility and those which preach social perfectibility. Each, of course, involves the other, and the dispute between them revolves around which is to be given temporal priority. It is the old war between the yogi and the commissar. For some reason ideologies which base their program on proposed changes in the social structure are regarded as more respectable than those which claim to act directly on the individual. Converts to the former are usually more sober and less hysterical than those who take as their

---

5. This is a sentence fragment, and should be connected to previous sentence. Use a colon after "fallacy."

6. A nice turn of phrase.

7. Example of a "dropped quotation." From the *Tao te Ching* by Lao Tzu. We need a note.

bible Korzybski's "Science and Sanity" or Ouspensky's "Tertium Organum." They are also much more hypocritical. The latter individuals, at least, are ready to admit that part of the cause of their misery may lie somewhere within themselves and are not inclined to charge all their unhappiness to a social system which has more than enough to answer for already.

This is not to deny that changes in the social order can or should be made, but merely to assert that such changes are inevitably trivial. *Nothing that counts can be changed.* Our patterns of behavior and the character of the consciousness which accompanies them were decided by factors beyond our control long before we achieved maturity. Our happiness is largely independent of the constitution of society.[8]

Social panaceas do have a certain surface plausibility but they are nevertheless unworkable. The nature of existence is such as to preclude forever the realization of the biblical ideal: "And each man shall sit in his own garden, under his own fig-tree and none shall make him afraid"[9] for "the evil we suffer is not from our environment but from ourselves—these hands. We have no strength to bear anything, unable to bear pain, impotent to enjoy, intolerant of everything."[10]

8. Starting with the italicized sentence, this part of the paragraph is the paper's thesis. Perhaps a bit too grandiose, too sweeping? The assumed unity with the reader implied by first person plural works against this thesis.

9. Micah 4:4.

10. This is also a quotation from the Bible, but it is not accurate.

The most magnificent attempt to provide a basis for an infantilism is that of I. A. Richards in *The Principles of Literary Criticism*. This book is an attempt to demonstrate that the mind grows and that it does so through the influence of minds more highly developed than itself;[11] the minds of artists. However, this influence is not a direct one as between teacher and pupil but is accomplished through the intermediation of symbols, that is, works of art.[12] That the experiences communicated by works of art have lasting effects in the form of modified behavior and consciousness is Richards's central and most revolutionary contention. In spite of this it has gone unchallenged while less important claims like the utilitarian theory of value and the denial of discontinuity between life and art have been extensively criticized.

A corollary of this view that art induces order is necessarily the thesis that artists are superior beings, since they could hardly be expected to do for others what they could not accomplish for themselves. Richards quotes with approval Shelley's statement in "The Defence of Poetry": "That he is the wisest, the happiest and the best inasmuch as he is a poet is equally incontrovertible. The greatest poets have been

11. Only a comma or em-dash, not a semicolon, needed here.

12. Paragraph needs to be developed.

men of the most spotless virtue, of the most consummate prudence, and if we look into the interior of their lives, the happiest of men."[13]

Shelley allowed himself to be carried away by his enthusiasm here, for he could easily have maintained a less vulnerable proposition and still have made his point. He could have said, for instance, that the poet's moments of inspiration make up in their intensity for all his hours of unhappiness, and that his creations compensate his contemporaries for his personal shortcomings. But as his statement stands it is unacceptable. For how are we to reconcile it with all we know of artists that bears witness that they are as miserable and despicable as most men?[14] To conceal this fact helps no one.

While, on the other hand, where there is no illusion, there can be no disillusion. Were we to restrict ourselves to those works of art which were created by men whose conduct we would imitate and whose happiness we could envy, we would soon run out of matter. However, aware as we are of the tormenting dichotomy between our own behavior and our hidden selves, we will judge others accordingly.[15] The world being what it is, we can't afford to cut ourselves off

13. A page reference would help here.

14. This is a rhetorical question. In general, to be avoided in discursive essays—they lead to padding.

15. This is slightly cryptic. It might be expanded or rephrased or both.

from any possible sources of consolation. The artist is no better off than other men. He feels pain where others do not. Is he to be envied because he secretes his own anesthetic?[16]

Richards's view that the modifications of cerebral structure caused by the arts is highly debatable. The evidence would seem to indicate that such improvement in experience or behavior that results from art is temporary and requires constant renewal. As Freud writes, "art affects us but as a mild narcotic and can provide no more than a temporary refuge for us from the hardships of life. Its influence is not strong enough to make us forget real misery."[17]

This is not to minimize its importance. It is our greatest comfort; but working in the hot sun is rendered more bearable by the memory of shade, not because of any inherent capacity to "organize our minds" that this experience possesses, but because the fact of its existence promises occasional surcease.[18] So it is with art. "The arts," Richards writes, "are our storehouse of recorded values. They spring from and perpetuate hours in the lives of exceptional people when their control and command of experience is at its highest, hours when the varying possibilities of existence are

---

16. Another striking and quite strange verbal formulation.

17. Freud is being quoted as if he were the final authority. He is not. One shouldn't end paragraph on quote.

18. Another interesting formulation —an analogy that suggests the author has experienced great pain.

most clearly seen and the different activities which may arise are most exquisitely reconciled, hours when habitual narrowness of interests or confused bewilderment are replaced by intricately wrought composure. In the arts we find the record in the only form in which these things can be recorded of the experiences which have seemed most worth having to the most sensitive and discriminating persons."[19] It is difficult to say just how and why a reading of Jaroslav Hašek's *The Good Soldier Schweik* should make military life more bearable, but it does. A line like "Mieux cette tete-la que pas de tout"[20] can do more to reconcile us to our physical nonconformity and more healthily than any attempt to convince ourselves of a correlation between genius and dysplasticity.[21] This would seem to bear out Richards's claim, but the corroboration is only apparent. It does not follow from these isolated moments of adjustment a new orientation will spring. As the work of art recedes from us in time, the old response comes sneaking back.[22]

Richards exposed the so-called aesthetic mode of perception, and so put an end to the posturing of sensitive, quivering aesthetes. His book contains expositions of mental

---

19. Quotations of more than forty words should be set off from the rest of the paper.

20. You should never drop in foreign phrases and not translate them. This means "better this head than none at all."

21. Word means "abnormal development."

22. Hard to follow what the author is getting at here.

faculties such as memory and imagination which rival those of William James. Some of his chapters produce that tremendous lucidity of mind which he attributes to good art. Nevertheless his central thesis is anti-stoical, and must be rejected. Its adoption would impede resignation to reality.

Beliefs manifest themselves as attitudes, tendencies to behave in certain ways. They are not, however, identical with those attitudes, since attitudes exist for which there are no corresponding conscious beliefs. Beliefs are merely steps taken by the mind to insure the development of certain attitudes. It is in this manner that our behavior becomes self-directed. Ideally we should approach any situation with a great stock of attitudes and utilize that which seems most appropriate. But such flexibility is impossible of attainment. Many attitudes are contradictory to one another. The most we can do is to choose beliefs which will engender attitudes that are least often inappropriate, that is, which most conform to reality.[23]

A belief is infantile when the actions it leads to expose the holder to frustration or when those it debars from him would cause satisfaction. The spawning grounds of such beliefs are the atypical states of mind.

23. Again, these paragraphs seem to contain interesting ideas, but they are at too high a level of abstraction.

It has been said that a book is the documentation of a simple sentence. In the same sense a philosophy is the documentation of a single experience. This comes about in the following manner. A man has an experience an element of which is the conviction that it is somehow more real than his day-by-day existence. He feels that he has momentarily penetrated the veil that shrouds reality and grasped its very essence. This experience he makes the nucleus of his cosmology. Its nature determines his life-style. However, he usually claims for this belief a universal validity. He feels that it is true not only for himself but for all men. He differs from the artists in that he is not content merely to communicate his experience but attempts to construct an objective foundation for it. The metaphysician is then a shamefaced poet who incorporates an argument into his vision. He does this in order that he may continue to believe in the absence of inspiration. In so doing, however, he acts to his detriment, for if the belief is maintained after the collapse of the situation which brought it about, his behavior becomes as inappropriate as that of Don Quixote among the windmills. This is always to some degree inevitable, for whichever attitudes we may

adopt, there are bound to occur situations in which they will
be inappropriate.[24]

These atypical states of mind are pockets of unreality,
and the belief that they are somehow more real than our
ordinary existence and that it is an eradicable peculiarity
or our nature that renders their occurrence so rare is an
infantilism.[25] In stating that it is our ordinary existence which
is real, I am committing myself to a statistical criterion of
reality. I am maintaining that what is recurrent and relatively
stable is real. If "real" means anything it means this. An
hallucination or mirage is "unreal" because it fails to persist
when different conditions obtain.

There are feelings which except for brief happy gaps do
persist, and it is these feelings which may be safely equated
with reality. It is rarely that an honest act of introspection
fails to discover at least one of them. Even when not fully
developed, intimations of their presence color consciousness.
These feelings are fear, hate, self-contempt, and isolation.[26]
They are not aberrations but responses to facts of existence;
the fact that we are helpless before nature and must submit
to pain or any other affliction she[27] chooses to put upon us,

24. A much more fully developed paragraph.

25. A key term in this paper, "infantilism" needs sharper definition.

26. This seems unduly and unrealistically pessimistic. Why are no positive states included here?

27. Written in 1950, this paper subscribes to the idea that nature is female. I would avoid this.

that we are in constant conflict with our fellows who constitute obstacles to the fulfillment of our desires, that we aspire
to standards we can never meet, and finally that even for the
most loved among us a point exists beyond which we stand
alone. Social pressures conspire to make recognition of these
truths extremely difficult.

The attacks on the proposition that might makes right[28]
are often of authoritarian origin. They are attempts of the
"ins" to cast the stigma of immorality on the revolutionary
"outs" and on their own wielding of power an aura of legitimacy. That freedom is a function of power is a principle the
truth of which those who have done any thinking of the
matter are convinced. Yet they find it impossible to act upon.
Why is this?

Moral standards are not spontaneously generated.
Conscience is an alien, a conquering alien, which after years
of garrison duty is on familiar terms with the natives. These
come to sentimentalize their relationships to it, forgetting
that its loyalty lies elsewhere. There are men who can't speak
a word or make a gesture without betraying to the world
the absolute contempt in which they hold themselves. Like

28. This is certainly familiar enough,
but it needs to be more clearly
connected to ideas of previous
paragraph.

Dostoyevsky's Underground Man, they ask: "With people who know how to revenge themselves and stand up for themselves generally, how is it done?"[29] The subtle methods of intimidation by which independence is maintained in human society are not for such. Yet the only other path of escape from underground is barred to them. It is not fear of possible consequences that keeps them from violence. Nothing can be done to such men that they don't do to themselves. The reason for their inaction is that society has made them into their own warders.

C. K. Ogden remarks somewhere apropos of the disadvantages attendant on the study of psychology that "we may be such as we should hate to know who we are."[30] We have passed that stage. It takes but little insight into one's own nature (provided one is not masochistic enough to insist on the moral authority of others) to be convinced of human depravity. Duplicity is the basis of all our relationships with equals.[31] Only with our inferiors can we be honest. This honesty consists in the open avowal of our egoism, the hypocritical pose of selflessness being no longer necessary. Consideration for others is always the result of coercion.

29. We need a source here (though it's clear that it's *Notes from the Underground*, this needs to be stated).

30. I cannot find this quotation. You never want to cite a source by saying, "X says somewhere that ..." Try to locate the source. Extensive Googling of Ogden and keywords yielded nothing.

31. A somewhat harsh judgment, one that most people would disagree with. Perhaps acknowledge that possibility.

Others do not exist for themselves but as instruments. We differ only in the degree of subtlety with which we manipulate them and in the extent of our awareness as to what we are really doing. Long years of practice have rendered the falsification of experience automatic with most. No sooner has something happened than they are busy "remolding it nearer to the heart's desire."[32]

Once one accepts empiricist premises, solipsist conclusions inevitably follow. The position outlined by Ayer in "Language, Truth and Logic" which he is so careful to distinguish from solipsism is, in fact, solipsism. However, Ayer's refutation of the analogical argument by which many positivists attempt to justify their belief in the sentiency of others is valid, and therefore they too are logically committed to solipsism. To assert that a being is conscious is to assert that its existence is independent of the observer's and that when he is not aware of it, it is aware of itself. These assertions are by any criteria of verifiability meaningless. But all this is more or less irrelevant according to the greater or lesser degree to which psychological solipsism is dependent on logical solipsism; that is, on the nature of the relationship

32. This needs to be attributed to someone. John Dewey or Edward Fitzgerald?

between the fact of isolation and the feeling of isolation. It is probable that a logical confutation of solipsism, if there can be such, would leave untouched the feeling of absolute and utter aloneness from whence it springs.[33]

The empiricist holds a view in accordance with which he can't behave for five consecutive minutes. We must not be dismayed by the fact that on returning home he embraces his wife and children and asks of these agitations in his nervous system: Are you happy? Does it hurt? Do you love Daddy? and other meaningless questions. For these men are, like Hume, logical and not temperamental solipsists.

"As in looking upward each beholder thinks himself the center of the sky; so nature formed her individuals that each must see himself as the center of being."[34] This observation, though a banal commonplace, is the central fact of human existence.

The manner in which I conceive the awareness of this fact to affect an individual is as follows. On first coming face to face with it he is seized by a feeling of immense vertigo, but it passes and life goes on. If he ever again thinks of the matter it is in terms of Russell's solipsist who wondered why

33. The whole paragraph seems to be making an interesting point, but it never gets around to it.

34. From Johann Lavater. Needs a note and also further explanation.

everyone was not a solipsist. But as he becomes increasingly aware of the egoistic motivation of all human behavior, he becomes convinced of the truth of his original insight until he reaches the stage where Lavater's aphorism or any other proof of the universality of this sensation ceases to comfort. The problem of evil and that of isolation become one: "Naught loves another as itself / Nor venerates another so / Nor is it possible to Thought / A greater than itself to know."[35] To be an outsider because of physical configuration or psychological idiosyncrasy is tragic enough, but to be an outsider because there is nothing to be inside of—an aura of terror surrounds this idea. Nietzsche's dictum becomes: Everyone is dead; all is permitted!

With all his will he suppresses this idea sometimes so successfully that months pass during which the illusion of contact with others will maintain itself. But for all his attempts to stifle it a voice intermittently makes itself heard, a voice telling him that he is all alone; all, and therefore alone. From here there are several directions in which he can go. He can continue to suppress this idea and project his despair onto some feature of the external world which he can ultimately

35. Set off and also identify source of quotation.(in this case, William Blake's "A Little Boy Lost.")

hope to eradicate. Thus the fanatical revolutionary with nothing to fear but victory, is born.

Or he can acknowledge this insight after having concocted a new opiate. Thus is created the mystic to whom the fact of human isolation is rendered bearable by his belief that through the assiduous practice of certain techniques he may transcend this isolation, merging himself with the "oneness of the universe." The mystic is looked upon with scorn by his more enlightened brethren, the militantly unsuperstitious, but it is the scorn of the alcoholic for the drug addict. Mystics are unlike the proverbial ostrich in that they risk a peek before burrowing even deeper than their less courageous fellows.[36]

But there is still another course. He can admit this fact—the isolation of each from each—and create new values with which it can co-exist. It is this third course which I would urge. We have emancipated ourselves from the belief in the benevolence of the universe to become enslaved in the belief in the solidarity of humans. Of the fact that we have merely exchanged infantilisms few of us are aware. This new infantilism is much more plausible but at the same time much

36. It's not clear whether this is all about Nietzsche or about someone else.

less comforting than the old. In spite of this fact it is one whose rejection is tremendously more difficult.

The abandonment of God entailed resignation to our mortality. The abandonment of man will entail resignation to our aloneness.[37] We have hardly adjusted ourselves to the "neutralization of nature" and so it seems all the more gratuitous to be called upon to make the even more difficult adjustment to the isolation of man, but only in so doing can we make ourselves free. The awareness of our freedom, the freedom of someone adrift in a boat which has slipped its moorings, instills in us a panic that only the realization that the harbor was illusory can quell. It is not a question of having the courage to live without illusions—it is rather the old story of Pandora's Box. The old view of the world is like Humpty Dumpty shattered beyond repair. We can't tuck the bugle call back into the bugle; and even if we could, are we so sure that what we've heard is last post and not reveille?[38]

---

37. Well put. Concise and powerful.

38. A strong closing image, though with four metaphorical expressions of the situation (unmoored boat, Pandora, Humpty-Dumpty, the bugle) piling on top of one another, the concluding paragraph is a little hard to figure out. And in general, the paper needs rewriting and polishing—an overall reorganization —with introduction of more con arguments (overall a far too one-sided view offered here), fuller documentation of quoted material (including a Works Cited page), and more fully-developed paragraphs. But it is filled with powerfully evocative language and aperçus. Even though it should be rewritten so that its points come out more fully and clearly, this essay has at its core what we are all looking for: an imaginative argument.

Works Cited

Adams, James. *Conceptual Blockbusting.* Perseus, 1990.

Asner, Gene. Letter. *New York Times.* 24 Sept. 2004, p. A26.

Bain, Ken. *What the Best College Teachers Do.* Harvard UP, 2004.

Baker, Sheridan. *The Practical Stylist.* 7th ed., Harper, 1990.

Barry, Dave. "College Admissions." *Dave Barry's Bad Habits: A 100% Fact-Free Book,* Owl Books, Henry Holt, 1987, pp. 200–203.

Becker, Alida. "The Inventor, His Wife, Her Lover, and a Tomato." Review of *Ira Foxglove,* by Thomas McMahon, *New York Times Book Review,* 21 Mar. 2004, p. 10.

Becker, Carl. *Heavenly City of the Eighteenth Century Philosophers.* Yale UP, 1992.

Bell, Susan. "Revisioning *The Great Gatsby.*" *Tin House,* Summer 2004, pp. 148–57.

Benedict, Ruth. *Patterns of Culture.* NAL, 1934.

Bennett, Deborah J. *Logic Made Easy: How to Know When Language Deceives You.* W. W. Norton, 2004.

Berry, Wendell. *Standing by Words.* Counterpoint, 2011.

Bing, Xu. *Book from the Ground: From Point to Point.* MIT P, 2013.

Black, David M. "People, Places, and Things." *Road and Track,* Oct. 2004, p. 21.

Bleich, David. *Subjective Criticism.* Johns Hopkins UP, 1998.

Booth, Wayne, et al. *The Craft of Research.* U of Chicago P, 1995.

Bowling for Columbine. Directed by Michael Moore, performances by Michael Moore, Charlton Heston, Dick Clark, and George W. Bush, United Artists, 2002.

Brown, Goold. *The Institutes of English Grammar.* William Wood, 1863.

Buranen, Lise. "But *I* Wasn't Cheating: Plagiarism and Cross-Cultural Mythology." *Perspectives on Plagiarism and Intellectual Property in a Postmodern World,* edited by Lise Buranen and Alice M. Roy, State U of New York P, 1999, pp. 63–74.

Carroll, Lewis. *Alice's Adventures in Wonderland and Through the Looking Glass.* Penguin, 1962.

Carroll, Noël. *The Philosophy of Horror, or Paradoxes of the Heart.* Routledge, 1990.

Ch'ien, Evelyn Nien-Ming. *Weird English.* Harvard UP, 2005.

Chismar, Douglas E. "Theodore Lipps, Aesthetic Empathy, and the Self-Other Problem." *Journal of Comparative Literature and Aesthetics,* vol. 17, no. 1–2, 1994, pp. 17–24.

Christensen, Clayton M. *The Innovator's Dilemma: The Revolutionary Book That Will Change the Way You Do Business.* HarperCollins, 2011.

Cioffi, Frank L. *One Day in the Life of the English Language: A Microcosmic Usage Handbook.* Princeton UP, 2015.

Columbia Encyclopedia. Edited by Paul Legassé, 6th ed., New York: Columbia UP, 2000.

Cooper, Allen. "Was Melania Trump's Speech Plagiarized from Michele Obama?" *USA Today,* 16 July 2016, Usatoday.com.

de Bono, Edward. *Lateral Thinking: Creativity Step by Step.* Harper, 1973.

Denham, Sir John. *The Poetical Works of Sir John Denham.* Edited by Theodore Howard Banks, Jr., Yale UP, 1928.

Dickens, Charles. *Hard Times.* 1854. Edited by George Ford and Sylvère Monod, W. W. Norton, 1966.

Doolittle, Hilda. *H.D.: Collected Poems, 1912–1944.* Edited by Louis Martz, New Directions, 1983.

Dougherty, Peter J. "The Wealth of Notions: A Publisher Considers the Literature of Globalization." *Chronicle Review,* 16 July 2004. http://www.chronicle.com/article /The-Wealth-of-Notions-a/19862.

Du Bois, W.E.B. *Writings.* Edited by Nathan Huggins, Library of America, 1986.

Dubrow, Heather. "Thesis and Antithesis: Rewriting the Rules on Writing." *Chronicle of Higher Education,* 6 Dec. 2002, p. B13.

Edmundson, Mark. "The Risk of Reading: Why Books Are Meant to Be Dangerous." *New York Times Magazine,* 1 Aug. 2004, pp. 11–12.

Elbow, Peter. *Writing without Teachers.* 1973. Oxford UP, 1998.

Eliot, T. S. *Selected Prose of T. S. Eliot.* Edited by Frank Kermode, Harcourt, 1975.

Emerson, Ralph Waldo. *Essays and Lectures.* Edited by Joel Porte, Library of America, 1983.

Felaco, Linda. Letter. *Atlantic Monthly,* Oct. 2004, p. 29.

Finkel, Don. *Teaching with Your Mouth Shut.* Heinemann, 2000.

Fish, Stanley. *How to Write a Sentence and How to Read One.* Harper, 2011.

Frank, Jerome. "On Lawsuits as Inquiries into the Truth, from *Courts on Trial.*" *The World of Law: The Law as Literature,* edited by Ephraim London, Simon and Schuster, 1960, pp. 731–53.

Franklin, Ben. "The Autobiography." *Benjamin Franklin: Writings,* edited by J. A. Leo Lemay, Library of America, 1987, pp. 1305–1469.

Franzen, Jonathan. "My Father's Brain: What Alzheimer's Takes Away." *New Yorker,* 10 Sept. 2001. www.newyorker.com /magazine/2001/09/10/my-fathers-brain.

Frazier, Charles. "Introduction." *The Book of Job,* King James Version, Grove, 1999, vii–xvii.

Frost, Robert. "Fire and Ice." *Robert Frost: Collected Poems, Prose, & Plays,* edited by Richard Poirier and Mark Richardson. Library of America, 1995, p. 204.

Gelbspan, Ross. "Cool the Rage." *Orion,* July/ Aug. 2004, p. 11.

Goffman, Erving. *Stigma: Notes on the Management of Spoiled Identity.* Simon and Schuster, 1963.

Gold, Barry Steven. "Insect Bites and Stings." *The Merck Manual of Diagnosis and Therapy,* edited by Mark H. Beers and Robert Berkow, 17th ed., Merck, 1999, p. 2650.

———. "Insect Bites and Stings." *The Merck Manual of Diagnosis and Therapy,* edited by Mark H. Beers and Robert Berkow, 18th ed., Merck, 2006, pp. 2639–40.

Goldman, Adam. "The Comet Ping Pong Gunman Answers Our Reporter's Questions." *New York Times,* 7 Dec. 2016. https://www .nytimes.com/2016/12/07/us/edgar-welch -comet-pizza-fake-news.html.

Goldsmith, Kenneth. "The Case for Plagiarism from a Celebrated Poet Who Has Made a Career Out of It." *Qz.com,* 21 July 2016.

Gorrell, Donna. *A Writer's Handbook from A to Z.* Allyn and Bacon, 1964.

Gould, James. "Science Writing." Unpublished paper.

Gould, James, and Peter J. Arduino, Jr. "Is Tonic Immobility Adaptive?" *Animal Behaviour,* vol. 32, no. 3, Aug. 1984, pp. 921–23.

Graves, Robert, and Alan Hodge. *The Reader over Your Shoulder: A Handbook for Writers of Prose.* Macmillan, 1943.

Gurr, Ted Robert. *Why Men Rebel.* Princeton UP, 1970.

Hall, Donald. *Writing Well.* 9th ed., Addison, 1997.

Hap, Bela. "Structuralist Meta-Analysis." Translated by Gyula Kodolanyi. *Essaying Essays: Alternative Forms of Exposition,* edited by Richard Kostelanetz, Out of London Press, 1975, p. 310.

Harari, Yuval Noah. *Homo Deus: A Brief History of Tomorrow.* HarperCollins, 2017.

Harvey, Gordon. *Writing with Sources.* Hackett, 2000.

Hawking, Stephen. "Findings." *Harper's,* Oct. 2004, p. 104.

Hemingway, Ernest. *Complete Poems.* Edited by Nicholas Gerogiannis, U of Nebraska P, 1992.

Huyssen, Andreas. *Present Pasts: Urban Palimpsests and the Politics of Memory.* Stanford UP, 2003.

Hwang, Heemyung. Letter. *USA Today,* 29 Dec. 2008.

J.C. "Reader's Guide." *Times Literary Supplement,* 27 Feb. 2017. https://www .the-tls.co.uk/articles/private/readers-guide/

James, Henry. *The Art of Fiction and Other Essays.* Oxford UP, 1948.

———. "Hawthorne." *Henry James: Literary Criticism: Essays on Literature; American Writers; English Writers,* edited by Leon Edel, Library of America, 1984, pp. 315–457.

James, William. *The Letters of William James.* 2 vols., edited by Henry James, Atlantic Monthly Press, 1920.

———. *The Varieties of Religious Experience. William James: Writings, 1902–1910,* edited by Bruce Kuklick, Library of America, 1987.

Kafalenos, Emma. "The Power of Double Coding to Represent New Forms of Representation: *The Truman Show, Dorian Gray,* "Blow-Up," and Whistler's *Caprice in Purple and Gold.*" *Poetics Today,* vol. 24, no. 1, Spring 2003, pp. 1–33.

Kasner, Edward, and James Newman. *Mathematics and the Imagination.* Simon and Schuster, 1940.

Keats, John. *A Critical Edition of the Major Works.* Edited by Elizabeth Cook, Oxford UP, 1990.

Kostelanetz, Richard, ed. *Essaying Essays: Alternative Forms of Exposition.* Out of London Press, 1975.

Kulish, Nicholas. "Not Plagiarism but Mixing and Matching, Says Best-Selling German Author, 17." *New York Times,* 12 Feb. 2010, late ed., p. A4.

Kuhn, Thomas. *The Structure of Scientific Revolutions.* 2nd ed., U of Chicago P, 1970.

Lanham, Richard A. *A Handlist of Rhetorical Terms.* 2nd ed., U of California P, 1991.

Lipsyte, Robert. "Athletes Offer Straight Talk about Cancer." *New York Times,* 25 Nov. 2001, late ed., sec. 5, p. 11.

MacPherson, Robin. *University English.* Wydawnictwa Szkolne i Pedagogiczne, 1994.

Mahler, Jonathan. "Search Party." *New York Times Magazine,* 1 Jan. 2017, pp. 9–11.

Marius, Richard. *A Writer's Companion.* McGraw-Hill, 1995.

Mattenson, Lauri M. "Teaching Student Writers to Be Warriors." *Chronicle Review,* 6 Aug. 2004, pp. B10–B11.

Menand, Louis. "Comp Time." *New Yorker,* 11 Sept. 2000.

Merkin, Daphne. "Secrets of the Soul: Is Psychoanalysis Science or Is It Toast?" Review of *Secrets of the Soul* by Eli Zaretsky, *New York Times Book Review,* 5 Sept. 2004, pp. 9–10.

Merwin, W. S. *Collected Poems, 1952–1993.* Edited by J. D. McClatchy, Library of America, 2013.

Mill, John Stuart. *On Liberty.* 1859. Hackett, 1978.

Miller, Laura. "Imagine." *New York Times Book Review,* 5 Sept. 2004, p. 23.

Miner, Horace. "Body Ritual among the Nacirema." *Apeman, Spaceman: Anthropological Science Fiction,* edited by Leon Stover and Harry Harrison, Doubleday, 1968, pp. 238–42.

Mitchell, Luke. "The Osama Endorsement." *Harper's,* Oct. 2004, p. 89.

Muir, John. *Nature Writings.* Edited by William Cronon, Library of America, 1997.

Nabokov, Vladimir. *Novels (1955–1962)*. Edited by Brian Boyd, Library of America, 1996.

O'Gorman, Joe. "In Battle of QBs, Pennington Has Last Laugh." *The Trentonian*, 29 Dec. 2008.

O'Rourke, P. J. "The Art of Policy: 'To Hell with Lipitor.'" *Atlantic Monthly*, Oct. 2004, p. 56.

Orwell, George. *The Orwell Reader: Fiction, Essays, and Reportage by George Orwell*. Harcourt, Brace, 1949.

———. *Shooting an Elephant and Other Essays*. Secker and Warburg, 1950.

Piercy, Marge. "To Be of Use." *Poemhunter. com*, https://www.poemhunter.com/poem /to-be-of-use/.

Posner, Richard. *The Little Book of Plagiarism*. Knopf, 2009.

Raftery, Brian. "Now Playing: Cheap-and-Schlocky Blockbuster Ripoffs." *Wired.com*, 21 Dec. 2009.

Ramsey, Frank P. *Philosophical Papers*. Edited by D. H. Mellor, Cambridge UP, 1990.

Rawlings, Wendy. "Food and Worker Safety across the Globe: A Nervous and Incomplete Case Study." *2016: Pushcart Prize XL: Best of the Small Presses*, edited by Bill Henderson, Pushcart Press, 2016, pp. 351–60.

Richards, I. A. *Principles of Literary Criticism*. Harcourt, 1925.

Robertson, William O. "Poisoning." *Merck Manual of Diagnostics and Therapeutics*, edited by Mark H. Beers and Robert Berkow, Merck, 1999, pp. 2619–55.

Sanders, Scott. "Invisible Men and Women: The Disappearance of Character in Science Fiction." *Science Fiction Studies*, vol. 4, no. 1, 1977, pp. 14–24.

Scholes, Robert, and Karl Klaus. *Elements of the Essay*. Oxford UP, 1969.

Sirc, Gregory. *English Composition as a Happening*. Utah State UP, 2002.

Shteyngart, Gary. *Super Sad True Love Story: A Novel*. Random House, 2011.

Slater, Lauren. "The Trouble with Self-Esteem." *New York Times Magazine*, 3 Feb. 2002, pp. 44–47.

Sohn, Amy G. "The Elements of Sexual Style." *New York Times Book Review*, 26 Sept. 2004, p. 31.

Sontag, Susan. *Against Interpretation and Other Essays*. 1966. Picador, 2001.

Stoppard, Tom. *Jumpers*. Grove, 1972.

———. *Rosencrantz and Guildenstern Are Dead*. Grove, 1994.

Szymborska, Wisława. "A Tale Retold." *Poezje/ Poems*. Translated by Magnus J. Krynski and Robert A. Maguire, Wydawnictwo Literackie, 1989, p. 49.

Taylor, Edward. *The Poems of Edward Taylor*. Edited by Donald E. Stanford, Yale UP, 1960.

Trapani, Gina. "Master Da Vinci's Streamwriting Technique." *Lifehacker.com*, 31 May 2006. http://lifehacker.com/177301/master -da-vincis-streamwriting-technique.

Turner, Jenny. "The Amis Papers." Review of *The War against Cliché: Essays and Reviews, 1971–2000*, by Martin Amis, *New York Times Book Review*, 23 Dec. 2001, p. 10.

Updike, John. "Hub Fans Bid Kid Adieu." *Baseball: A Literary Anthology*, edited by Nicholas Davidoff, Library of America, 2002, pp. 301–17.

Van Leer, David. "Hester's Labyrinth: Transcendental Rhetoric in Puritan Boston." *New Essays on The Scarlet Letter*, edited by Michael J. Colacurcio, Cambridge UP, 1985, pp. 57–100.

Wallace, David Foster. "Consider the Lobster." *Gourmet*, Aug. 2004, pp. 50–64.

Weinstein, Arnold. *A Scream Goes through the House: What Literature Teaches Us about Life*. Random House, 2003.

Wells, Colleen. "Roadkill Rod." *Orion*, July/Aug. 2004, p. 10.

Winchester, C. T. *Some Principles of Literary Criticism*. Macmillan, 1914.

Windolf, Jim. "Cultural Studies: Nothing Good to Eat." *New York Times*, 24 Sept. 2015, p. D6.

Wittgenstein, Ludwig. *Philosophical Investigations*. Translated by G.E.M. Anscombe, Macmillan, 1958.

Woolf, Virginia. *A Room of One's Own, Three Guineas*. Oxford UP, 1992.

"Wrist Watch Industry Statistics." *Statisticbrain*, 1 Aug. 2016. http://www.statisticbrain .com/wrist-watch-industry-statistics/.

Yates, Brock. "Someone Needs to Rewrite Racing Rules." *Car and Driver*, Sept. 2004, p. 26.

Index

Hap, Bela, example of writing by, 237–39
Harari, Yuval Noah, 258
Harvey, Gordon, 94
Hašek, Jaroslav, *The Good Soldier Schweik*, 337
hasty generalization (logical fallacy), 218
Hawthorne, Nathaniel: biography by Henry James of quoted, 23; on novel (*The Scarlet Letter*) by, 84–85
H.D. (Hilda Doolittle, pseud.), 97–99; considerations if writing about, 70–71. *See also* "Pool, The"
Hegemann, Helene, 248–49, 250
Heisenberg Uncertainty Principle, 78, 88
Hemingway, Ernest, 158–59
Hengel, Daniel, 280, 281
Herum, John, 228
Heston, Charlton, in *Bowling for Columbine*, 40
Hoban, Russell, style of, 29
Hodge, Alan, and Robert Graves, *The Reader over Your Shoulder*, 93
"Hub Fans Bid Kid Adieu" (Updike), writing style of passage from, 236–37
Hurston, Zora Neale, use of metaphor by in *Their Eyes Were Watching God*, 209
Huyssen, Andreas, language use of, 38, 41, 43
Hwang, Heemyung, letter to editor by, 190–91
hypallage (figure of speech), 208, 210n4; Fitzgerald's use of, 212; Rawlings's use of, 242nn73, 74, and 77; Updike's use of, 237n46; Wallace's use of, 241n70
hyperbole (figure of speech), 208
hypotaxis, avoiding, 225–26

idea, generation of, 258
infeeling, 99–102
informative writing, 15
Internet: evaluating sources found on, 49, 105–08; Goldsmith on, 249, 257; plagiarism enabled by, 176, 255, 264; as source for research, 106
interpretation: as explanation, 20; as invention strategy, 49; Susan Sontag and, 20
invention: and freewriting, 176; of new forms, 163–66; in research, 104–05; in writing, 45–49
Isaac, Brad, 170
italics, avoiding use of, 10

James, Henry: on allegory, 23; later style of, 226–27
James, William: in contrast with I.A. Richards, 338; on English "spelt spontaneously," 29–30; example of writing by, 231–32
Job, The Book of: Frazier on, 239–40; Szymborska on, 239
Johnson, Justin, use of hypallage by, 208
Johnson, Samuel, belletristic writing of, 15
journalism, 15–16; 28
Joyce, James, style of, 29

Kahn, Louis I., 68, 72; quoted by Dubrow, 61
Kasner, Edward, and James Newman, example of writing by, 234–35
Keats, John, "negative capability" and, 68–69
knowledge: advancement of, 115; in humanistic discourse, 80; as subjective, 144–45, 258
Kübler-Ross, Elisabeth, on five stages of death and dying, 161
Kuhn, Thomas, on paradigm formation, 116–18

language use: inappropriate, 27, 223–24; Lydia Morgan on, 325–30
Lanham, Richard A., 206–09
Lao Tzu, *Tao Te Ching*, 332
Lateral Thinking (de Bono), 48, 266

Lavater, Johann, 344–45
Lincoln, Abraham, W.E.B. Du Bois on, 232–33
Lipps, Theodore, 100
Lipsyte, Robert, paragraphing of, 133–34
logical fallacies, 214–20, as "cheating at argument," 9, 214; damage to society of, 259; persuasive value of, 220. *See also individual fallacies*
Lombardi, Vince, on winning, 260
lyrical essay. *See narrative essay*

MacPherson, Robin, on style, 221–22
macro-questions, 93–95, 105; conclusion and, 101
Marius, Richard, and "blueprint thesis," 71
Mathematics and the Imagination (Kasner and Newman), writing style of passage from, 234–35
Mattenson, Lauri M., on student attitudes toward writing, 259–60
Maxwell, James Clerk, and "Maxwell's Demon," 92
McLuhan, Marshall, 21
McMahon, Thomas, on ideas, 154–55, 265
meander (streamwriting), 174, 176; examples of, 178–83; used in teaching, 305
Medium Is the Massage, The (McLuhan), 21
Menand, Louis, 13
Merck Manual, paragraph incoherence within, 136–38
metaphor, 210, 243; Benedict's use of, 233n20, 234nn22 and 23; in clichés, 223; F.S. Cioffi's use of, 347n38; Du Bois's use of, 232n14; as figure of speech, 208; Fitzgerald's use of, 212–13; Goffman's use of, 235n36, 236n41; William James's use of, 231n1; Kasner and Newman's use of, 235n25; Nabokov's use of, 230; Orwell's use of, 235n33; Szymborska's use of, 239nn56 and 58; Updike's use of, 236n45
Micah, the book of, 333
Michelson, Peter, 291
micro-questions: audience objections as, 99; Carroll on, 95–96; conclusion and, 147, 149; H.D.'s "The Pool" (poem) analyzed via, 97
Mill, John Stuart: on cultural entrapment, 265–66; on percent of argument devoted to opposition, 99–101, 188, 268
mindstreaming (streamwriting), 175
Miner, Horace, "Body Ritual among the Nacirema" as creative nonfiction and, 151
"Modest Proposal, A" (Swift), 150
Montaigne, Michel de, belletristic writing and, 15
Moore, Michael: in *Bowling for Columbine*, 40–41
Morgan, Lydia, "The Ethics of Language Exposure: The Way We Talk to Our Babies" (undergraduate paper), 325–30
motive: for writing, 32–34; G. Harvey and, 94; in revised letter to editor, 203n1
Muir, John, hinge-structure paragraph of, 125–26
My Favorite Martian (TV show), 286
"my puppy syndrome," 310–11

Nabokov, Vladimir, as stylist, 229, 230, 270
Nachgeschichte (after-story), as invention strategy, 48
narrative essay: as creative nonfiction, 152–53; defined by Scholes and Klaus, 152
"negative capability" (Keats), 68–69
Newman, James, and Edward Kasner, example of writing by, 234–35
"New-Write," 2; 51–52

New York Times: headline as example of climax in, 207–08; on letters to editor in, 191
nominalizations: on avoidance of in writing, 223, 228; as used by William James, 232n10
nonalphabetic text assignment, 294–95
non sequitur (logical fallacy), 219

Obama, Michelle, 88, 248
Ogden, C. K., 342
O'Gorman, Joe, 189–90
"ooze," paragraph transitions and, 128–29
oral reports, 290
Orwell, George, 259, 261; example of writing by, 235; windowpane metaphor and, 228
outlines, use of, 52–55
outside-the-box thinking, suggestion on how to accomplish, 156–58
oxymoron: defined, 13; examples of, 234n26, 240n60; thesis as, 65

paradigm, as defined by Thomas Kuhn, 116–18
paragraph: coherence and cohesiveness within, 131–38; conclusion of, 127; development of, 129–31, 198–99; ideal length of, 130–31; Lipsyte example of, 133–34; *Merck Manual* example of, 136–38; old information v. new information in, 132–34; the "ooze" and, 128–29; as paper in miniature, 124; topic sentence in, 124–28; transitions within and between, 128–29
parallel tale, as invention strategy, 48–49
Parrish, Cindy, 294
passive voice: avoiding use of, 63–64, 225–26; used by Ruth Benedict, 233n16; in scientific writing, 38, 230; used by William James, 231n2
"patch-writing," 250
patterns: and classroom dynamics, 287, 293; discovery of, 94, 113; finding breaks within, 157
Patterns of Culture (Benedict), writing style of passage from, 233–34
pedagogies, reanimating, 282–97
penumbral suspicions, as way to get started writing, 49
Piercy, Marge, "To Be of Use" (poem), 174, 176
plagiarism, 247–57
"Politics and the English Language" (Orwell), 235; writing style of passage from, 259
polyptoton (figure of speech), 209; example of, 210nn2 and 3; Goffman's use of, 236n40
polysyndeton (figure of speech), 207, 209, 210n4; Frazier's use of, 240n63; Updike's use of, 236n43; Wallace's use of, 241n71
"Pool, The" (poem by H.D.): as judged by I. A. Richards, 70, 75–76; micro-questions about, 97–99; Nina B. on, 76–77; pseudo-theses about, 71–75; sample opening of paper on, 77–79
Pope, Alexander, use of antanagoge by, 207
Posner, Richard, on plagiarism, 251
post hoc ergo propter hoc (logical fallacy), 218
prepositional phrases, on avoidance of in writing, 222
"prewriting," and writing process, 45–57
Prince, Gerald, and "disnarration," 48–49
problem, as synonym for macro-question, 54, 94
problem solving, teaching method described, 274–75
Procrustes, and the blueprint thesis, 71–72
prolepsis, as way to develop argument, 89–92, 100
proposal, as genre of argument, 19

Proust, Marcel, Weinstein's analysis of novel by, 42
provocation, teaching method described, 274, 276
pseudo-thesis, 69–75; "blueprint thesis" as subtype of, 69, 71–72; description or summary as subtype of, 69, 71; "okey-dokey" thesis as subtype of, 69, 73–74; zany thesis as subtype of, 69, 74–75
Purvis, Rosalie, 254–55

question, as connected to thesis, 7–8. *See also* macro-questions; micro-questions
questioning, 7, 92–93, 144
quotation: ending paragraphs on, 224; as used in writing, 118–23

Ramon, Justin, "The Glymphiad" (undergraduate paper), 317–24
Ramsey, Frank Plumpton: on meaning as potential, 80; on "nothing to discuss," xiv
Rawlings, Wendy, 242–43
Rawls, John: other political philosophers and, 165; "veil of ignorance" and, 20, 64, 163–65
red herring (logical fallacy), 216–17
research paper, 103–23; databases and, 109; discovery as element of, 113–15; documentation in, 118–20; "dropped quotation" in, 121; "fake news" and, 110–13; identifiers as used in, 121–22; internet and, "106–08; macro-question for, 122–23; miscellaneous suggestions about, 122–23; narrowing topic for, 109–10; notecards and, 106; splitters and lumpers and, 104
rewriting, 45; 56–57; 187–204
rhetoric, empty, 205, 241
Richards, I. A., on "The Pool," 70, 75–76; *Principles of Literary Criticism*, 333–37
Robles, Mario Ortiz, 42–43
rules of usage, the, 28
Russell, Bertrand, 345
Ryan, Jeri, 248

Sanders, Scott, opening sentence of essay by, 84
Scarlet Letter, The (Hawthorne): outline topics in paper on, 54; Van Leer on, 85; theses about, 84
Scholes, Robert, and Carl Klaus, definition of narrative essay by, 152
"secret spring" (opening streamwrite in a series), 171–72
Shakespeare, William: hypallage used by, 208; Keats on, 68; plagiaristic quality of, 256; revision by Tom Stoppard of, 48
Shelley, Percy Bysshe, 334–45
simile (figure of speech), 208–09
slang, avoiding use of, 224. *See also* colloquial language
slippery slope (logical fallacy), 219–20
Sontag, Susan, *Against Interpretation*, 20
sources, external, 18
spelling, imaginative (William James), 29–30
Sperber, Murray, on destructive "critical machine," 24
Star Wars, Yoda's use of anastrophe in, 207
Steele, Richard, belletristic writing of, 15
Stein, Gertrude, language of, 29
Stevens, Wallace, 6
Stigma (Goffman): "moral career" and, 249; writing style of passage from, 235–36
Stoppard, Tom: *Jumpers* and, 8; *Rosencrantz and Guildenstern Are Dead* and, 48
streamwrite of consciousness, 172